# Miniseries Production

Andrew Parry

Published by Andrew Parry, 2024.

MINISERIES PRODUCTION

**First edition. September 25, 2024.**



ISBN: 979-8227457738

Written by Andrew Parry.

# Table of Contents

# Introduction: Opportunities for Screenplay Writers

We are living in what can only be described as the golden age of the miniseries. Once a niche format relegated to historical dramas and literary adaptations, the miniseries has undergone a renaissance, emerging as one of the most exciting and dynamic forms of storytelling in the modern television landscape. For screenplay writers, this evolution presents an unprecedented array of opportunities to craft compelling, tightly woven narratives that can resonate with global audiences.

The rise of streaming platforms and the shift in viewing habits have played a significant role in this transformation. Audiences today crave diverse, high-quality content that they can consume on their own terms, and the miniseries format is uniquely positioned to meet this demand. Unlike traditional long-running series, miniseries offer writers the chance to tell complete stories with a clear beginning, middle, and end, all within a limited number of episodes. This allows for a depth of storytelling that is often not possible in feature films or ongoing television shows.

For screenwriters, the miniseries format opens up a world of creative possibilities. It allows you to explore complex characters, intricate plots, and nuanced themes without the constraints of a two-hour film or the need to stretch a story over multiple seasons. You can take risks, experiment with structure, and delve into topics that might be too challenging or unconventional for other formats. The miniseries gives you the freedom to create powerful, self-contained narratives that can stand on their own as complete works of art.

Moreover, the demand for high-quality miniseries has never been greater. Streaming platforms like Netflix, HBO Max, Amazon Prime Video, and Hulu are in constant search of original content to attract and retain subscribers. This has led to a surge in production budgets and a willingness to invest in bold, innovative storytelling. As a screenwriter, this means more opportunities to get your work produced, as well as the potential to work with top-tier directors, actors, and production teams who are drawn to the creative possibilities of the miniseries format.

In this book, we will explore the unique opportunities and challenges of writing for the miniseries format. We will delve into the elements that make a great miniseries, from conceptualization and structuring to character development and thematic depth. We will examine the influence of streaming platforms on the industry, the importance of visual storytelling, and the ways in which you can balance creative vision with commercial success.

Whether you are an experienced screenwriter looking to expand your repertoire or a new writer eager to break into the industry, the miniseries offers a fertile ground for innovation and expression. By mastering the art of the miniseries, you can create stories that captivate audiences, leave a lasting impact, and contribute to the ongoing evolution of television.

Welcome to the golden age of the miniseries.

# Starting with the End in Mind: Crafting the Series Conclusion

When embarking on the journey of writing a television miniseries, one of the most powerful strategies you can employ is to start with the end in mind. Crafting the series conclusion first allows you to establish a clear destination, guiding every decision you make throughout the writing process. This approach ensures that your story remains cohesive, focused, and impactful, leading to a conclusion that resonates deeply with your audience.

The ending of a miniseries is often what stays with viewers long after the credits roll. It's the final note of your narrative symphony, the culmination of all the themes, character arcs, and plot developments you've carefully woven together. A strong, well-thought-out conclusion provides closure, answers lingering questions, and leaves your audience with a sense of satisfaction. However, achieving this requires more than just wrapping up loose ends. It's about delivering an emotional and narrative payoff that feels both inevitable and surprising.

To begin crafting your series conclusion, consider the core themes of your story. What message or exploration of human nature are you trying to convey? The end should encapsulate these themes, offering a resolution that aligns with the story's overarching purpose. For example, if your miniseries is a tale of redemption, the conclusion should demonstrate the protagonist's final step toward or away from redemption. If it's a story about power and corruption, the ending might depict the ultimate consequence of the characters' choices regarding these themes.

Next, think about your characters' journeys. The protagonist's arc is central to the conclusion, but the arcs of supporting characters should also reach a satisfying resolution. Reflect on where each character started and how they've evolved over the course of the series. How do their final actions or fates reflect the changes they've undergone? A well-crafted conclusion often ties back to the characters' initial motivations, fears, and desires, showing how they've grown—or, in some cases, how they've tragically remained the same.

In addition to character arcs, the resolution of your series should address the central conflict. This is where starting with the end in mind becomes particularly advantageous. By knowing the outcome of the conflict, you can effectively build tension and stakes throughout the series, leading to a climax that feels both thrilling and meaningful. The conflict's resolution should feel earned, a direct result of the characters' actions and decisions, rather than a contrived or convenient plot twist.

As you develop your conclusion, consider the pacing and structure of the final episodes. A common pitfall in miniseries writing is rushing the ending, which can leave viewers feeling unsatisfied or even cheated. To avoid this, plan out the buildup to the conclusion carefully. Allow enough time for the climax to unfold naturally, and for the aftermath to be fully explored. This doesn't mean you need to drag out the ending, but rather that you give each element of the conclusion—emotional, narrative, and thematic—its due time on screen.

Another key aspect of crafting the series conclusion is ensuring that it aligns with the tone and style you've established throughout the series. If your miniseries has maintained a dark, brooding atmosphere, a suddenly light-hearted or overly sentimental ending may feel jarring.

Conversely, if your series has been more light-hearted or optimistic, a bleak or nihilistic ending could alienate your audience. The conclusion should feel like a natural extension of the story you've been telling, reinforcing the mood and tone that have kept your viewers engaged.

Once you have a clear vision for the conclusion, you can begin working backward to map out the rest of the series. This method allows you to plant seeds early on that will blossom in the finale, creating a sense of cohesion and inevitability. Foreshadowing is an invaluable tool here—subtle hints or symbols introduced in the first episodes can pay off in the final moments, rewarding attentive viewers and adding layers of meaning to the story.

Finally, it's essential to remember that the conclusion of a miniseries is not just an ending—it's also a beginning of sorts. It's the moment where your audience reflects on the journey they've just experienced, and it's the last opportunity you have to leave a lasting impression. Whether your ending is open-ended, leaving some questions unanswered, or neatly tied up, it should resonate with the themes and emotions you've explored throughout the series.

In conclusion, crafting the series conclusion with intention and care is crucial to the success of your television miniseries. By starting with the end in mind, you ensure that every element of your story works in service of that final moment, creating a cohesive, powerful narrative that stays with your audience long after the credits have rolled. As you move forward in your writing process, keep your ending in sight, letting it guide your decisions and inspire your creativity. The result will be a miniseries that feels both inevitable and unforgettable, a story that truly resonates with its viewers.

# Building the Story Backwards: Structuring the Narrative

Building a story backwards may seem like an unconventional approach to structuring a narrative, but it's an incredibly effective method for crafting a television miniseries. This technique involves starting with the end in mind and then working your way back to the beginning, ensuring that every plot point, character decision, and thematic element aligns with your ultimate conclusion. By structuring your narrative in this way, you create a cohesive and tightly woven story that feels both purposeful and compelling.

The first step in building a story backwards is to clearly define your ending. This is more than just deciding how the series will conclude; it's about understanding the emotional and narrative impact you want to leave with your audience. What is the final image or moment that will resonate most deeply with viewers? What themes will be crystallized in these closing scenes? Once you have a firm grasp of your ending, you can begin to plot the steps that lead to this moment.

One of the key benefits of working backwards is that it allows you to create a strong, inevitable progression toward your conclusion. Every scene, every character arc, and every plot twist is designed to build toward the final outcome. This method helps to eliminate any narrative flabbiness—those extraneous subplots or scenes that might distract from the central story. Instead, your series becomes a streamlined journey with a clear destination, where each element serves a specific purpose.

To start structuring your narrative backwards, begin by identifying the major plot points that must occur to lead to your ending. These might include the climax, key character decisions, and significant turning points. Once these major moments are established, you can begin to fill in the gaps, working your way back to the series' beginning. This process might feel a bit like reverse engineering a mystery: you know where you need to end up, and now you're figuring out how all the pieces fit together to get there.

As you work backwards, pay special attention to character development. Just as the plot should progress toward your ending, so too should your characters' arcs. Consider where your characters are at the series' conclusion—how have they changed, what have they learned, and what challenges have they overcome? Now, think about what needs to happen in the narrative for them to reach this point. This approach ensures that your characters' journeys feel organic and satisfying, as each step in their development is a direct response to the events of the story.

Building the story backwards also allows you to strategically plant seeds throughout the series that will pay off in the finale. By knowing where the story is headed, you can introduce subtle hints, foreshadowing, and thematic elements early on that will come full circle by the end. These narrative echoes create a sense of cohesion and depth, making the story feel richer and more rewarding for viewers. For example, a seemingly innocuous detail in the first episode might take on greater significance when revisited in the final episode, giving the audience a satisfying "aha" moment.

Another advantage of this approach is that it helps you manage pacing more effectively. Since you already know the climactic moments and the resolution, you can control the build-up, ensuring that the tension and stakes increase at the right moments. This prevents the story from dragging in the middle or feeling rushed toward the end. Instead, the narrative maintains a steady, engaging rhythm that keeps viewers hooked from start to finish.

When structuring your narrative backwards, it's important to remain flexible. While having a clear plan is essential, you should also be open to discovering new possibilities as you work through the story. Sometimes, as you fill in the details, you might realize that a different path would be more effective or that a character's journey could take an unexpected turn. Embrace these moments of discovery, as they can lead to even more compelling storytelling. However, always check these new developments against your planned ending to ensure they still align with the overall vision.

As you approach the beginning of your series, you'll need to consider how to set up the story in a way that naturally leads to the progression you've planned. The opening episodes should introduce the characters, the world, and the central conflict in a way that hints at the journey to come. However, because you're working backwards, you can ensure that these introductions are not just engaging but also strategically aligned with the conclusion. This creates a sense of symmetry in your storytelling, where the beginning and end of the series feel intrinsically connected.

Finally, remember that building a story backwards is as much about crafting a narrative with a strong spine as it is about creating an emotional experience for your audience. The structure should support the emotional beats of the story, guiding viewers through the highs and lows of the characters' journeys. By working backwards, you can ensure that these emotional beats hit at just the right moments, leading to a powerful and memorable conclusion.

In conclusion, structuring your narrative by building the story backwards is a highly effective strategy for writing a television miniseries. It allows you to create a cohesive, well-paced story with a strong sense of purpose and direction. By starting with the end in mind and carefully mapping out the steps that lead there, you can craft a series that feels both inevitable and surprising, providing viewers with a rich and rewarding experience from beginning to end. This approach not only strengthens the narrative but also enhances character development, thematic depth, and emotional impact, ensuring that your miniseries leaves a lasting impression.

# The Core Idea: Defining Your Miniseries Concept

The foundation of any successful television miniseries lies in a strong, clear core idea. This core idea is the heart of your miniseries, the central concept around which every aspect of your story will revolve. Defining this concept is one of the most critical steps in the creative process, as it will guide your narrative choices, character development, and thematic exploration. A well-defined core idea provides a solid framework for your series, ensuring that it remains focused, engaging, and resonant with your audience.

To begin defining your miniseries concept, you first need to identify the central theme or message you want to explore. This could be a universal human experience, a particular moral or philosophical question, or a unique perspective on a specific issue. The theme should be something that you are passionate about, as this passion will fuel your writing and help you create a compelling narrative. Ask yourself: What do I want to say with this story? What emotions or thoughts do I want to evoke in my audience? The answers to these questions will help you hone in on your core idea.

Once you have a theme in mind, consider how it can be translated into a story that is both engaging and suited to the miniseries format. The miniseries structure—typically consisting of a limited number of episodes—lends itself well to stories that are complex and layered but also have a clear beginning, middle, and end. Your core idea should be something that can be fully explored within this timeframe, allowing you to delve deeply into the characters, setting, and plot without overstaying your welcome.

At this stage, it's also important to consider the genre and tone of your miniseries. The genre will help shape how your core idea is presented and how the audience will engage with it. Whether it's a historical drama, a sci-fi thriller, a dark comedy, or a character-driven drama, the genre will dictate the narrative conventions and audience expectations you'll need to navigate. Similarly, the tone—whether it's light-hearted, serious, gritty, or whimsical—will influence the way your core idea is communicated and how it resonates emotionally with viewers.

With your theme, genre, and tone in mind, it's time to distill your concept into a clear and concise premise. This premise should capture the essence of your miniseries in a single sentence or two. It's the elevator pitch that encapsulates what your series is about and why it matters. For example, if your theme is about the moral complexities of power, your premise might be something like: "A high-ranking official navigates the treacherous waters of political intrigue and corruption, struggling to maintain their integrity as they climb the ranks." This premise immediately tells us what the story is about, who the central character is, and hints at the moral dilemmas that will be explored.

The strength of your core idea also depends on its originality and relevance. While it's true that there are no entirely new stories, the way you approach your theme, the unique perspective you bring to the table, and the specific details of your world and characters are what will make your miniseries stand out. Think about how your concept offers a fresh take on familiar ideas, or how it addresses issues that are particularly relevant to today's audience. Originality doesn't necessarily mean inventing something entirely new; it can also mean combining existing elements in a novel way or exploring a well-worn theme from a different angle.

As you refine your core idea, it's also crucial to consider its scalability and adaptability. A strong miniseries concept should be able to sustain interest over the course of multiple episodes, offering enough depth and complexity to keep the audience engaged from start to finish. This means that your core idea should be rich enough to generate multiple subplots, character arcs, and narrative twists, while still maintaining a clear through-line.

Additionally, consider how your concept might evolve during the writing process. While it's important to start with a strong, well-defined idea, you should also remain open to new possibilities and discoveries as you develop the story.

Another key aspect of defining your miniseries concept is understanding your target audience. Who are you writing for? What are their expectations, and how can you meet or subvert them in a way that enhances the storytelling experience? Knowing your audience will help you tailor your concept to their interests and preferences, ensuring that your miniseries resonates with the people who are most likely to watch it. This doesn't mean pandering to the audience, but rather being aware of the cultural context in which your series will be received and finding ways to connect with viewers on a meaningful level.

Once you've solidified your core idea, it's time to start expanding on it, exploring the different ways it can be brought to life in your miniseries. This involves fleshing out the characters who will embody your themes, the world in which your story will take place, and the plot that will drive the narrative forward. However, throughout this process, always keep your core idea at the forefront of your mind. It should be the guiding light that informs every creative decision, ensuring that your series remains cohesive and true to its central vision.

In conclusion, defining your miniseries concept is a critical step that lays the foundation for the entire writing process. A strong core idea provides a clear direction for your narrative, characters, and themes, ensuring that your miniseries is focused, engaging, and resonant. By starting with a well-defined concept, you set the stage for a story that not only captures the audience's attention but also leaves a lasting impact. As you move forward with your writing, let this core idea guide you, providing a solid anchor that keeps your series grounded in its purpose and potential.

# Balancing Big Budget and Small Budget Productions

When writing a television miniseries, one of the most significant considerations is how to balance the realities of budget constraints with your creative vision. Whether you're working with a large or small budget, understanding how to navigate these financial parameters is crucial for ensuring that your story is not only compelling but also feasible to produce. Striking the right balance between big-budget aspirations and small-budget limitations can make the difference between a successful miniseries and one that falls short of its potential.

First, it's important to recognize that budget constraints are not necessarily a bad thing. In fact, they can be a source of creative inspiration, pushing you to think outside the box and come up with innovative solutions that might not have occurred to you otherwise. Whether you're working with a generous budget or a more modest one, the key is to make the most of what you have while staying true to the core of your story.

When planning your miniseries, start by assessing the scope of your narrative. Consider the scale of the settings, the number of characters, and the complexity of the plot. A big-budget production might allow for elaborate set designs, extensive special effects, and a large ensemble cast, while a smaller budget might require a more intimate, character-driven story set in fewer locations. Understanding the scale of your story will help you determine how to allocate resources effectively and where you might need to make adjustments.

One of the most effective ways to balance big-budget and small-budget considerations is to focus on the strengths of your story. Identify the elements that are essential to the narrative and invest in those areas. For example, if your miniseries hinges on powerful performances and character development, prioritize casting talented actors who can bring depth and nuance to their roles. If the story relies on a particular setting or atmosphere, consider allocating more of the budget to location scouting or set design to create an immersive environment. By concentrating your resources on the most important aspects of your story, you can ensure that your miniseries has a strong foundation, regardless of budget.

Another key strategy is to be strategic with your use of special effects and action sequences. While big-budget productions often feature elaborate CGI and high-octane action scenes, these elements can quickly drain a small budget. However, this doesn't mean you need to abandon these ideas altogether. Instead, consider how you can achieve similar effects with more practical, cost-effective methods. For example, practical effects, clever camera angles, and creative editing can often be just as impactful as expensive CGI, if not more so. Additionally, you can use suggestion and implication to convey the scale of events without actually showing them, allowing the audience's imagination to fill in the gaps.

When working with a smaller budget, it's also important to be mindful of the number of locations and sets used in your miniseries. Each new location or set design adds to the overall cost of production, so consider how you can tell your story using a limited number of settings. One approach is to use multipurpose locations—spaces that can be dressed or shot differently to represent various places within the story. This not only saves money but also allows for a more streamlined production process.

In terms of casting, big-budget productions often have the advantage of attracting well-known actors, which can boost the visibility and appeal of the miniseries. However, small-budget productions can also benefit from thoughtful casting choices. Emerging talent or lesser-known actors can bring fresh energy and authenticity to the roles, often at a lower cost. Additionally, a smaller, more focused cast can create a more intimate and intense viewing experience, which can be particularly effective in character-driven dramas.

Balancing budget considerations also involves making smart choices about the length and structure of your miniseries. A shorter series with fewer episodes might allow for higher production values within each episode, while a longer series might require spreading resources more thinly. Consider how the story you want to tell aligns with the budget available—can it be effectively told in fewer episodes, or does it require a longer format to do it justice? Finding the right balance here will help you create a miniseries that feels complete and satisfying without overextending your resources.

Collaboration with the production team is another crucial aspect of balancing budget and creative vision. Working closely with directors, producers, and other key personnel can help you identify cost-saving opportunities without sacrificing quality. For example, an experienced director might have ideas for shooting certain scenes more efficiently, or a producer might suggest alternative locations that offer similar visual impact at a lower cost. Open communication and collaboration can lead to creative solutions that enhance the overall production while staying within budget. When faced with budget limitations, it's also essential to embrace the art of compromise. While it's natural to want to bring every aspect of your vision to life, some elements may need to be scaled back or reimagined to fit within the financial constraints. Rather than viewing these compromises as sacrifices, think of them as opportunities to refine and focus your story. Often, the most memorable and impactful moments in a miniseries come from creative problem-solving and working within limitations.

Finally, remember that the quality of a miniseries is not solely determined by its budget. Audiences are drawn to compelling stories, well-developed characters, and emotional resonance, all of which can be achieved regardless of budget. By focusing on the core elements that make your story unique and engaging, you can create a miniseries that resonates with viewers, whether you're working with a Hollywood-sized budget or a more modest one.

In conclusion, balancing big-budget and small-budget productions requires a combination of strategic planning, creative problem-solving, and a clear understanding of your story's priorities. By making thoughtful choices about where to allocate resources, embracing practical effects and multipurpose locations, and collaborating closely with your production team, you can bring your vision to life in a way that is both financially feasible and artistically satisfying. Whether you're working with a large or small budget, the key is to stay true to the heart of your story, ensuring that it shines through in every aspect of the production.

# Writing for Impact: Crafting Visual Moments

In television miniseries, visual storytelling is just as important, if not more so, than the dialogue and plot. Crafting powerful visual moments is essential for creating a lasting impact on your audience, as these moments often linger in the minds of viewers long after the series ends. Writing for impact means thinking beyond the words on the page and imagining how scenes will play out visually. It involves leveraging the full spectrum of cinematic tools—composition, lighting, camera movement, and more—to create moments that are both emotionally resonant and visually striking.

When crafting visual moments, it's crucial to start with the core of your story: the emotions, themes, and character dynamics that drive the narrative. These elements should inform the visual language of your miniseries. For example, if your story is about isolation, you might use wide, empty landscapes or sparse, desaturated interiors to reflect the character's inner world. If your theme revolves around power and control, you might employ tight framing or sharp contrasts in lighting to convey tension and dominance. By aligning your visual choices with the thematic heart of your story, you create a cohesive and immersive viewing experience.

One of the most effective ways to create impactful visual moments is through the careful use of symbolism and imagery. Symbols—objects, colors, or even specific visual motifs—can add layers of meaning to your scenes. A recurring visual motif, such as a specific color or object that appears at key moments, can tie together different parts of the narrative and deepen the audience's understanding of the characters and themes. For instance, a recurring shot of a locked door might symbolize the protagonist's emotional barriers, with the door finally opening at a crucial moment of character development. These visual symbols can be subtle, yet they leave a lasting impression, enriching the storytelling experience.

Another technique for crafting visual moments is to consider the composition of each shot. The way you frame a scene can drastically alter its emotional impact. A character shown in a wide shot, dwarfed by their surroundings, can evoke feelings of loneliness or insignificance, while a close-up of a character's face during a moment of intense emotion can draw the audience into their inner world. Experimenting with different angles, perspectives, and compositions can help you find the most powerful way to tell each part of your story. For example, a high-angle shot looking down on a character can make them appear vulnerable, while a low-angle shot looking up can make them seem powerful or threatening.

Lighting is another critical element in creating visually impactful moments. The quality, direction, and color of light can set the tone for a scene and influence how the audience perceives it. Harsh, direct lighting can create sharp shadows and a sense of danger or mystery, while soft, diffused lighting can evoke warmth, nostalgia, or tranquility. Similarly, the use of color in lighting can convey different emotions—blue tones might suggest melancholy or coldness, while warm tones like red or orange can evoke passion, anger, or comfort. By thinking about how lighting can enhance the mood and atmosphere of your scenes, you can create visuals that resonate more deeply with viewers.

Camera movement is another tool that can enhance the impact of your visual moments. The way the camera moves—or doesn't move—can influence how the audience experiences the action. A slow, deliberate zoom can build tension or draw attention to a particular detail, while a sudden, jarring camera shake can heighten a moment of chaos or fear.

Tracking shots that follow a character can create a sense of immersion, making the audience feel as though they are part of the action. Conversely, a static camera can create a feeling of stillness or inevitability, particularly in moments of contemplation or revelation. By being deliberate with camera movements, you can control the pacing and emotional rhythm of your scenes.

In addition to these technical elements, the use of silence and sound can also contribute to the impact of visual moments. Sometimes, the absence of sound can be just as powerful as its presence. A scene that is completely silent, save for the ambient noise of the setting, can heighten tension and focus the viewer's attention on the visual elements. On the other hand, strategic use of sound effects or music can enhance the emotional weight of a visual moment. For example, the slow, echoing footsteps of a character approaching a crucial decision can build suspense, while a sudden crescendo of music can punctuate a dramatic reveal. By carefully considering the relationship between sound and visuals, you can create moments that are both visually and aurally memorable.

To craft truly impactful visual moments, it's also important to think about pacing and timing. The buildup to a visual climax is just as important as the moment itself. A well-timed reveal, where the camera lingers just long enough before showing something important, can create a powerful sense of anticipation. Conversely, cutting away too quickly or revealing too much too soon can diminish the impact. Balancing the timing of these moments—when to show something and when to hold back—can significantly enhance the emotional effect of your visual storytelling.

One final consideration is the emotional journey of your characters. Visual moments should not exist in isolation; they should be integrated into the character's development and the overall narrative arc. Think about how a particular visual moment reflects or catalyzes a change in your character. A visually stunning scene should also carry emotional weight, whether it's a moment of realization, transformation, or conflict. By grounding these moments in the characters' emotional journeys, you ensure that they are not just beautiful images but also meaningful parts of the story.

In conclusion, writing for impact in a television miniseries requires a deep understanding of how visual elements can enhance storytelling. By carefully crafting visual moments—through symbolism, composition, lighting, camera movement, and sound—you can create scenes that resonate on multiple levels, leaving a lasting impression on your audience. These moments should be more than just visually striking; they should also serve the story, reflecting the themes and emotional journeys of your characters. When done effectively, these visual moments can elevate your miniseries, turning it into a memorable and impactful viewing experience that stays with the audience long after the final credits roll.

# From Idea to Plot: Mapping Out the Miniseries

Taking a miniseries from an initial idea to a fully developed plot is a process that requires careful planning, creativity, and a deep understanding of storytelling. Mapping out your miniseries involves transforming your core concept into a structured narrative that will captivate audiences from the first episode to the last. This process is about creating a roadmap that guides the development of your characters, the unfolding of your plot, and the exploration of your themes. By mapping out your miniseries, you ensure that every element of the story works together to create a cohesive and engaging experience.

The first step in this process is to revisit your core idea, the central concept that you've defined for your miniseries. This idea serves as the foundation for everything that follows, so it's essential to keep it at the forefront of your mind as you begin to build out the plot. Ask yourself: What is the essence of my story? What message or experience do I want to convey to the audience? Understanding the heart of your idea will help you make decisions about the direction of the plot and the development of your characters.

Once you've solidified your core idea, the next step is to start brainstorming the major beats of your story. These are the key moments that define the arc of your miniseries—events that will drive the narrative forward and shape the characters' journeys. In a miniseries, these beats are typically spread across a limited number of episodes, so it's important to ensure that each one is significant and contributes to the overall story. As you brainstorm, think about the progression of the plot: What happens at the beginning? How does the conflict escalate? What are the turning points that will keep the audience engaged? And most importantly, how does the story resolve?

One effective method for mapping out these major beats is to use the classic three-act structure, which can be easily adapted for a miniseries format. In this structure, the first act introduces the world, characters, and central conflict; the second act develops the conflict, introducing complications and escalating tension; and the third act brings the story to a climax and resolution.

For a miniseries, you might consider each act corresponding to a set of episodes, with the climax and resolution unfolding in the final episodes. This structure provides a clear framework that helps you organize your ideas and ensure that the story builds to a satisfying conclusion.

After identifying the major beats, it's time to start fleshing out the plot in more detail. This involves thinking about the individual episodes and how they contribute to the overall narrative. Each episode should have its own mini-arc—a beginning, middle, and end—that contributes to the larger story. As you outline each episode, consider how it advances the plot, deepens the characters, and explores the themes you've established. This is also the time to think about pacing: How will you balance action with quieter moments of character development? How will you maintain tension and keep the audience engaged from one episode to the next?

Character development is a crucial part of mapping out your miniseries. Your characters are the driving force behind the plot, and their actions, decisions, and growth will shape the direction of the story. Start by outlining the arcs of your main characters: Where do they begin at the start of the series, and where do they end up by the conclusion?

What challenges and conflicts do they face along the way? How do their relationships with other characters evolve? By plotting out these character arcs in tandem with the plot, you ensure that the narrative feels organic and that the characters' journeys are integral to the story.

In addition to the main plot and character arcs, consider the subplots that will enrich your miniseries. Subplots are secondary storylines that complement the main plot and often provide additional insight into the characters or themes. They can also serve to break up the pacing of the main narrative, providing variety and keeping the audience engaged. When developing subplots, think about how they can intersect with the main plot, creating moments of tension or revelation that enhance the overall story. However, be mindful not to introduce too many subplots, as they can detract from the focus of the miniseries if not carefully managed.

As you continue to map out the plot, it's important to think about the themes you want to explore. Themes are the underlying ideas or messages that give your story depth and resonance. Whether it's a commentary on society, an exploration of human nature, or a meditation on a particular moral dilemma, your themes should be woven into the fabric of the plot and character development. Consider how each episode and plot point can reflect or enhance these themes, making them an integral part of the narrative rather than an afterthought.

Another critical aspect of plotting your miniseries is considering the pacing of the story. Pacing refers to the rhythm of the narrative—how quickly or slowly the plot unfolds, how tension builds, and how moments of intensity are balanced with quieter scenes. Good pacing keeps the audience engaged, preventing the story from dragging or feeling rushed. As you map out the plot, think about how to vary the pacing to create a dynamic viewing experience. For example, you might start with a slower, more deliberate pace to establish the world and characters, then gradually increase the tempo as the conflict escalates, culminating in a fast-paced climax.

Once you've mapped out the major beats, episodes, and character arcs, it's time to review the overall structure of your miniseries. This is your opportunity to step back and look at the big picture: Does the plot flow logically from one episode to the next? Are the character arcs satisfying and well-integrated into the narrative? Does the pacing keep the audience engaged? Are the themes consistently explored throughout the series? By answering these questions, you can identify any gaps or inconsistencies in the plot and make adjustments before moving on to the writing phase.

In conclusion, mapping out a miniseries is a meticulous but rewarding process that involves transforming your core idea into a structured and engaging plot. By carefully planning the major beats, character arcs, and thematic elements, you create a roadmap that guides the development of your story, ensuring that every episode contributes to the overall narrative. This process not only helps you stay organized but also allows you to craft a miniseries that is cohesive, compelling, and emotionally resonant. As you move from idea to plot, keep your creative vision in mind, and let it guide you in building a story that will captivate and inspire your audience.

# Character Foundations: Developing the Protagonist

The protagonist is the beating heart of your miniseries, the character around whom the entire narrative revolves. Developing a compelling and multi-dimensional protagonist is crucial to creating a story that resonates with viewers and keeps them engaged from beginning to end. The protagonist is more than just the main character; they are the lens through which the audience experiences the world of your miniseries, and their journey often reflects the central themes and conflicts of the story. In this chapter, we'll explore the process of building a strong foundation for your protagonist, focusing on their backstory, motivations, flaws, and growth.

The first step in developing your protagonist is to establish their backstory. This is the history that shapes who they are at the beginning of your miniseries—the experiences, relationships, and events that have influenced their personality, beliefs, and behavior. A well-developed backstory provides context for the protagonist's actions and decisions, making them more relatable and understandable to the audience. As you create your protagonist's backstory, consider the following questions: What defining moments in their past have shaped their current worldview? What personal traumas or triumphs have left a lasting impact? How do their past experiences influence their goals, fears, and relationships?

While it's important to develop a rich backstory, remember that not all of it needs to be explicitly revealed to the audience. Instead, use the backstory to inform the character's actions and dialogue throughout the series. Subtle hints, references, or behaviors can give the audience insight into the protagonist's past without overwhelming them with exposition. This approach allows the backstory to add depth to the character while keeping the focus on the present narrative.

Next, consider the protagonist's motivations. These are the driving forces behind their actions—the desires, needs, and goals that propel them forward in the story. Understanding your protagonist's motivations is key to writing a character who feels authentic and relatable. Ask yourself: What does the protagonist want more than anything else? What are they willing to do to achieve it? Are their motivations driven by external factors (such as a quest for justice, revenge, or love) or internal needs (such as self-acceptance, redemption, or freedom)? A well-defined motivation not only gives the protagonist a clear direction but also creates a sense of urgency and stakes, making the audience invested in their journey.

However, a protagonist's motivations should not be static. Over the course of the miniseries, they may evolve as the character learns, grows, and faces new challenges. This evolution is a crucial part of the protagonist's character arc—the journey they undergo from the beginning of the series to the end. A strong character arc is one where the protagonist is changed by the events of the story, emerging as a different person than they were at the start. This change can be positive (growth, self-discovery, redemption) or negative (corruption, loss, disillusionment), depending on the themes and tone of your miniseries.

In addition to motivations, it's important to define your protagonist's flaws. Flaws are the imperfections, weaknesses, or internal conflicts that make your character human and relatable. A flawless protagonist is often less interesting and harder for the audience to connect with because they lack the struggles and vulnerabilities that define real people.

When developing your protagonist, think about what flaws might complicate their journey:

Do they have a fear of failure that holds them back?

Are they overly ambitious, leading to ethical compromises?

Do they struggle with trust, making it difficult for them to form meaningful relationships?

These flaws should be integral to the character's arc, influencing their decisions and creating obstacles they must overcome.

Flaws also provide opportunities for growth. As the protagonist confronts their flaws throughout the miniseries, they may learn valuable lessons, change their behavior, or come to terms with their limitations. This process of confronting and overcoming flaws is often at the heart of the character's development, adding depth and emotional resonance to the story. It also creates tension and conflict, both internal and external, which keeps the audience engaged.

Another important aspect of developing the protagonist is their relationships with other characters. These relationships are crucial in revealing different facets of the protagonist's personality and in driving the plot forward.

Consider the dynamics between your protagonist and the supporting characters:

Who are their allies?

Who are their adversaries?

How do these relationships challenge or support the protagonist?

The protagonist's interactions with others should reveal their strengths, weaknesses, and complexities, adding layers to their character.

The antagonist, in particular, plays a significant role in shaping the protagonist's journey. A well-developed antagonist is not just an obstacle for the protagonist to overcome, but a character who challenges the protagonist's beliefs, motivations, and values. This conflict between protagonist and antagonist can drive much of the narrative tension in your miniseries. The antagonist should be a foil to the protagonist, highlighting their flaws and pushing them to grow or change in some way.

While it's important to focus on the protagonist's development, it's equally important to ensure that they remain relatable and sympathetic, even if they make mistakes or have morally ambiguous traits. The audience should be able to see themselves in the protagonist, or at least understand and empathize with their struggles. This connection is what keeps viewers invested in the character's journey, rooting for their success or redemption.

Finally, as you develop your protagonist, think about how they embody the themes of your miniseries. The protagonist's journey should reflect the central ideas and messages you want to convey. For example, if your miniseries explores themes of identity and self-discovery, the protagonist's arc might involve coming to terms with who they truly are and rejecting the expectations placed upon them by others. If the theme is about the corrupting influence of power, the protagonist might start as an idealistic character who gradually becomes more ruthless as they gain power. By aligning the protagonist's development with the thematic core of your miniseries, you create a story that is not only compelling but also meaningful.

In conclusion, developing a strong protagonist is a crucial step in creating a successful television miniseries. By carefully crafting their backstory, motivations, flaws, relationships, and character arc, you lay the foundation for a character who is complex, relatable, and deeply engaging. The protagonist's journey should be at the heart of your story, driving the plot forward and exploring the themes that are central to your miniseries. As you develop your protagonist, keep in mind that they are the audience's guide through your story, and their growth and development are what will ultimately make your miniseries resonate with viewers.

# The Antagonist's Journey: Creating a Compelling Adversary

In any compelling narrative, the antagonist plays a crucial role in shaping the protagonist's journey, providing the conflict and obstacles that drive the story forward. A well-developed antagonist is not just a villain to be defeated; they are a fully realized character with their own motivations, desires, and complexities. In many cases, the antagonist's journey is just as important as the protagonist's, as it mirrors, contrasts, or challenges the protagonist's path. Crafting a compelling adversary involves understanding their role in the story, exploring their backstory, motivations, and flaws, and ensuring that their presence elevates the overall narrative.

To begin creating a compelling antagonist, it's essential to understand their function within the story. The antagonist's primary role is to oppose the protagonist, creating conflict that drives the narrative. However, this opposition should be more than just a simple obstacle. A great antagonist challenges the protagonist on multiple levels—physically, emotionally, intellectually, and morally. They force the protagonist to confront their own flaws, question their beliefs, and grow in response to the challenges they face. The more complex and formidable the antagonist, the more satisfying the protagonist's journey becomes.

One of the first steps in developing your antagonist is to give them a clear and compelling motivation. Just like the protagonist, the antagonist needs a reason for their actions, a driving force that propels them through the story. This motivation should be rooted in their backstory—events and experiences that have shaped their worldview and led them to oppose the protagonist. Consider what the antagonist wants to achieve, why they want it, and how far they are willing to go to get it. A well-motivated antagonist is not evil for the sake of being evil; rather, they believe they are justified in their actions, even if those actions are harmful or destructive.

It's also important to consider the antagonist's perspective. In their own story, they are often the hero, the protagonist of their own narrative. This perspective adds depth and complexity to the character, making them more than just a one-dimensional villain. For example, an antagonist might believe that their actions are necessary for the greater good, even if they involve morally questionable decisions.

By exploring the antagonist's perspective, you can create a character who is relatable and even sympathetic, despite their opposition to the protagonist. This complexity can make the conflict between the protagonist and antagonist more engaging and thought-provoking.

A compelling antagonist should also have their own character arc—a journey that mirrors, contrasts, or complements the protagonist's arc. This arc could involve the antagonist becoming more ruthless or desperate as the story progresses, or it could involve moments of doubt, vulnerability, or even redemption. The antagonist's journey should be dynamic, showing how they are affected by the events of the story and how their relationship with the protagonist evolves. This arc adds layers to the character and makes their eventual confrontation with the protagonist more meaningful.

Flaws are another essential element of a well-developed antagonist. Just as the protagonist has flaws that complicate their journey, the antagonist should have weaknesses or vulnerabilities that affect their decisions and actions. These flaws can humanize the antagonist, making them more relatable and less like a caricature. For example, an antagonist driven by a desire for power might be plagued by insecurity or a fear of failure, leading them to make reckless or self-destructive choices. These flaws can also create opportunities for the protagonist to gain the upper hand, adding tension and uncertainty to the story.

The relationship between the protagonist and antagonist is at the heart of many great stories. This relationship should be complex and multifaceted, reflecting the deeper themes of the narrative. In some cases, the antagonist might be a dark mirror of the protagonist—a character who embodies what the protagonist could become if they made different choices. In other cases, the antagonist might represent a specific challenge or fear that the protagonist must overcome. By carefully crafting the dynamic between the protagonist and antagonist, you can create a relationship that is both adversarial and deeply intertwined, where the actions of one character profoundly impact the other.

It's also important to consider how the antagonist fits into the larger thematic framework of your miniseries. The antagonist should embody or challenge the central themes of the story, serving as a catalyst for exploring these themes in greater depth. For example, if your miniseries explores themes of power and corruption, the antagonist might be a powerful figure who has been corrupted by their authority, challenging the protagonist to confront their own relationship with power. By aligning the antagonist with the thematic core of the story, you ensure that their role is integral to the narrative and that their conflict with the protagonist resonates on a deeper level.

When creating a compelling antagonist, it's also helpful to consider their relationships with other characters. The antagonist's interactions with the protagonist, as well as with supporting characters, can reveal different aspects of their personality and motivations. These relationships can add depth to the antagonist's character and create additional layers of conflict within the story. For example, an antagonist who has a complicated relationship with a close ally or a tragic past involving a loved one can become more nuanced and sympathetic, adding emotional complexity to their actions.

As you develop your antagonist, remember that they should be a force to be reckoned with—someone who poses a genuine threat to the protagonist and creates real stakes in the story. A weak or underdeveloped antagonist can undermine the tension and drama of the narrative, making the protagonist's journey feel less significant.

To avoid this, ensure that your antagonist is formidable, with skills, resources, or influence that make them a credible and challenging opponent. This doesn't necessarily mean that the antagonist needs to be physically powerful; they might be intellectually brilliant, socially influential, or morally manipulative. The key is to create an adversary who pushes the protagonist to their limits and forces them to grow in response.

Finally, consider the antagonist's resolution in the story. How does their journey end, and what impact does it have on the protagonist and the overall narrative? The resolution of the antagonist's arc should be satisfying and consistent with the themes and tone of the miniseries. Whether the antagonist is defeated, redeemed, or left in ambiguity, their resolution should feel earned and provide closure to their role in the story. A well-crafted ending for the antagonist can leave a lasting impression on the audience, reinforcing the impact of the conflict and the growth of the protagonist.

In conclusion, creating a compelling antagonist involves more than just crafting a villain for the protagonist to defeat. It requires building a fully realized character with their own motivations, flaws, and arc, whose journey is integral to the overall narrative. A great antagonist challenges the protagonist in meaningful ways, creating conflict that drives the story and explores its deeper themes. By carefully developing the antagonist's backstory, perspective, and relationships, you can create a character who is not only a formidable adversary but also a crucial part of what makes your miniseries compelling and memorable.

# Action and Pacing: Maintaining Momentum

Action and pacing are vital elements in crafting a television miniseries that keeps viewers engaged and invested from start to finish. These elements work hand in hand to ensure that the story flows smoothly, maintaining momentum while allowing for moments of reflection and character development. Striking the right balance between action-packed sequences and quieter, more introspective scenes is key to creating a dynamic and engaging narrative that holds the audience's attention throughout the entire series.

The first step in effectively managing action and pacing is to understand the rhythm of your story. Every narrative has a natural ebb and flow, a rhythm that guides the progression of events and the emotional journey of the characters. Action sequences typically represent the peaks in this rhythm, moments of heightened tension, conflict, or drama that push the plot forward and reveal key aspects of the characters. These sequences are often where the stakes are at their highest, and the characters are forced to confront significant challenges.

To maintain momentum, it's important to space out these action sequences strategically throughout the miniseries. Think of them as anchor points that keep the narrative moving and the audience engaged. Too much action in quick succession can overwhelm the viewer and make the story feel frantic or exhausting. On the other hand, too little action can cause the pacing to drag, leading to a loss of interest. By alternating between action and quieter scenes, you can create a balanced rhythm that keeps the audience on their toes while also allowing time for character development and thematic exploration.


When crafting action sequences, consider how they serve the overall narrative and the development of the characters. Action for the sake of action can feel gratuitous and may detract from the story's impact. Instead, each action sequence should be purposeful, advancing the plot or revealing something new about the characters. For example, a fight scene might not only showcase the protagonist's physical abilities but also highlight their moral dilemma or internal struggle. A chase scene might reveal the antagonist's relentless pursuit or the protagonist's desperation. By infusing action with meaning, you create sequences that are not only exciting but also emotionally and thematically resonant.

The pacing of your miniseries is closely tied to how you handle these action sequences. Pacing refers to the speed at which the story unfolds—the timing of events, the length of scenes, and the overall structure of the narrative. Good pacing keeps the audience engaged by varying the tempo of the story, creating a dynamic and immersive experience. To achieve this, it's important to think about the pacing on both a macro and micro level.

On a macro level, consider the pacing of the entire series. How does the story build from one episode to the next? Where are the major turning points, and how do they affect the overall flow of the narrative? A well-paced miniseries gradually escalates the tension, leading to a climax that feels earned and satisfying. The pacing should allow for peaks and valleys, moments of intensity followed by periods of calm where the characters—and the audience—can catch their breath. This variation in pacing creates a sense of rhythm and progression, making the climax more impactful when it finally arrives.

On a micro level, consider the pacing within individual scenes and episodes. This involves the timing of dialogue, the length of shots, and the transitions between scenes. Quick cuts and rapid-fire dialogue can create a sense of urgency or chaos, while longer takes and slower pacing can build tension or allow for deeper emotional connection. Pay attention to how each scene flows into the next—abrupt changes in pacing can be jarring unless they're intentional and serve a specific purpose. For example, a sudden cut from a slow, contemplative scene to a fast-paced action sequence can heighten the impact of the action, catching the audience off guard and pulling them into the moment.

In addition to managing the rhythm of the story, it's important to consider how action sequences are visually and thematically integrated into the narrative. Action scenes should not exist in isolation; they should be woven into the fabric of the story, reflecting the themes and character arcs you've established. For example, if your miniseries explores themes of survival and sacrifice, the action sequences might involve characters making difficult choices under pressure, with each decision reflecting the larger themes at play. This integration ensures that the action feels like a natural part of the story rather than a detour from it.

Another key aspect of maintaining momentum is ensuring that the stakes are consistently high throughout the miniseries. High stakes create tension and urgency, compelling the audience to keep watching to see how the characters will navigate the challenges they face. These stakes can be physical (life and death situations), emotional (the risk of losing a loved one or failing to achieve a personal goal), or moral (making a choice that goes against the character's values). By raising the stakes as the story progresses, you maintain momentum and keep the audience invested in the outcome.

It's also important to consider the pacing of character development alongside the pacing of the plot. As the action escalates, the characters should evolve in response to the events they experience. This evolution might involve growing stronger, more determined, or more morally conflicted. The key is to ensure that the characters' internal journeys are paced in a way that feels organic and reflective of the challenges they face. For example, a character who starts off hesitant or unsure might become more decisive and confident as they survive each action sequence, while another character might become increasingly disillusioned or desperate.

One effective technique for maintaining momentum is to use cliffhangers or unresolved questions at the end of episodes. These moments of suspense compel the audience to keep watching, eager to see how the situation will be resolved. However, it's important to balance these cliffhangers with moments of resolution, where the audience feels a sense of satisfaction or closure, even if it's temporary. This ebb and flow of tension and resolution is crucial for sustaining momentum without exhausting the audience.

Finally, remember that action and pacing are not just about keeping the audience entertained—they're about serving the story. Every decision about pacing and every action sequence should be in service of the narrative, the characters, and the themes you're exploring. By focusing on the story's needs and maintaining a balance between action and character-driven moments, you can create a miniseries that is both thrilling and deeply engaging, keeping the audience hooked from the first episode to the last.

In conclusion, maintaining momentum in a television miniseries requires careful attention to action and pacing. By strategically placing action sequences, managing the rhythm of the story, and ensuring that each scene serves the overall narrative, you can create a dynamic and engaging viewing experience.

The key is to balance moments of intensity with periods of reflection, allowing the characters and the audience to process what's happening while keeping the story moving forward. With thoughtful planning and execution, you can craft a miniseries that captivates viewers, drawing them into a story that is both exciting and emotionally resonant.

# Setting the Scene: Designing the World of Your Miniseries

The setting of a television miniseries plays a crucial role in shaping the story, defining its atmosphere, and grounding the audience in the world you've created. Whether your miniseries is set in a gritty urban environment, a fantastical otherworld, or a historical era, the design of your world will significantly influence how the story unfolds and how the audience experiences it. Setting the scene involves more than just choosing a location; it's about creating a fully realized world that supports the narrative, enhances the themes, and provides a rich backdrop for the characters' journeys.

The first step in designing the world of your miniseries is to consider how the setting aligns with the core idea and themes of your story. The setting should be more than just a backdrop; it should be an integral part of the narrative that reflects and enhances the story's themes. For example, if your miniseries explores themes of isolation and survival, a remote, harsh environment might serve as a powerful metaphor for the protagonist's internal struggles. If your story is about power and corruption, a bustling, decaying metropolis might reflect the moral decay of its inhabitants. By aligning the setting with the thematic core of your story, you create a world that feels purposeful and resonant.

Once you've determined the thematic role of the setting, it's time to flesh out the details that will bring the world to life. This involves thinking about the physical, cultural, and social aspects of the setting, as well as how they influence the characters and plot. Start by considering the physical environment: What does this world look like? Is it a sprawling city with towering skyscrapers, a quiet rural town surrounded by forests, or a futuristic landscape filled with advanced technology? The physical details of the setting—such as architecture, climate, geography, and natural features—help to establish the mood and tone of the story.

In addition to the physical environment, consider the cultural and social dynamics of your world. What kind of society exists in this setting? What are the norms, values, and beliefs that shape the behavior of its inhabitants? Understanding the cultural context of your setting will help you create characters who feel authentic and grounded in their world. For example, if your miniseries is set in a dystopian future, the societal structure might be oppressive and hierarchical, influencing how the characters interact with each other and with the institutions around them. Alternatively, a setting in a close-knit, rural community might emphasize themes of tradition, family, and belonging.

As you develop the setting, think about how it influences the characters and their actions. The environment should have a direct impact on the story, shaping the challenges the characters face and the choices they make. For example, a character living in a harsh, unforgiving landscape might be hardened and resourceful, while a character in a more idyllic setting might struggle with complacency or a fear of change. The setting can also create external obstacles that drive the plot forward, such as a natural disaster, a political uprising, or a societal taboo.

The visual design of the setting is another critical aspect of world-building. This includes the color palette, lighting, and overall aesthetic of the world, which can significantly influence the mood and tone of the miniseries.

For example, a dark, muted color palette with shadowy lighting might create a sense of mystery or foreboding, while a bright, vibrant aesthetic might convey optimism or surrealism. The visual elements of the setting should be consistent with the story's themes and emotional tone, helping to immerse the audience in the world you've created.

When designing the world of your miniseries, it's important to pay attention to both the broad strokes and the finer details. The broad strokes involve the overall concept and aesthetic of the setting, while the finer details involve the small, specific elements that make the world feel lived-in and authentic. These details might include the texture of a character's clothing, the sound of footsteps on a cobblestone street, or the smell of food cooking in a marketplace. By incorporating sensory details, you can create a more immersive experience for the audience, allowing them to fully engage with the world of the story.

The history of the setting is another important element to consider. Even if the history is not explicitly mentioned in the miniseries, it can inform the design of the world and the behavior of the characters. Think about the events that have shaped the world—wars, revolutions, migrations, technological advancements—and how these events have influenced the current state of the setting. A world with a rich, well-developed history will feel more complex and realistic, adding depth to the story and providing opportunities for subtext and symbolism.

The setting can also play a dynamic role in the narrative, changing and evolving as the story progresses. For example, a city might start off as a symbol of hope and opportunity but gradually become a place of danger and despair as the protagonist's journey unfolds. Alternatively, a seemingly idyllic rural community might reveal darker, hidden secrets as the story progresses. By allowing the setting to evolve in response to the events of the narrative, you can create a more dynamic and engaging world that reflects the characters' growth and the story's escalating tension.

Interaction with the setting is another key element in world-building. Consider how your characters interact with their environment and how the environment, in turn, interacts with them. Do they navigate familiar, comforting spaces, or are they constantly thrust into unfamiliar, hostile territory? The way characters move through and engage with the setting can reveal important aspects of their personality and their relationship with the world around them. For example, a character who confidently navigates a chaotic cityscape might be seen as resourceful and adaptable, while a character who struggles to find their way might be portrayed as vulnerable or out of their depth.

Finally, it's important to remember that the setting is not just a physical space—it's also a psychological space. The environment can reflect the internal states of the characters, serving as an external manifestation of their emotions and thoughts. For example, a stormy, turbulent landscape might mirror a character's inner turmoil, while a calm, serene setting might reflect a moment of peace or resolution. By using the setting as a tool for emotional storytelling, you can create a deeper connection between the characters and the audience, making the world of your miniseries feel more intimate and impactful.

Setting the scene in a television miniseries involves much more than choosing a location; it requires creating a fully realized world that supports and enhances the narrative. By carefully designing the physical, cultural, and social aspects of the setting, and by considering how the environment influences the characters and plot, you can create a world that is both immersive and integral to the story. The setting should not only reflect the themes and mood of the miniseries but also evolve and interact with the characters, creating a dynamic backdrop that adds depth and complexity to the narrative.

# Themes that Resonate: Weaving Deeper Meanings into the Story

Themes are the underlying ideas and messages that give a story depth and resonance. In a television miniseries, themes can elevate the narrative from mere entertainment to a thought-provoking exploration of complex ideas, engaging the audience on both an emotional and intellectual level. Weaving deeper meanings into the story involves identifying the core themes you want to explore and integrating them seamlessly into the plot, characters, and setting. When done effectively, these themes can provide a unifying thread that ties together the various elements of your miniseries, creating a rich and meaningful viewing experience.

The first step in weaving themes into your miniseries is to identify the central ideas you want to explore. These themes should be closely aligned with the core concept of your story and reflect the questions or issues you're most interested in examining. Common themes might include love, power, identity, justice, sacrifice, or redemption, but they can also be more specific or nuanced, such as the impact of technology on human relationships, the cost of ambition, or the nature of truth. Whatever themes you choose, they should be relevant to the characters' journeys and the overall narrative arc.

Once you've identified your themes, the next step is to think about how they can be integrated into the various elements of the story. One of the most effective ways to do this is through your characters. Each character in your miniseries should, in some way, embody or grapple with the central themes. For example, if one of your themes is the corrupting influence of power, your protagonist might start out as an idealistic figure who gradually becomes more morally compromised as they gain power. Meanwhile, the antagonist might represent the extreme end of this theme, having already succumbed to corruption. By placing your characters in situations that force them to confront the thematic issues, you create a narrative that naturally explores these deeper meanings.

Character relationships are another powerful tool for exploring themes. The dynamics between characters—whether they are allies, adversaries, or something in between—can highlight different aspects of the themes you're exploring. For instance, if your miniseries is centered around the theme of loyalty versus betrayal, you might create a central relationship where one character's loyalty is tested, leading to a dramatic betrayal that impacts the entire story. The fallout from this betrayal can then be used to further explore the consequences of loyalty and trust within the broader narrative.

The plot itself is another avenue for weaving themes into your story. The events of the miniseries should reflect and reinforce the themes, creating a sense of cohesion and purpose. For example, if your theme is the cost of revenge, the plot might involve a character's single-minded pursuit of vengeance, with each step they take bringing them closer to a tragic or hollow victory. The choices the characters make and the obstacles they encounter should all be tied back to the central themes, creating a narrative that feels both tightly constructed and deeply meaningful.

In addition to characters and plot, the setting can also play a crucial role in exploring themes. The environment in which your story takes place can reflect the thematic concerns of the narrative, adding another layer of meaning. For example, a dystopian setting might reinforce themes of control, freedom, or survival, while a lush, idyllic landscape might contrast with darker themes of hidden corruption or underlying despair. The way characters interact with their environment can also reflect their relationship to the themes—perhaps a character's struggle to navigate a hostile world mirrors their internal struggle with fear or doubt.

Symbolism is another powerful tool for weaving themes into your miniseries. Symbols are objects, actions, or visual motifs that represent larger ideas or concepts. By carefully choosing symbols that reflect your themes, you can add layers of meaning to your story. For example, a recurring image of a broken mirror might symbolize the theme of fractured identity, while a persistent storm might represent turmoil or conflict. The key to effective symbolism is subtlety—symbols should enrich the narrative without overpowering it or feeling too on-the-nose.

Dialogue is another area where themes can be explored. What your characters say—and what they leave unsaid—can reveal their perspectives on the themes at play. Through dialogue, you can introduce different viewpoints on the thematic issues, allowing characters to debate, reflect on, or question the ideas at the heart of the story. However, it's important to avoid heavy-handed exposition; instead, let the themes emerge naturally through the characters' conversations, actions, and decisions.

Another way to weave themes into your miniseries is through the use of motifs—recurring elements that reinforce the central ideas. These motifs can be visual, auditory, or narrative, and they help to create a sense of unity and coherence within the story. For example, if your theme is the passage of time, you might use motifs like clocks, aging, or changing seasons to underscore this idea. Each time the motif appears, it can deepen the audience's understanding of the theme and its relevance to the characters' journeys.

It's also important to consider how the themes evolve over the course of the miniseries. As the story progresses, the characters' understanding of the themes—and the audience's understanding—should deepen and become more complex. The themes might be introduced in a straightforward way at the beginning of the series, but as the plot unfolds and the characters face new challenges, the themes should be explored from different angles, revealing their nuances and contradictions. By the end of the series, the themes should have been fully explored, leaving the audience with a deeper understanding of the issues at hand.

Finally, remember that themes should be woven into the story in a way that feels organic and natural. While it's important for the themes to be present and meaningful, they should not overshadow the characters or the plot. The best thematic storytelling is subtle, allowing the themes to emerge naturally from the narrative rather than being imposed on it. This approach creates a story that is rich in meaning but also engaging and entertaining, resonating with the audience on multiple levels.

In conclusion, weaving deeper meanings into your miniseries involves integrating themes into every aspect of the story—from characters and plot to setting and dialogue. By carefully crafting a narrative that reflects and explores these themes, you create a miniseries that is not only compelling but also thought-provoking and emotionally resonant. The themes should be an integral part of the story, guiding the characters' journeys, influencing the plot, and enriching the world of the miniseries. When done effectively, this approach creates a story that resonates with viewers long after the final episode, leaving them with something to think about and reflect on.

# The Hero's Odyssey: Crafting a Transformational Journey

The Hero's Odyssey, also known as the Hero's Journey, is a timeless narrative structure that has been used in storytelling across cultures and eras. At its core, the Hero's Odyssey is about transformation—a character's journey from the ordinary to the extraordinary, from ignorance to knowledge, from weakness to strength. This structure is particularly powerful in a television miniseries, where the extended format allows for deep character development and a complex, evolving narrative. Crafting a transformational journey for your protagonist involves not only following the traditional stages of the Hero's Odyssey but also adapting them to fit the unique needs of your story and the themes you wish to explore.

The Hero's Odyssey typically begins with the protagonist in their ordinary world, a familiar setting where they are comfortable but unchallenged. This stage is crucial for establishing the character's baseline—their strengths, weaknesses, fears, and desires. It gives the audience a sense of who the protagonist is before the journey begins, making the transformation that follows all the more impactful. As you craft this stage, consider what aspects of the protagonist's life will be upended by the journey. What is missing in their life that the journey will help them discover? What flaws or limitations will the journey force them to confront?

The journey begins in earnest with the "Call to Adventure," an event or realization that disrupts the protagonist's ordinary world and propels them into the unknown. This call is often a challenge or a crisis that the protagonist cannot ignore—something that forces them out of their comfort zone and sets the plot in motion. The Call to Adventure should be compelling and urgent, creating a sense of necessity that drives the protagonist forward. It's important to clearly define what is at stake for the protagonist—what they stand to lose if they refuse the call and what they hope to gain by accepting it.

Often, the protagonist initially refuses the call, a stage known as the "Refusal of the Call." This hesitation can stem from fear, self-doubt, or a reluctance to leave the safety of the ordinary world. This stage adds depth to the protagonist's character, showing their vulnerability and making their eventual decision to embark on the journey more meaningful. The Refusal of the Call also builds tension, as the audience understands the stakes and eagerly anticipates the protagonist's choice. When crafting this stage, consider what internal conflicts or external pressures might cause the protagonist to hesitate. How do these conflicts foreshadow the challenges they will face on their journey?

Once the protagonist accepts the call, they often encounter a "Mentor" figure who provides guidance, tools, or knowledge that will help them on their journey. The Mentor can be a literal character—a wise elder, a seasoned warrior, or a trusted friend—or it can be symbolic, representing the protagonist's inner wisdom or a new understanding they gain. The Mentor stage is an opportunity to introduce important themes and set the stage for the protagonist's transformation. It's also a chance to explore the relationships that will shape the protagonist's journey, whether the Mentor is a supportive ally or a challenging figure who pushes the protagonist to grow.

As the protagonist crosses the threshold into the unknown, they enter the "Special World" of the journey—a place that is unfamiliar, dangerous, and full of new challenges. This is where the bulk of the action takes place, as the protagonist faces trials, makes allies and enemies, and begins to change in response to their experiences.

The Special World should be a stark contrast to the ordinary world, reflecting the new and heightened stakes of the journey. It's important to design this world in a way that tests the protagonist's strengths and exposes their weaknesses, forcing them to confront their deepest fears and desires.

Throughout the journey, the protagonist will face a series of tests and obstacles that challenge their abilities and resolve. These trials are often physical, but they can also be emotional or moral, testing the protagonist's values and beliefs. Each test should bring the protagonist closer to the ultimate goal of the journey while also pushing them further from their old self. This stage of the Hero's Odyssey is where the protagonist's transformation begins in earnest, as they learn new skills, gain new insights, and grow in ways they never anticipated. When crafting these trials, consider how each one contributes to the protagonist's growth and how it prepares them for the final challenge.

The climax of the Hero's Odyssey is the "Ordeal," a major crisis or confrontation that represents the protagonist's greatest challenge. This is the moment where everything is on the line, and the protagonist must draw on everything they have learned to overcome the obstacle. The Ordeal is often a life-or-death situation, either literally or metaphorically, and it forces the protagonist to confront their deepest fears. This stage should be intense and emotionally charged, as the protagonist faces the possibility of failure and the consequences that would follow. The Ordeal is also a turning point in the protagonist's transformation—whether they succeed or fail, they will never be the same after this moment.

Following the Ordeal is the "Reward," where the protagonist achieves the goal of the journey or gains something of great value. This reward might be a literal object, such as a treasure or a weapon, or it might be something intangible, such as knowledge, wisdom, or self-acceptance. The Reward stage is a moment of triumph, but it is also a moment of reflection, as the protagonist realizes what they have gained and what they have lost. This stage should feel like a culmination of the protagonist's efforts, but it should also set the stage for the final act of the journey—the Return.

The final stages of the Hero's Odyssey involve the protagonist's return to the ordinary world, now changed by their experiences. This return is not always easy—there may be final challenges to overcome, and the protagonist may struggle to reintegrate into their old life. However, the protagonist is now equipped with the knowledge and strength they gained on their journey, allowing them to face these challenges with newfound confidence. The Return should feel like a resolution, bringing the protagonist's journey full circle while also showing how they have been transformed by their experiences.

The last stage of the Hero's Odyssey is the "Return with the Elixir," where the protagonist brings back something of value to their ordinary world. This "elixir" might be a literal object, a new understanding, or a changed perspective. It represents the culmination of the protagonist's journey and the lasting impact of their transformation. The Return with the Elixir is a powerful moment, as it shows the protagonist's growth and the way their journey has enriched both themselves and their world. This stage also provides closure, allowing the audience to see the full arc of the protagonist's transformation.

While the Hero's Odyssey provides a classic framework for storytelling, it's important to remember that this structure is not a rigid formula. Each story is unique, and the stages of the Hero's Odyssey can be adapted, combined, or even subverted to suit the needs of your miniseries. The key is to focus on the transformational journey of your protagonist—how they grow, change, and ultimately achieve a new understanding of themselves and their world. Each stage of the journey should challenge the protagonist, forcing them to confront their fears, grow in new ways, and ultimately achieve a deeper understanding of themselves and their world. The Hero's Odyssey is a powerful tool for storytelling, and when used effectively, it can elevate your miniseries into a memorable and impactful viewing experience.

# The Pilot Episode

The pilot episode of a television miniseries is perhaps the most critical component of the entire series. It's your first and best chance to capture the audience's attention, introduce them to your world, and set the tone for the rest of the story. A successful pilot episode lays the foundation for the narrative arc, establishes key characters, and hooks viewers with a compelling premise that makes them eager to continue watching. Crafting a pilot that accomplishes all of this requires careful planning, strategic storytelling, and a clear understanding of what makes your miniseries unique.

The first task in creating an effective pilot episode is to start with a strong, attention-grabbing opening. The opening moments of the pilot are crucial—they set the tone, establish the genre, and give the audience their first impression of the world and characters. Whether it's a dramatic action scene, a poignant character moment, or a mysterious event, the opening should immediately engage viewers and pique their curiosity. It's important to create a sense of urgency or intrigue that compels the audience to keep watching, while also hinting at the larger story that will unfold over the course of the series.

As you craft the opening, consider how you can introduce the core elements of your miniseries—its themes, tone, and style—in a way that is both engaging and informative. For example, if your miniseries is a tense political thriller, you might open with a high-stakes negotiation or a covert operation gone wrong. If it's a character-driven drama, you might begin with an emotionally charged scene that reveals the protagonist's central conflict. The goal is to give the audience a taste of what's to come while also setting the stage for the rest of the episode.

After the opening, the next priority is to introduce your key characters, particularly the protagonist. The pilot episode is where the audience meets the characters for the first time, and it's essential to make a strong impression. This doesn't mean revealing everything about the characters right away, but rather giving the audience enough information to understand who they are, what drives them, and what challenges they might face. The protagonist should be introduced in a way that immediately establishes their personality, strengths, weaknesses, and motivations. Consider how you can show the audience who the protagonist is through their actions, decisions, and interactions with other characters. In addition to the protagonist, it's important to introduce the central antagonist or conflict that will drive the story. The pilot episode should clearly establish what the protagonist is up against, whether it's a person, a system, or an internal struggle. This conflict doesn't need to be fully explored in the pilot, but it should be introduced in a way that creates tension and raises questions. The audience should understand the stakes and be invested in seeing how the protagonist will navigate the challenges ahead. By setting up the central conflict early on, you create a sense of direction and purpose for the series, giving viewers a reason to keep watching.

The world-building in the pilot episode is another crucial element. The setting of your miniseries—whether it's a specific time period, a fantastical realm, or a realistic present-day environment—should be established in a way that feels immersive and authentic. The audience needs to understand the rules of this world, the social dynamics, and the key locations that will be central to the story. However, it's important to balance world-building with pacing; you don't want to overwhelm the audience with too much information at once. Instead, focus on showing key aspects of the world through the characters' interactions and the unfolding plot. Use visual and auditory cues, such as costume design, architecture, and soundscapes, to subtly convey the world's unique qualities.

The plot of the pilot episode should introduce the main story arc while also providing a self-contained narrative that is satisfying on its own. This means that the pilot should have a clear beginning, middle, and end, with its own mini-arc that resolves by the episode's conclusion. However, it should also leave enough unanswered questions and unresolved tensions to make the audience want to come back for more. One effective approach is to end the pilot with a cliffhanger or a major revelation that shifts the story in a new direction, raising the stakes and deepening the intrigue. This leaves the audience eager to see what happens next.

In terms of pacing, the pilot episode should move at a brisk pace that keeps the audience engaged while also allowing for moments of character development and world-building. It's important to find the right balance between action and exposition, ensuring that the story progresses without feeling rushed or overloaded with information. Each scene should serve a clear purpose, whether it's advancing the plot, deepening the characters, or establishing the setting. By keeping the pacing tight and focused, you can maintain the audience's attention and build momentum for the rest of the series.

Another key element of a successful pilot episode is tone. The tone of the pilot sets the emotional and stylistic foundation for the entire miniseries, whether it's dark and gritty, light-hearted and whimsical, or somewhere in between. The tone should be consistent throughout the episode and reflective of the series as a whole. This includes the visual style, dialogue, music, and overall atmosphere. The tone should also resonate with the themes you're exploring, reinforcing the emotional impact of the story. For example, a miniseries dealing with themes of loss and redemption might have a somber, reflective tone, while a story about adventure and discovery might have a more upbeat and optimistic tone.

One final consideration in crafting the pilot episode is the hook—what makes your miniseries stand out and why the audience should invest their time in it. The hook is the unique element or combination of elements that sets your story apart from others in the same genre. It could be a unique premise, an intriguing character dynamic, or a fresh take on a familiar theme. Whatever it is, the hook should be clearly established in the pilot, giving the audience a reason to keep watching. This might be something as simple as a compelling mystery that needs solving, or as complex as a multi-layered character with a dark secret. The pilot episode of a television miniseries is your chance to capture the audience's attention and set the stage for the rest of the story. By starting with a strong, engaging opening, introducing key characters and conflicts, building an immersive world, and establishing a clear tone and pacing, you can create a pilot that hooks viewers and makes them eager to see what happens next. The pilot should provide a satisfying narrative on its own while also leaving enough unanswered questions and unresolved tensions to draw the audience into the series. With careful planning and execution, the pilot episode can be a powerful tool for launching your miniseries and ensuring its success.

# Series Arcs: Ensuring Consistent Progression

Series arcs are the backbone of a television miniseries, providing the overarching structure that ties together individual episodes and ensures consistent narrative progression from start to finish. These arcs encompass the main storyline, character developments, thematic exploration, and subplots, all of which must be carefully managed to create a cohesive and compelling viewing experience.

Ensuring consistent progression in your series arcs involves planning, balancing various narrative elements, and maintaining a clear focus on the story's direction. This chapter will explore how to effectively craft and sustain series arcs that keep the audience engaged and invested throughout the entire miniseries.

The first step in ensuring consistent progression in your series arcs is to clearly define the main arc—the central storyline that will drive the narrative from the first episode to the last. This main arc should be rooted in the core concept of your miniseries and aligned with the protagonist's journey. It's the thread that ties all the episodes together, guiding the overall direction of the story. Start by identifying the key events and turning points that will shape this arc, such as the inciting incident, major conflicts, and the climax. These moments should be spaced strategically throughout the series, ensuring that the narrative builds momentum and tension as it progresses.

A well-crafted main arc also requires a clear understanding of the story's beginning, middle, and end. The beginning should establish the world, characters, and central conflict, setting the stage for the journey ahead. The middle is where the tension escalates, challenges are faced, and characters undergo significant development. The end should bring the arc to a satisfying resolution, providing closure to the main conflict and completing the protagonist's journey. By mapping out these key stages in advance, you create a blueprint for the series that ensures the story progresses logically and cohesively.

In addition to the main arc, character arcs are a crucial component of consistent progression in a miniseries. Each of your key characters, particularly the protagonist, should have their own arc—a personal journey of growth, change, or discovery that unfolds alongside the main storyline. These character arcs should be carefully integrated with the main arc, with each episode contributing to the characters' development in meaningful ways. For example, if your protagonist starts as a reluctant hero who gradually embraces their role, each episode should present challenges and experiences that push them closer to accepting their destiny. This progression should feel natural and organic, with the character's decisions and actions driving the narrative forward.

To maintain consistency in character arcs, it's important to track the emotional and psychological states of your characters throughout the series. Consider how each event and interaction affects them, and ensure that their reactions and growth are believable and consistent with their established personalities. This attention to detail helps create characters that feel real and relatable, making their journeys more impactful for the audience. It's also important to allow for moments of reflection and introspection, where characters can process their experiences and the audience can see the changes taking place within them.

Subplots are another important element in creating a rich and layered series arc. Subplots can add depth to the main narrative, explore secondary characters, and provide variety in pacing and tone. However, it's essential to ensure that subplots are closely connected to the main arc and contribute to the overall progression of the story. Subplots should never feel like distractions or filler; they should enhance the main narrative by exploring different aspects of the themes or providing additional context for the characters' decisions. For example, a subplot involving a secondary character's struggle with loyalty might parallel the protagonist's own moral dilemmas, creating a thematic resonance that enriches the story.

One of the challenges in managing series arcs is balancing the need for episodic satisfaction with the need for overarching consistency. Each episode should have its own internal structure, with a clear beginning, middle, and end, and should provide some level of resolution or progression. However, it's important to avoid making each episode feel too self-contained; the events of one episode should have consequences that carry over into subsequent episodes, contributing to the overall arc.

This sense of continuity is key to maintaining the audience's investment in the story, as they see how each episode builds on what came before and sets the stage for what's to come.

To achieve this balance, consider using cliffhangers or unresolved questions at the end of episodes. These moments of suspense can keep the audience engaged and eager to see how the story will unfold, while also ensuring that each episode feels like a vital piece of the larger puzzle. However, it's important to use cliffhangers judiciously; too many unresolved endings can frustrate viewers if they feel like they're being strung along without any real progression. Instead, aim for a mix of resolution and anticipation, where some storylines or character arcs are advanced or resolved within an episode, while others are left open to be explored further.

Thematic consistency is another crucial aspect of maintaining series arcs. The themes of your miniseries should be woven throughout the narrative, influencing the characters, plot, and setting. As the story progresses, these themes should deepen and evolve, reflecting the changes in the characters and the escalating stakes of the plot. For example, a theme of redemption might start with a character seeking forgiveness for a past mistake, but as the series progresses, the theme could expand to explore the complexities of atonement, the difficulty of self-forgiveness, and the impact of one's actions on others. By consistently revisiting and expanding on the themes, you create a narrative that feels cohesive and meaningful.

Finally, it's important to remain flexible and open to discovery as you develop your series arcs. While planning is essential, the creative process often leads to unexpected ideas and developments that can enrich the story. Be willing to adapt your arcs as needed, allowing the characters and plot to evolve in ways that feel organic and true to the story. However, ensure that any changes or additions still align with the overall direction and themes of the series, maintaining the consistency and cohesion of the narrative. Ensuring consistent progression in your series arcs involves careful planning, thoughtful character development, and a clear focus on the main storyline and themes. By defining the key stages of the main arc, tracking character growth, integrating subplots, and balancing episodic satisfaction with overarching continuity, you can create a miniseries that is both compelling and cohesive. The series arcs should guide the narrative from beginning to end, providing a sense of direction and purpose that keeps the audience engaged and invested in the story. With attention to detail and a commitment to thematic and narrative consistency, you can craft a miniseries that resonates with viewers and delivers a satisfying and memorable viewing experience.

# Conflict as Catalyst: Driving the Narrative

Conflict is the engine that drives any compelling story, and in a television miniseries, it serves as the catalyst that propels the narrative forward, shapes character development, and sustains audience engagement. Whether it's an external clash between opposing forces or an internal struggle within a character, conflict creates tension, raises stakes, and compels characters to take action. Understanding how to effectively use conflict to drive the narrative is essential for crafting a miniseries that is both dynamic and emotionally resonant.

The first step in using conflict as a narrative catalyst is to clearly define the central conflict of your miniseries. This conflict should be closely tied to the core themes and central premise of your story, providing a clear and compelling challenge for the protagonist. The central conflict can take many forms—it might be a battle between good and evil, a struggle for power, a fight for survival, or a quest for redemption. Whatever the nature of the conflict, it should be significant enough to impact the protagonist's life in a profound way, forcing them out of their comfort zone and into action.

In addition to the central conflict, it's important to layer in secondary conflicts that add complexity and depth to the narrative. These conflicts can arise from subplots, character relationships, or thematic explorations, and they should interact with the central conflict in meaningful ways. For example, a protagonist who is fighting to save their family from an external threat might also be grappling with internal guilt over a past mistake, creating a conflict between their desire to protect others and their fear of failing them. By weaving together multiple layers of conflict, you create a rich and nuanced narrative that keeps the audience engaged on multiple levels.

Character-driven conflict is particularly powerful because it directly ties the narrative tension to the emotional and psychological stakes of the story. When crafting character-driven conflict, consider what your protagonist wants most and what stands in their way. The conflict should arise from the protagonist's goals, desires, and fears, forcing them to confront obstacles that challenge their beliefs and push them to grow. This type of conflict is often more nuanced and complex than purely external conflicts, as it involves the characters' internal struggles, moral dilemmas, and personal relationships.

For example, if your protagonist is driven by a desire for justice, the conflict might arise from their need to balance this desire with the consequences of their actions. They might face moral quandaries about how far they're willing to go to achieve their goals, or they might struggle with the impact of their pursuit of justice on their relationships with others. By making the conflict personal and tied to the protagonist's character arc, you create a more compelling and relatable narrative that resonates with the audience.

External conflict, on the other hand, often provides the immediate and tangible challenges that the protagonist must overcome. This type of conflict can take the form of physical obstacles, antagonistic forces, or societal pressures that threaten the protagonist's goals. External conflicts are essential for maintaining momentum and driving the plot forward, as they create the circumstances that force the protagonist to act. However, it's important to ensure that external conflicts are not just arbitrary obstacles—they should be closely connected to the central themes and character development, adding layers of meaning to the narrative.

One effective way to create external conflict is to introduce a formidable antagonist who directly opposes the protagonist's goals. The antagonist should be a well-developed character in their own right, with their own motivations, desires, and conflicts. A strong antagonist not only provides a worthy adversary for the protagonist but also serves as a mirror, reflecting the protagonist's strengths, weaknesses, and moral choices. The conflict between the protagonist and antagonist should escalate throughout the series, culminating in a final confrontation that tests the protagonist's resolve and brings the central conflict to a head.

In addition to character-driven and external conflicts, consider how environmental and situational conflicts can add tension and complexity to the narrative. These conflicts might involve the setting itself, such as a harsh and unforgiving landscape that the characters must navigate, or a societal structure that imposes limitations on the characters' actions. Environmental and situational conflicts can create a sense of urgency and danger, raising the stakes for the protagonist and forcing them to adapt to changing circumstances. These types of conflicts also provide opportunities to explore themes such as survival, resilience, and the impact of environment on human behavior.

As you develop the conflicts in your miniseries, it's important to think about how they evolve over the course of the narrative. Conflict should not remain static—it should escalate, deepen, and take on new dimensions as the story progresses. The challenges faced by the protagonist in the early episodes should be different from those they encounter later on, as the stakes increase and the consequences of their actions become more severe. This progression keeps the narrative dynamic and prevents the story from becoming repetitive or predictable.

One way to ensure that conflict drives the narrative effectively is to use it as a tool for character development. The way characters respond to conflict reveals their true nature, forcing them to make difficult choices that shape their journey. Consider how each conflict in your miniseries can serve as a turning point for the characters, pushing them to confront their fears, question their beliefs, or redefine their goals. These moments of conflict-driven growth are essential for creating a satisfying character arc and for keeping the audience emotionally invested in the story.

Another key aspect of using conflict as a catalyst is to balance tension with moments of release. While constant conflict can create a sense of urgency, it's also important to allow for quieter moments where characters can reflect on their experiences and where the audience can process the events of the story. These moments of release provide contrast and help to build anticipation for the next wave of conflict. By carefully pacing the ebb and flow of conflict, you can create a narrative rhythm that keeps the audience engaged without overwhelming them.

Finally, consider how the resolution of conflict impacts the overall narrative and themes of your miniseries. The way conflicts are resolved should feel earned and consistent with the story's tone and message. Whether the resolution is triumphant, tragic, or ambiguous, it should provide closure to the central conflict while also leaving the audience with something to think about. The resolution of conflict is often where the themes of the story come into sharp focus, as the characters' choices and the consequences of their actions reveal the deeper meanings behind the narrative. Conflict is a powerful catalyst for driving the narrative of a television miniseries. By carefully crafting character-driven, external, environmental, and situational conflicts, and by ensuring that these conflicts evolve and escalate throughout the series, you can create a dynamic and compelling story that keeps the audience engaged. Conflict not only propels the plot forward but also serves as a tool for character development and thematic exploration, making it an essential element of any successful miniseries.

# Resolution and Closure: Satisfying the Audience

Resolution and closure are critical elements in the conclusion of a television miniseries, providing the audience with a sense of satisfaction and fulfillment after the journey they've experienced. A well-crafted resolution ties up the narrative threads, resolves the central conflicts, and offers emotional and thematic closure that resonates with viewers. However, achieving this balance can be challenging, as it requires addressing the major plot points, delivering on character arcs, and reinforcing the themes, all while ensuring that the ending feels both inevitable and, ideally, somewhat surprising. In this chapter, we'll explore how to create a satisfying resolution and closure that leaves your audience both content and reflective.

The first step in crafting a satisfying resolution is to revisit the central conflicts and questions that have driven the narrative. These are the issues that have kept the audience engaged, and they deserve careful consideration in the final episodes. The resolution should provide clear answers or conclusions to these conflicts, whether through a climactic confrontation, a dramatic reveal, or a poignant moment of realization. However, it's important to strike a balance between clarity and ambiguity. While the audience should feel that the main narrative has reached a conclusion, some questions can be left open to interpretation, allowing viewers to reflect and engage with the story on a deeper level.

When resolving the central conflicts, consider the arc of the protagonist and how their journey has prepared them for this moment. The resolution should reflect the growth and changes the protagonist has undergone throughout the series. For example, if your protagonist has been on a journey of self-discovery, the resolution might involve them finally embracing their true identity or making peace with their past. If the story has been about a battle for justice, the resolution should address whether justice is achieved and at what cost. The key is to ensure that the protagonist's actions and decisions in the resolution are consistent with their character development, creating a sense of narrative and emotional coherence.

In addition to resolving the main plot, the resolution should also address the character arcs of key supporting characters. While the protagonist's journey is central, the fates of other characters should not be overlooked. Consider how their stories intersect with the protagonist's and how their arcs contribute to the overall themes of the series. For example, a secondary character who has struggled with loyalty might find resolution in making a final, decisive act of allegiance or betrayal. These moments of resolution for supporting characters add richness and depth to the narrative, providing a more complete sense of closure.

Thematic closure is another essential component of a satisfying resolution. Throughout your miniseries, you've likely explored various themes—such as redemption, power, love, or sacrifice—that have given the story depth and resonance. The resolution is the moment where these themes should come into full focus, offering the audience a final reflection on the ideas that have been woven throughout the narrative. This thematic closure can be achieved through dialogue, symbolism, or the resolution of character arcs. For instance, a theme of redemption might be highlighted in the protagonist's final act of selflessness, while a theme of power might be underscored by the consequences of a character's ultimate decision.

When crafting the resolution, it's important to consider the emotional impact on the audience. The ending should evoke a strong emotional response, whether it's joy, sadness, relief, or a mix of complex emotions. This emotional closure is what makes the resolution feel satisfying and memorable. To achieve this, focus on the key emotional beats of the story—moments of triumph, sacrifice, loss, or reconciliation—and ensure that they are given the space and weight they deserve in the final episodes. Music, cinematography, and pacing all play crucial roles in enhancing the emotional impact of these moments.

While it's important to provide closure, the resolution should also leave room for the audience to reflect and interpret the story in their own way. This is where the balance between closure and ambiguity comes into play. Some of the most powerful resolutions are those that offer a clear conclusion while also leaving certain elements open to interpretation. For example, a character's final decision might be left ambiguous, allowing the audience to ponder the implications. This approach can make the resolution more thought-provoking and allow the story to linger in the minds of viewers long after the credits roll.

Another consideration in crafting the resolution is the tone and style of the miniseries. The ending should be consistent with the tone that has been established throughout the series, whether it's hopeful, dark, bittersweet, or triumphant. A sudden shift in tone at the end can feel jarring and undermine the emotional and narrative coherence of the story. Instead, aim for an ending that feels like a natural culmination of the journey, one that is true to the story's essence and the emotions it has evoked along the way.

In some cases, a miniseries may benefit from an epilogue—a final scene or sequence that offers a glimpse into the characters' lives after the main events of the story. An epilogue can provide additional closure, showing how the characters have moved on or how the world has changed as a result of the events that unfolded. This can be particularly effective in stories with a strong focus on character development or in narratives that leave certain questions unanswered in the main resolution. However, an epilogue should be used sparingly and only if it genuinely adds value to the story. It should not feel like an afterthought or an unnecessary extension of the narrative.

Finally, consider how the resolution reflects the overall message or moral of the story. The ending is your last chance to communicate the deeper meanings and takeaways of your miniseries. Whether it's a cautionary tale, a story of hope, or a meditation on human nature, the resolution should reinforce the message you want to leave with your audience. This doesn't mean spelling out the message explicitly, but rather allowing it to emerge naturally through the resolution of the plot, characters, and themes.

In conclusion, crafting a satisfying resolution and closure for a television miniseries involves tying together the narrative threads, resolving central conflicts, and providing emotional and thematic closure. The resolution should reflect the growth of the protagonist, address the arcs of key supporting characters, and bring the central themes into focus. It should evoke a strong emotional response while also leaving room for reflection and interpretation. By staying true to the tone and style of the series and considering the overall message you want to convey, you can create a resolution that resonates with the audience and provides a fitting conclusion to the journey they've experienced. A well-crafted resolution not only satisfies the audience in the moment but also leaves a lasting impression, ensuring that your miniseries is remembered long after it has ended.

# Visual Storytelling: Show, Don't Tell

Visual storytelling is one of the most powerful tools in a filmmaker's arsenal, especially in a television miniseries where the visual medium can be used to convey complex ideas, emotions, and themes without relying heavily on dialogue or exposition. The principle of "show, don't tell" is at the heart of effective visual storytelling. It encourages you to use images, actions, and symbols to communicate meaning, allowing the audience to engage more deeply with the story by interpreting visual cues and making connections on their own. In this chapter, we'll explore how to harness the power of visual storytelling to create a rich, immersive narrative experience that resonates with viewers.

The first step in mastering visual storytelling is to understand the unique strengths of the visual medium. Unlike written stories, where description and dialogue are the primary tools, film and television rely heavily on images to convey meaning. A single shot can communicate layers of information, from a character's emotional state to the underlying themes of the story. To effectively "show, don't tell," it's important to think about what each scene is trying to convey and how you can use visual elements—such as composition, color, lighting, and movement—to communicate that information without relying on dialogue.

One of the most fundamental aspects of visual storytelling is composition—how elements are arranged within the frame. Composition can direct the audience's attention, convey relationships between characters, and create a specific mood or atmosphere. For example, placing a character in the center of the frame with a lot of space around them can emphasize their isolation or vulnerability, while a close-up on a character's face can draw the audience into their emotional world. The use of leading lines, symmetry, and framing devices (like doorways or windows) can also add depth to the storytelling, guiding the audience's eye to important details or creating a sense of confinement or freedom.

Color is another powerful tool in visual storytelling. Different colors evoke different emotions and can be used to symbolize various themes or character states. Warm colors like red, orange, and yellow often convey energy, passion, or danger, while cool colors like blue, green, and purple can suggest calm, sadness, or mystery. The deliberate use of color can help reinforce the narrative and themes of your miniseries. For example, a character who undergoes a significant transformation might be associated with a particular color palette that changes as their journey progresses. Alternatively, contrasting colors might be used to highlight conflict or duality within the story.

Lighting plays a crucial role in shaping the mood and tone of a scene. Harsh, high-contrast lighting can create a sense of tension or danger, while soft, diffused lighting can evoke warmth or tranquility. The direction of light can also influence how the audience perceives a character—light from below can create a sinister or mysterious effect, while light from above or the side can add depth and drama to a character's face. In addition to setting the mood, lighting can be used to symbolize themes or ideas. For example, a character stepping out of the shadows and into the light might symbolize a moment of revelation or moral clarity.

Movement within the frame, both of the camera and of the characters, is another key element of visual storytelling. Camera movements like pans, tilts, and tracking shots can add dynamism to a scene, emphasize certain actions, or reveal new information. For example, a slow zoom in on a character can build suspense or indicate that they are deep in thought.

Meanwhile, the way characters move within the frame—whether they are running, walking, or standing still—can convey their emotional state and intentions. A character who is constantly in motion might be restless or anxious, while a character who remains still might be calm, contemplative, or even paralyzed by fear.

Symbolism is a powerful aspect of visual storytelling, where objects, settings, or actions are imbued with deeper meaning. Symbols can be used to reinforce themes, foreshadow events, or provide insight into a character's psyche. For example, a broken mirror might symbolize a fractured identity, a recurring image of a bird might represent freedom, or a door that remains closed might signify an opportunity or truth that is out of reach. The key to effective symbolism is subtlety—symbols should enrich the narrative without being overly obvious or heavy-handed. When used well, they can add layers of meaning that reward attentive viewers.

Another important technique in visual storytelling is the use of visual motifs—repeated images or patterns that reinforce a particular theme or idea. A visual motif might be a specific object, color, or framing technique that recurs throughout the series, creating a sense of cohesion and emphasizing certain aspects of the story. For example, a motif of reflective surfaces might be used to explore themes of self-perception and identity, while a recurring shot of a character looking out of a window might symbolize their longing for something beyond their current situation. By repeating these visual elements, you can subtly reinforce the themes and emotional undercurrents of the narrative.

The mise-en-scène, which refers to the arrangement of everything that appears in the frame—sets, props, actors, costumes, and lighting—also plays a crucial role in visual storytelling. Every element within the mise-en-scène should be carefully considered and purposeful, contributing to the story in some way. For example, a cluttered, chaotic set might reflect a character's mental state, while a minimalist, orderly environment might suggest control or repression. The choice of props and costumes can also provide insight into characters' backgrounds, personalities, and relationships. A well-designed mise-en-scène creates a rich visual environment that enhances the narrative and provides context for the characters' actions.

Editing is another powerful tool in visual storytelling. The way scenes are cut together can influence the pacing, create tension, or highlight connections between characters and events. For example, quick cuts between different locations can create a sense of urgency or chaos, while a long, unbroken take can build suspense or allow the audience to fully immerse themselves in a moment. Cross-cutting between two parallel actions can create dramatic tension, as the audience anticipates how the two threads will intersect. The rhythm of the editing should be in harmony with the emotional and narrative beats of the story, guiding the audience's experience of the unfolding drama.

Finally, silence and sound are key components of visual storytelling. Sometimes, what's not said can be as powerful as what is spoken. Silence can create tension, highlight a character's isolation, or focus attention on a specific visual detail. Conversely, sound—whether it's the ambient noise of a setting, a piece of music, or a specific sound effect—can enhance the emotional impact of a scene. For example, the distant sound of a ticking clock might build tension in a suspenseful moment, while the absence of sound might underscore the gravity of a character's realization. By thoughtfully combining visuals with sound (or the lack thereof), you can create a more immersive and emotionally resonant experience for the audience.

In conclusion, visual storytelling is about using the visual language of film and television to convey meaning, evoke emotions, and engage the audience on a deeper level. By focusing on composition, color, lighting, movement, symbolism, motifs, mise-en-scène, editing, and sound, you can create a rich and immersive narrative that "shows" rather than "tells." This approach not only makes your miniseries more visually compelling but also allows the audience to actively engage with the story, interpreting visual cues and making connections on their own. When done effectively, visual storytelling can elevate your miniseries, making it a memorable and impactful experience that resonates long after the final credits roll.

# Dialogue Dynamics: Making Words Count

Dialogue is a crucial component of any television miniseries, serving as a primary means of character expression, plot advancement, and thematic exploration. In a medium where every word counts, effective dialogue can elevate a scene, making it memorable and impactful. Crafting dialogue that feels authentic, sharp, and purposeful requires a keen understanding of character voice, pacing, and the underlying subtext that drives conversations. In this chapter, we'll explore how to make dialogue dynamic and meaningful, ensuring that every line contributes to the overall narrative and engages the audience.

The first step in creating dynamic dialogue is to establish distinct voices for each character. Every character in your miniseries should speak in a way that reflects their background, personality, and emotional state. This involves considering factors such as their education level, cultural background, profession, and personal experiences. A character who is a seasoned detective might speak in short, clipped sentences, with a tone of authority and pragmatism, while a younger, more idealistic character might use more expressive language, reflecting their passion and naivety. By giving each character a unique voice, you make the dialogue more engaging and help the audience connect with and differentiate between the characters.

Character voice is also influenced by the relationships between characters. People speak differently depending on who they're talking to—a character might be formal and reserved with a superior, casual and teasing with a friend, or vulnerable and open with a loved one. Understanding these dynamics allows you to craft dialogue that not only reveals character but also deepens relationships and builds tension. For example, a conversation between two characters who are rivals might be laced with sarcasm or thinly veiled hostility, while a dialogue between allies might be more supportive and collaborative. The way characters speak to each other should reflect their relationship and the history they share, adding layers of meaning to the words.

Another important aspect of dynamic dialogue is subtext—the underlying meaning or emotion that is not directly stated but implied. Subtext allows you to convey complex emotions, hidden agendas, or unspoken tensions without spelling everything out for the audience. This makes the dialogue more engaging, as viewers are invited to read between the lines and interpret the true meaning behind the words. For example, a character who says, "I'm fine," when they're clearly upset might be using subtext to mask their true feelings. The audience can sense the discrepancy between what the character says and what they really mean, creating dramatic tension. To use subtext effectively, think about what the characters are really feeling or thinking and how they might express those emotions indirectly through dialogue.

Pacing is another critical element in making dialogue count. The rhythm of a conversation can influence the tension and emotional impact of a scene. Quick, overlapping dialogue can create a sense of urgency or chaos, while slower, measured exchanges can build suspense or emphasize the weight of a conversation. Varying the pacing within a scene can also enhance the dynamics between characters—moments of rapid back-and-forth can give way to a pregnant pause, highlighting a shift in the emotional tone or signaling an important realization. When crafting dialogue, pay attention to the flow of the conversation and how it contributes to the overall mood and pacing of the scene.

In addition to pacing, silence is a powerful tool in dialogue dynamics. Sometimes, what is left unsaid can be more impactful than what is spoken. A character's decision to remain silent, or a pause in the conversation, can convey hesitation, uncertainty, or a shift in power dynamics. Silence can also be used to build tension, allowing the audience to anticipate what might be said next.

For example, a long pause before a character responds to a difficult question can create suspense, as the audience wonders how they will answer. By strategically using silence in your dialogue, you can add depth and tension to the scene.

Conflict is a driving force in dynamic dialogue. Whether it's an argument, a negotiation, or a disagreement, conflict in conversation creates tension and drama, propelling the narrative forward. Characters in conflict often reveal their true motivations and vulnerabilities, making these moments rich with subtext and emotional weight. However, not all conflict needs to be overt—subtle conflicts, such as differing perspectives or unspoken resentments, can be just as compelling. When writing dialogue with conflict, consider the stakes for each character and how their goals or desires clash, leading to a confrontation that is both engaging and revealing.

Exposition is often necessary in storytelling, but it can easily bog down dialogue if not handled carefully. To make exposition dynamic, integrate it naturally into the conversation rather than delivering it as a monologue or a "data dump." Characters should have a reason for sharing information, whether it's to persuade, warn, or challenge another character. For example, instead of a character simply stating, "The city is in danger," they might say, "I saw the flames from miles away—there's no way we can save everyone." This approach not only conveys the necessary information but also adds urgency and emotional context, making the exposition more engaging.

Another technique for making dialogue count is the use of repetition and callbacks. Repetition can emphasize a particular idea or emotion, creating a sense of rhythm and resonance in the conversation. For example, a character who repeatedly says, "I have no choice," might be trying to convince themselves of their decision, revealing their inner conflict. Callbacks—when a character references something said earlier in the series—can create continuity and depth, reinforcing themes or character development. These techniques can make dialogue more memorable and impactful, giving weight to certain lines or ideas.

Humor is another tool that can add dynamism to dialogue, providing contrast to more serious moments and revealing character traits. Well-timed humor can diffuse tension, create camaraderie between characters, or highlight a character's wit and intelligence. However, humor should be consistent with the tone of the miniseries and the character's personality—forced or out-of-place humor can undermine the emotional impact of a scene. When used effectively, humor can make dialogue more engaging and endear characters to the audience.

Finally, when crafting dialogue, always keep in mind the overall narrative and themes of your miniseries. Dialogue should not only serve the immediate needs of the scene but also contribute to the larger story. This means that conversations should advance the plot, develop characters, and reinforce the themes you're exploring. Every line of dialogue should have a purpose, whether it's to reveal something new about a character, create tension, or foreshadow future events. By ensuring that your dialogue is purposeful and connected to the broader narrative, you make each word count and create a more cohesive and impactful story.

In conclusion, dynamic dialogue is essential for creating a television miniseries that is engaging, emotionally resonant, and memorable. By giving each character a distinct voice, using subtext and conflict, varying pacing and silence, and making exposition natural and purposeful, you can craft dialogue that is sharp, authentic, and full of meaning. Remember that dialogue is not just about conveying information—it's about revealing character, building relationships, and driving the narrative forward. When every word counts, your dialogue can elevate the storytelling, making your miniseries a rich and compelling experience for the audience.

# Building Tension: The Art of Suspense in a Miniseries

Building tension and creating suspense are essential elements in crafting a compelling television miniseries. Suspense keeps the audience on the edge of their seats, eagerly anticipating what will happen next, while tension provides the emotional pull that drives the story forward. The art of suspense lies in carefully balancing what the audience knows with what they don't know, creating a sense of uncertainty and anticipation that compels viewers to keep watching. In this chapter, we'll explore techniques for building tension and sustaining suspense throughout your miniseries, ensuring that your narrative remains engaging and thrilling from beginning to end.

The foundation of suspense is the careful control of information—what the audience knows, what the characters know, and what is hidden from both. One of the most effective ways to create suspense is to give the audience more information than the characters have. This technique, often referred to as dramatic irony, allows the audience to anticipate events or outcomes that the characters are unaware of, creating a sense of impending doom or excitement. For example, if the audience knows that a character is walking into a trap, the tension builds as they watch the character unknowingly move closer to danger. The key to dramatic irony is to maintain the tension by gradually revealing information and keeping the audience in a state of anticipation.

Another powerful tool for building tension is the use of pacing. The rhythm of your story—how quickly or slowly events unfold—can significantly influence the level of suspense. Slow, deliberate pacing can heighten tension by allowing the audience to fully absorb the details of a scene and anticipate what might happen next. For example, a slow camera movement toward a closed door, paired with ominous music, can create a sense of dread as the audience wonders what lies beyond. On the other hand, quick, rapid pacing can create a sense of urgency and chaos, making the audience feel as though events are spiralling out of control. By varying the pacing throughout your miniseries, you can keep the audience engaged and build suspense in different ways.

The use of cliffhangers is a classic technique for creating suspense and keeping the audience hooked from episode to episode. A cliffhanger is a moment of unresolved tension or uncertainty at the end of an episode that leaves the audience eager to see what happens next. It could be a sudden twist, a revelation, or a character in immediate danger. The key to an effective cliffhanger is to leave the audience with just enough information to spark their curiosity, but not enough to satisfy it. This creates a powerful incentive for viewers to tune in to the next episode. However, it's important to balance cliffhangers with moments of resolution; if every episode ends with a cliffhanger, the audience may become frustrated or desensitized to the tension.

Foreshadowing is another technique that can be used to build tension and create suspense. By planting subtle hints or clues early in the series, you can prepare the audience for events that will occur later, creating a sense of inevitability and anticipation. For example, a seemingly innocuous detail, such as a character's casual mention of a fear of heights, might foreshadow a later scene where that fear becomes a critical plot point. Foreshadowing not only builds tension but also adds depth and complexity to the narrative, rewarding attentive viewers who pick up on the clues.

The manipulation of time is a powerful way to create suspense. Techniques such as flashbacks, flash-forwards, and parallel timelines can add layers of tension by revealing information out of chronological order. For example, a flash-forward that shows the protagonist in a dire situation can create suspense as the audience wonders how they ended up there and whether they will survive.

Similarly, intercutting between two parallel storylines—such as a character searching for something while another character is unknowingly moving closer to it—can create a sense of urgency and tension as the two threads converge. The key to using time manipulation effectively is to maintain clarity while heightening the sense of anticipation.

Silence and sound are also crucial elements in building tension. Silence can be just as powerful as sound in creating suspense, as it forces the audience to focus on the visual elements and heightens their awareness of what might happen next. A sudden silence in the midst of a tense scene can signal that something significant is about to occur, making the audience hold their breath in anticipation. Conversely, sound—whether it's the creak of a floorboard, the ticking of a clock, or a distant siren—can create a sense of unease and heighten the tension. The strategic use of sound and silence can manipulate the audience's emotions and build suspense in unexpected ways.

Character development plays a vital role in building tension. The more the audience cares about the characters, the more invested they are in the outcome of the story. By creating complex, relatable characters with clear goals, motivations, and vulnerabilities, you increase the emotional stakes of the narrative. The tension rises when characters are placed in situations that challenge their beliefs, push them to their limits, or force them to make difficult decisions. For example, a character who is hiding a dark secret might experience mounting tension as the truth threatens to come out, creating suspense for the audience as they wonder if and when the secret will be revealed.

Visual storytelling is another effective way to build tension. The use of lighting, shadows, camera angles, and composition can all contribute to the sense of suspense in a scene. For example, a character moving through a dimly lit corridor, with shadows obscuring what's ahead, creates a sense of uncertainty and danger.

The placement of objects or characters within the frame can also create tension—such as showing a character in the foreground while something ominous looms in the background, just out of focus. By carefully crafting the visual elements of each scene, you can build tension without relying on dialogue or exposition.

The manipulation of expectations is a key technique in creating suspense. Audiences are often familiar with genre conventions and narrative tropes, which can be used to your advantage. By setting up certain expectations and then subverting them, you can surprise the audience and heighten the tension. For example, a scene that appears to be leading to a predictable outcome might take an unexpected turn, catching the audience off guard and increasing the suspense. This technique keeps the audience engaged, as they realize that nothing is certain and that the story could go in any direction.

Finally, the resolution of tension and suspense is just as important as building it. The payoff must be satisfying and consistent with the narrative and character arcs. If tension is built up over several episodes, the resolution should provide a sense of closure, whether it's a triumphant victory, a tragic loss, or an unexpected twist. However, it's also important to leave room for new tensions to emerge, keeping the audience invested in the ongoing story. The key is to balance the resolution of current suspense with the introduction of new conflicts, ensuring that the narrative remains dynamic and engaging.

In conclusion, building tension and creating suspense in a television miniseries requires a careful balance of pacing, information control, character development, and visual storytelling. By using techniques such as dramatic irony, foreshadowing, cliffhangers, and time manipulation, you can create a sense of anticipation that keeps the audience engaged and eager to see what happens next.

The art of suspense lies in maintaining this delicate balance, ensuring that the tension builds gradually while providing satisfying resolutions along the way. When done effectively, suspense can elevate your miniseries, making it a thrilling and unforgettable experience for viewers.

# Character Arcs: Evolution and Transformation

Character arcs are the emotional and psychological journeys that characters undergo throughout a television miniseries. These arcs are crucial to creating a compelling narrative, as they allow characters to evolve and transform in response to the events of the story. A well-crafted character arc not only adds depth to individual characters but also enriches the overall narrative, making the story more engaging and emotionally resonant. In this chapter, we'll explore the key elements of character arcs, how to effectively develop them, and how they can enhance the themes and narrative of your miniseries.

The first step in creating a compelling character arc is to establish a clear starting point for the character. This involves defining who the character is at the beginning of the miniseries—their personality, beliefs, goals, and flaws. This baseline is essential because it provides a contrast to the character's eventual transformation, allowing the audience to see how far they've come by the end of the story. For example, a character might start as an idealistic novice who believes in the inherent goodness of people, or as a cynical loner who trusts no one. By clearly establishing the character's initial state, you set the stage for their journey of evolution and transformation.

Central to any character arc is the concept of change. A character arc is, at its core, about transformation—how a character evolves in response to the challenges they face. This transformation can be positive, as a character overcomes their flaws and grows into a better version of themselves, or it can be negative, as they succumb to their weaknesses and spiral downward. The key to a successful character arc is to ensure that the change feels earned and organic. The character's transformation should be a direct result of the experiences they go through, the choices they make, and the conflicts they face. This makes the arc more believable and impactful for the audience.

To create a dynamic character arc, it's important to introduce internal and external conflicts that challenge the character's beliefs and force them to grow. Internal conflicts are those that occur within the character's mind—struggles with self-doubt, fear, guilt, or desire. These conflicts often stem from the character's flaws or unresolved issues from their past. External conflicts, on the other hand, involve the challenges the character faces in the outside world, such as antagonistic forces, societal pressures, or physical obstacles. By intertwining internal and external conflicts, you create a more complex and layered arc that resonates on both an emotional and narrative level.

A key element of character arcs is the midpoint, often referred to as the "crisis point" or "turning point." This is the moment when the character reaches a critical juncture in their journey—typically a point of no return where they must confront their deepest fears or make a life-altering decision. The midpoint is crucial because it forces the character to face the consequences of their actions and propels them toward their eventual transformation. For example, a character who has been avoiding responsibility might be forced to step up and take charge in a crisis, or a character who has been driven by revenge might realize that their quest is leading them down a destructive path. The midpoint is a pivotal moment that shapes the rest of the character's arc.

As the character progresses through their arc, it's important to show the gradual nature of their transformation. Change rarely happens overnight, and a character's evolution should be depicted as a process with ups and downs.

This might involve moments of growth and insight, followed by setbacks or relapses into old habits. For example, a character who is learning to trust others might take a step forward by confiding in someone, only to later revert to their distrustful ways when they feel betrayed. This back-and-forth dynamic adds realism to the arc and makes the character's ultimate transformation more satisfying.

The climax of the character arc often coincides with the climax of the miniseries, where the character is tested to their limits and must make a decisive choice that reflects their growth. This moment is the culmination of the character's journey, where they either overcome their flaws and achieve a personal victory, or succumb to their weaknesses and face the consequences. The climax should be emotionally charged and thematically resonant, providing a clear resolution to the character's arc. For example, a character who has been grappling with forgiveness might finally let go of their anger and extend an olive branch to an adversary, or a character who has been driven by ambition might sacrifice their goals to save someone they care about.

After the climax, the resolution of the character arc provides closure and shows the impact of the character's transformation. This is the point where the audience sees how the character has changed as a result of their journey—whether they've found peace, gained wisdom, or embraced a new perspective. The resolution should also reflect the themes of the miniseries, reinforcing the messages you've been exploring throughout the story. For example, if your miniseries is about the cost of vengeance, the resolution might show a character who has learned the value of forgiveness and chooses a different path.

While the protagonist's arc is often the most prominent, it's important to consider the arcs of supporting characters as well. These secondary arcs can add depth to the narrative and provide additional layers of meaning. Supporting characters might have parallel arcs that mirror the protagonist's journey, contrasting arcs that highlight different themes, or intersecting arcs that influence the protagonist's decisions. By developing strong arcs for your supporting characters, you create a richer and more interconnected narrative that keeps the audience engaged.

It's also worth noting that not all character arcs need to follow a traditional trajectory of growth or decline. Some characters may experience a flat arc, where they remain largely unchanged but influence the world around them. For example, a character with a strong moral compass might inspire others to change, even as they stay true to their principles. Alternatively, a character might undergo a "circular" arc, where they end up back where they started but with a new understanding or perspective. These variations can add complexity to your storytelling and offer different ways to explore character and theme.

In addition to individual character arcs, consider how these arcs interact and intersect with each other. Relationships between characters—whether they're allies, rivals, or something in between—can drive character development and add tension to the narrative. A mentor's arc might be closely tied to the protagonist's growth, with the mentor's own experiences providing guidance or a cautionary tale. A romantic subplot might involve two characters whose arcs are intertwined, with each influencing the other's journey. By carefully weaving together the arcs of different characters, you create a more cohesive and emotionally resonant story. Character arcs are a vital component of a television miniseries, providing the emotional and psychological depth that makes a story engaging and memorable. The key is to ensure that each character's journey feels earned and organic, with the transformation reflecting the experiences and challenges they've faced. When done effectively, character arcs can elevate your miniseries, making it a powerful exploration of growth, change, and the human condition.

# The Role of Subplots: Adding Depth to the Story

Subplots play a crucial role in enriching a television miniseries, adding layers of complexity, depth, and nuance to the main narrative. While the central plot drives the core story, subplots offer opportunities to explore secondary characters, develop themes more fully, and create a more immersive world. When woven effectively into the narrative, subplots can enhance the overall storytelling, providing contrast, resonance, and a fuller emotional experience for the audience. In this chapter, we'll explore the importance of subplots, how to develop them, and how to integrate them seamlessly into the main narrative.

## The Purpose of Subplots

Subplots serve multiple functions within a miniseries, each contributing to the richness of the story. One of the primary purposes of a subplot is to provide additional layers of character development. While the main plot focuses on the protagonist and their central conflict, subplots allow for the exploration of secondary characters who might not be in the spotlight. These secondary characters can have their own arcs, struggles, and resolutions, adding depth to the narrative and giving the audience more perspectives to engage with.

Subplots also serve to develop themes in a more nuanced way. While the main plot might tackle the central theme head-on, subplots can explore different aspects or variations of that theme. For example, if the main plot deals with the theme of justice, a subplot might explore the personal cost of seeking justice, or the difference between legal justice and moral justice. By examining the theme from multiple angles, subplots can enrich the audience's understanding of the story's deeper meanings.

Another important function of subplots is to provide contrast and balance within the narrative. A miniseries that is relentlessly focused on one plotline can risk becoming monotonous or overwhelming. Subplots offer a way to vary the tone, pacing, and emotional intensity of the story. For instance, a subplot might provide comic relief in a predominantly serious drama, or a tender romance in a story full of tension and conflict. This contrast not only keeps the audience engaged but also highlights the main plot by providing moments of respite or reflection.

Subplots can also be used to foreshadow or reinforce the main narrative. A well-crafted subplot might mirror the central conflict on a smaller scale, subtly preparing the audience for developments in the main plot. Alternatively, a subplot might introduce a theme, character, or piece of information that becomes crucial later in the story. This interconnection between subplots and the main plot creates a sense of cohesion and intricacy, making the story feel more tightly woven and thought-out.

## Developing Effective Subplots

When developing subplots, it's important to ensure that they are meaningful and integral to the overall narrative. A subplot should not feel like an afterthought or filler; it should have its own internal structure, with a beginning, middle, and end, and it should contribute to the main plot or themes in some way. To achieve this, start by identifying the secondary characters who will drive the subplot. Consider what challenges or conflicts these characters might face and how these conflicts relate to the main story.

For example, if the main plot involves a protagonist seeking revenge, a subplot might follow a secondary character who struggles with forgiveness, offering a counterpoint to the protagonist's journey. The subplot can then develop its own arc, with the secondary character facing obstacles, making choices, and undergoing growth or change. By giving subplots their own structure and stakes, you ensure that they are engaging and contribute to the overall narrative.

Subplots should also be paced appropriately throughout the miniseries. Rather than dumping all the subplot's developments in a single episode, spread them out across the series, interweaving them with the main plot. This helps to maintain momentum and keeps the audience invested in multiple storylines at once. The pacing of subplots can also create opportunities for tension and suspense—just as the audience becomes fully engrossed in the main plot, you might shift focus to a subplot, delaying gratification and keeping viewers on the edge of their seats.

Another important consideration is how subplots interact with the main plot. Ideally, subplots should intersect with the main narrative in meaningful ways, whether through character interactions, thematic parallels, or plot developments. For instance, a subplot might involve a secondary character who provides crucial information or assistance to the protagonist, or it might introduce a complication that impacts the main story. These intersections create a sense of unity and cohesion, making the subplots feel essential rather than extraneous.

**Types of Subplots**

There are several types of subplots that can be used to enhance a miniseries, each serving different narrative functions. Some common types include:

**Character Arcs:** These subplots focus on the personal development of secondary characters. For example, a subplot might follow a supporting character's journey to overcome a personal flaw, reconcile with a loved one, or achieve a specific goal. Character arcs deepen the audience's connection to the cast and provide additional emotional depth to the story.

**Romantic Subplots:** Romance is a popular subplot that can add emotional complexity and stakes to the narrative. A romantic subplot might involve a will-they-won't-they dynamic, a love triangle, or a relationship tested by external conflicts. Romance can also provide contrast to the main plot, offering moments of tenderness in an otherwise tense or dark story.

**Thematic Subplots:** These subplots explore secondary themes or different aspects of the main theme. For instance, if the main theme is power, a thematic subplot might examine how power corrupts or how it can be used for good. Thematic subplots allow for a more nuanced exploration of the story's central ideas.

**Mystery or Investigation Subplots:** These subplots involve a secondary character or group of characters uncovering secrets, solving a mystery, or investigating a crime. This type of subplot can add suspense and intrigue, while also feeding into the main plot by revealing important information or creating new conflicts.

**Parallel Subplots:** A parallel subplot mirrors the main plot, often involving similar conflicts, themes, or character dynamics. The parallel subplot can offer a different perspective on the main story, highlight contrasts, or foreshadow future events. For example, a subplot about a minor character seeking redemption might mirror the protagonist's own quest for forgiveness.

**Conflict Subplots:** These subplots introduce secondary conflicts that create additional obstacles for the characters. Conflict subplots might involve rivalries, betrayals, or moral dilemmas that complicate the main plot and add tension. These subplots are particularly effective in heightening stakes and deepening character development.

**Integrating Subplots Seamlessly**

To integrate subplots seamlessly into your miniseries, it's essential to maintain a balance between the main plot and the subplots. The subplots should complement the main narrative, enhancing it without overshadowing it. One way to achieve this balance is by ensuring that each subplot has a clear connection to the main plot, whether through character interactions, thematic resonance, or plot intersections.

Transitions between the main plot and subplots should feel natural and fluid. Avoid abrupt shifts that might jar the audience out of the story; instead, look for organic points of connection where a subplot can emerge naturally from the events of the main plot. For example, a conversation between two characters in the main plot might segue into a scene that delves deeper into one character's subplot, creating a smooth narrative flow.

It's also important to resolve subplots in a way that feels satisfying and connected to the overall story. Subplot resolutions should align with the miniseries' climax or denouement, contributing to the final emotional and thematic impact. Whether a subplot concludes with a triumph, a tragedy, or an open-ended question, it should resonate with the broader narrative and leave the audience with a sense of completion.

In conclusion, subplots are a powerful tool for adding depth, complexity, and richness to a television miniseries. By developing meaningful subplots that complement the main narrative, you can create a more immersive and engaging story that resonates with the audience on multiple levels. Effective subplots provide additional layers of character development, thematic exploration, and emotional engagement, enhancing the overall storytelling and making your miniseries a more memorable and impactful experience.

# Balancing Character and Plot: A Harmonious Blend

Balancing character and plot is one of the most important—and often challenging—tasks in crafting a television miniseries. Both elements are crucial to a successful narrative: the plot provides the structure and momentum that drives the story forward, while the characters give the story heart, depth, and emotional resonance. A miniseries that prioritizes one over the other can feel either emotionally flat or narratively disjointed. Achieving a harmonious blend of character and plot ensures that the audience is not only engaged with the unfolding events but also deeply invested in the fates of the characters experiencing them. In this chapter, we'll explore strategies for balancing character and plot in a way that creates a cohesive and compelling story.

**Understanding the Interdependence of Character and Plot**

The first step in balancing character and plot is recognizing their interdependence. Characters should not exist in isolation from the plot, nor should the plot feel disconnected from the characters' experiences. Instead, the two elements should be intertwined, with each influencing and shaping the other. A strong plot arises naturally from the actions, decisions, and growth of the characters, while compelling character development is often driven by the challenges and events of the plot.

In other words, plot and character are two sides of the same coin: the plot provides the external framework that drives the narrative, while the characters provide the internal motivation that gives the plot meaning.

For example, a plot centered around a high-stakes heist is only as engaging as the characters involved—who they are, why they're taking the risk, and how the heist affects their relationships and personal journeys. Similarly, a character's internal struggle with guilt or ambition will be more compelling when it's reflected in the external events of the plot, such as a mission gone wrong or a moral dilemma.

**Developing Plot from Character**

One effective way to ensure a balance between character and plot is to develop the plot organically from the characters. This approach involves allowing the characters' goals, motivations, and flaws to drive the events of the story. When characters are fully realized and their actions are consistent with their established traits, the plot will feel more authentic and engaging.

To develop plot from character, start by clearly defining your characters' desires and motivations. What does each character want most, and what are they willing to do to achieve it? What internal conflicts or external obstacles stand in their way? Once these elements are established, consider how the characters' pursuit of their goals could lead to key plot developments. For example, a character's ambition might lead them to make a risky decision, sparking a chain of events that drives the plot forward. Similarly, a character's fear or flaw might cause them to make a mistake, creating a new conflict that propels the narrative.

By letting character motivations guide plot developments, you create a story that feels more cohesive and emotionally resonant. The audience becomes invested in the plot not just because of the events themselves, but because of how those events impact the characters they care about.

**Structuring the Plot to Serve Character Development**

Conversely, the plot should be structured in a way that facilitates meaningful character development. The events of the plot should challenge the characters, forcing them to confront their flaws, make difficult decisions, and ultimately grow or change. A well-structured plot will present the characters with a series of escalating obstacles that test their resolve and push them to their limits.

When structuring your plot, consider how each major event or conflict will impact the characters on a personal level. What internal or external pressure does the event create, and how will the character respond? How does this response lead to further complications or developments in the plot? For example, if a character is forced to choose between loyalty to a friend and loyalty to a cause, their decision could lead to a betrayal that drives the plot in a new direction, while also deepening the character's emotional journey.

The key is to ensure that the plot is not just a sequence of events, but a series of challenges that are directly connected to the characters' arcs. This approach creates a sense of momentum and purpose, as each plot point contributes to both the narrative and the characters' development.

## Balancing External and Internal Conflict

A harmonious blend of character and plot often involves balancing external and internal conflict. External conflict refers to the obstacles and challenges that arise from the outside world—such as antagonists, environmental dangers, or societal pressures—while internal conflict refers to the struggles within a character's mind and heart, such as fear, guilt, or desire.

A well-balanced miniseries will feature both types of conflict, with each influencing the other. For example, an external conflict might exacerbate a character's internal struggle, forcing them to confront their fears or make a difficult choice. Conversely, a character's internal conflict might drive them to take actions that create external obstacles, complicating the plot and increasing tension.

By interweaving external and internal conflict, you create a more complex and layered narrative. The plot becomes a vehicle for exploring the characters' inner worlds, while the characters' internal struggles add emotional depth to the external events. This balance ensures that the story is engaging on both a narrative and emotional level.

## Using Subplots to Enhance Character and Plot Balance

Subplots can also play a crucial role in balancing character and plot. Well-crafted subplots offer additional opportunities for character development and can also reinforce or contrast with the main plot. For example, a subplot might focus on a secondary character's journey, offering a different perspective on the main plot's themes. Alternatively, a subplot might introduce a parallel conflict that mirrors the protagonist's struggles, deepening the audience's understanding of the character's journey.

When developing subplots, it's important to ensure that they are integrated into the main narrative in a way that feels seamless and meaningful. Subplots should not detract from the main plot, but rather complement it by providing additional layers of depth and complexity. By carefully interweaving subplots with the main narrative, you can create a more balanced and cohesive story that engages the audience on multiple levels.

## Maintaining Pacing and Focus

One of the challenges in balancing character and plot is maintaining the pacing and focus of the narrative. It's important to strike a balance between advancing the plot and allowing for moments of character introspection and development. If the plot moves too quickly, character development may be sacrificed, making the story feel shallow or rushed. Conversely, if the narrative lingers too long on character exploration, the plot may lose momentum, causing the story to drag.

To maintain a balanced pace, consider alternating between plot-driven scenes and character-driven moments. For example, a high-stakes action sequence might be followed by a quieter scene where the characters reflect on what has just happened, revealing their fears or motivations. This ebb and flow between action and introspection helps to keep the narrative dynamic while ensuring that both character and plot are given the attention they deserve.

### Character-Driven vs. Plot-Driven Stories

It's worth noting that different miniseries may lean more heavily toward either character-driven or plot-driven storytelling, depending on the genre and the story being told. A character-driven miniseries focuses more on the internal journeys and relationships of the characters, with the plot serving as a backdrop to these developments. Examples might include dramas or psychological thrillers where the main focus is on the characters' emotional and psychological states.

On the other hand, a plot-driven miniseries places more emphasis on the events and actions that drive the story forward, with character development arising naturally from their responses to these events. Examples might include crime thrillers or adventure stories where the primary focus is on the unfolding mystery or quest.

While it's possible to lean more heavily toward one approach or the other, the most compelling stories often strike a balance, ensuring that the plot is engaging and the characters are fully realized. Regardless of whether your miniseries is more character-driven or plot-driven, the goal should always be to create a narrative where the characters and plot are in harmony, each enhancing the other.

Balancing character and plot is essential for creating a miniseries that is both narratively engaging and emotionally resonant. By recognizing the interdependence of character and plot, developing plot organically from character motivations, and structuring the plot to facilitate character development, you can create a cohesive and compelling story. Balancing external and internal conflict, using subplots to enhance the narrative, and maintaining pacing and focus are all key strategies for achieving this balance.

Ultimately, a harmonious blend of character and plot ensures that the audience is fully invested in the story—not just in what happens, but in who it happens to and why it matters. When character and plot work together in this way, your miniseries will resonate more deeply with viewers, leaving a lasting impression long after the final episode has aired.

# Writing Episodic Cliffhangers: Keeping the Audience Hooked

Episodic cliffhangers are one of the most effective tools for keeping an audience engaged and eager to continue watching a television miniseries. By ending each episode with a moment of suspense, uncertainty, or revelation, you create a powerful incentive for viewers to tune in to the next episode. Cliffhangers can be used to heighten tension, deepen intrigue, and maintain narrative momentum, ensuring that your miniseries remains compelling from start to finish. In this chapter, we'll explore the art of writing episodic cliffhangers, including different types of cliffhangers, how to structure them, and strategies for using them effectively without over-relying on them.

**Understanding the Purpose of Cliffhangers**

The primary purpose of a cliffhanger is to create a sense of anticipation and urgency that compels the audience to keep watching. A well-crafted cliffhanger leaves viewers with unanswered questions or unresolved tensions that they are eager to see resolved. This technique is especially important in a serialized format like a miniseries, where sustaining audience interest over multiple episodes is key to the story's success.

Cliffhangers also serve to heighten the emotional stakes of the narrative. By ending an episode at a critical moment, you amplify the tension and drama, making the audience more invested in the outcome. Additionally, cliffhangers can reinforce the overall themes of the miniseries, as the suspenseful moment often reflects the central conflicts or dilemmas faced by the characters.

**Types of Cliffhangers**

There are several different types of cliffhangers that can be used to keep the audience hooked. Each type serves a different narrative function and can be employed depending on the needs of the story:

**The Peril Cliffhanger:** This is the classic cliffhanger where a character is placed in immediate physical danger, and the episode ends before the outcome is revealed. For example, a protagonist might be hanging from a cliff (literally or figuratively), about to be attacked, or trapped in a life-threatening situation. The peril cliffhanger creates intense suspense and a strong desire to find out what happens next.

**The Revelation Cliffhanger:** This type of cliffhanger involves a shocking revelation or discovery that changes the course of the story. It could be a plot twist, the unveiling of a secret, or the discovery of a crucial piece of information. The revelation cliffhanger leaves the audience eager to see how this new information will impact the characters and the plot.

**The Decision Cliffhanger:** In this scenario, a character is faced with a significant decision or dilemma, and the episode ends before the choice is made. The audience is left wondering which path the character will take and what the consequences will be. This type of cliffhanger is particularly effective for deepening character development and highlighting internal conflict.

**The Emotional Cliffhanger:** This cliffhanger focuses on the emotional state of the characters, often ending an episode on a note of high emotional tension or uncertainty. It might involve a relationship at a breaking point, a character's breakdown, or a moment of intense emotional vulnerability. The emotional cliffhanger keeps the audience invested in the characters' personal journeys.

**The Mystery Cliffhanger:** This type of cliffhanger involves the introduction or deepening of a mystery that remains unresolved. It might involve a cryptic message, a missing person, or an unexplained event. The mystery cliffhanger draws the audience deeper into the story by raising questions that they are eager to see answered.

**The Procedural Cliffhanger:** Common in crime and legal dramas, this cliffhanger occurs when an episode ends with a key development in an ongoing investigation, trial, or case. The procedural cliffhanger keeps the audience hooked by advancing the procedural plotline while leaving the outcome uncertain.

**Structuring Effective Cliffhangers**

To write an effective cliffhanger, it's important to consider the structure of the episode and how the cliffhanger fits into the overall narrative. A cliffhanger should feel like a natural culmination of the episode's events, not an arbitrary or forced interruption. Here are some strategies for structuring cliffhangers:

**Build to the Cliffhanger:** The events leading up to the cliffhanger should gradually escalate tension and stakes, creating a sense of momentum that culminates in the cliffhanger moment. This build-up makes the cliffhanger more impactful and satisfying, as it feels like a logical progression of the story.

**Integrate the Cliffhanger with the Episode Arc:** The cliffhanger should be closely tied to the central conflict or theme of the episode. Whether it's a peril, revelation, or decision cliffhanger, it should resonate with the episode's main storyline, adding weight and significance to the suspenseful moment.

**Leave the Audience Wanting More:** The key to a successful cliffhanger is to end the episode at a point where the audience is desperate to know what happens next. This might involve leaving a question unanswered, a fate uncertain, or a relationship unresolved. The cliffhanger should create a strong emotional or intellectual pull that compels the audience to continue watching.

**Balance Resolution and Cliffhangers:** While cliffhangers are effective for maintaining suspense, it's important to balance them with moments of resolution. If every episode ends on a cliffhanger, the audience may feel frustrated or overwhelmed. By occasionally resolving a storyline or conflict, you give the audience a sense of satisfaction and provide breathing room before the next cliffhanger.

**Vary the Type and Intensity of Cliffhangers:** To keep the audience engaged, vary the type and intensity of cliffhangers from episode to episode. A mix of peril, revelation, decision, and emotional cliffhangers keeps the narrative dynamic and prevents predictability. Additionally, not every cliffhanger needs to be a high-stakes moment—sometimes, a quieter, more subtle cliffhanger can be just as effective in keeping the audience intrigued.

**Consider the Timing of the Cliffhanger:** The timing of the cliffhanger within the episode is crucial. Typically, cliffhangers are placed at the very end of an episode, but they can also occur in the final moments of a scene, with the episode ending shortly thereafter. The goal is to ensure that the cliffhanger is the last thing the audience experiences, leaving a lasting impression that draws them back for more.

**Using Cliffhangers Effectively**

While cliffhangers are a powerful tool, they should be used judiciously and strategically. Over-reliance on cliffhangers can lead to diminishing returns, where the audience becomes desensitized to the suspense or feels manipulated. Here are some tips for using cliffhangers effectively:

**Make Sure the Cliffhanger Serves the Story:** Every cliffhanger should serve a purpose in the larger narrative. It should advance the plot, deepen character development, or reinforce the themes of the miniseries. Avoid using cliffhangers as mere gimmicks—they should always contribute to the story in a meaningful way.

**Pay off the Cliffhanger:** The resolution of a cliffhanger is just as important as the cliffhanger itself. When the audience tunes in to the next episode, they should feel that the suspenseful moment was worth the wait. Whether the outcome is surprising, satisfying, or tragic, it should feel earned and consistent with the story's trajectory.

**Don't Overuse Cliffhangers:** While cliffhangers are effective for maintaining suspense, they lose their impact if overused. Instead of ending every episode with a cliffhanger, consider using them strategically at key moments in the series. This approach keeps the cliffhangers fresh and impactful, rather than predictable.

**Consider the Emotional Impact:** Cliffhangers should evoke a strong emotional response from the audience, whether it's anxiety, excitement, sadness, or anticipation. When crafting a cliffhanger, think about the emotional journey you want the audience to experience and how the cliffhanger will contribute to that journey.

**Align Cliffhangers with Character Arcs:** The most effective cliffhangers are those that are deeply connected to the characters' arcs. By ending an episode with a moment that challenges or transforms a character, you create suspense that is not only plot-driven but also emotionally resonant.

Episodic cliffhangers are a powerful tool for keeping the audience hooked, creating a sense of anticipation and urgency that compels viewers to keep watching. By understanding the different types of cliffhangers, structuring them effectively, and using them strategically, you can maintain narrative momentum and deepen audience engagement throughout your miniseries. The key is to ensure that cliffhangers are integrated into the story in a way that feels natural and meaningful, contributing to both the plot and character development. When done well, cliffhangers can elevate your miniseries, making it a thrilling and immersive experience that keeps viewers on the edge of their seats, eagerly awaiting the next episode.

# The Antagonist's Perspective: Giving the Villain a Voice

In any compelling story, the antagonist plays a crucial role, providing the conflict and challenges that drive the protagonist's journey. However, to create a truly memorable and impactful narrative, it's essential to give the antagonist more than just a one-dimensional role as the "villain." By exploring the antagonist's perspective and giving them a voice, you add depth and complexity to your story, making the conflict more nuanced and the overall narrative more engaging. In this chapter, we'll delve into the importance of understanding the antagonist's perspective, how to develop their motivations and backstory, and strategies for integrating their voice into your miniseries.

## The Importance of the Antagonist's Perspective

The antagonist's perspective is crucial because it provides the narrative with a counterbalance to the protagonist's journey. A well-developed antagonist with clear motivations and a distinct voice can elevate the story, making the conflict more engaging and the stakes higher. When the audience understands the antagonist's point of view, they are more likely to see the conflict as a clash of competing ideals or goals, rather than a simple battle between good and evil. This adds layers of complexity to the narrative, making it more thought-provoking and emotionally resonant.

Giving the antagonist a voice also humanizes them, making them more than just an obstacle for the protagonist to overcome. When the audience can empathize with the antagonist's motivations— even if they don't agree with them—they become more invested in the outcome of the conflict. This can create a more dynamic and unpredictable narrative, as the audience may find themselves torn between the protagonist and the antagonist, unsure of who will prevail.

## Developing the Antagonist's Motivations and Backstory

To give the antagonist a voice, start by developing their motivations and backstory. Every antagonist should have a clear reason for their actions, rooted in their personal history, beliefs, or desires. These motivations should be just as strong and well-defined as those of the protagonist, providing a foundation for the antagonist's behavior throughout the miniseries.

When crafting the antagonist's backstory, consider what events or experiences shaped their worldview. What led them to become the person they are when the story begins? Perhaps they experienced a significant loss, betrayal, or injustice that fueled their desire for revenge or power. Or maybe they have a deeply held belief that they are justified in their actions, even if those actions are harmful to others. By exploring the antagonist's past, you can create a more fully realized character whose actions are grounded in their personal history.

It's also important to consider the antagonist's goals and how they align with or oppose those of the protagonist. A strong antagonist should have their own agenda, one that puts them in direct conflict with the protagonist. However, their goals don't necessarily have to be evil or malicious; in fact, some of the most compelling antagonists are those who genuinely believe they are doing the right thing. For example, an antagonist who is trying to protect their family or community might come into conflict with the protagonist because they have different ideas about what is best.

## Exploring Moral Complexity

One of the most effective ways to give the antagonist a voice is by exploring moral complexity. Rather than painting the antagonist as purely evil, consider giving them a moral code or set of principles that guide their actions. This moral complexity can create a more nuanced and layered character, one who is driven by a sense of duty, honor, or justice, even if their methods are extreme or misguided.

For example, an antagonist who is a revolutionary leader might be fighting against a corrupt government, but their willingness to use violence and sacrifice innocent lives puts them at odds with the protagonist. The audience can understand the antagonist's desire for change, but they may struggle with the ethical implications of their actions. This moral ambiguity makes the conflict more interesting and forces the audience to grapple with difficult questions about right and wrong.

Another way to explore moral complexity is by highlighting the similarities between the protagonist and antagonist. In some cases, the antagonist might be a mirror image of the protagonist, representing what the protagonist could become if they made different choices. This parallelism can create a powerful dynamic, as the protagonist is forced to confront their own flaws and fears through their interactions with the antagonist.

## Giving the Antagonist a Voice in the Narrative

Once you've developed the antagonist's motivations and backstory, it's important to give them a voice in the narrative. This can be done in several ways, depending on the structure and style of your miniseries.

One approach is to provide the antagonist with their own point-of-view scenes, allowing the audience to see the story from their perspective. These scenes can offer insights into the antagonist's thoughts, feelings, and motivations, helping the audience understand their actions on a deeper level. For example, a scene where the antagonist reflects on a past trauma or reveals their true intentions to a confidant can add depth to their character and make them more relatable.

Dialogue is another powerful tool for giving the antagonist a voice. Through conversations with other characters, the antagonist can articulate their beliefs, justify their actions, and challenge the protagonist's worldview. These exchanges can create tension and conflict, as the protagonist and antagonist clash over their differing perspectives. For example, a confrontation between the protagonist and antagonist might involve a heated debate about morality, justice, or power, with each character defending their position and trying to sway the other.

Monologues can also be an effective way to give the antagonist a voice, especially in moments of introspection or revelation. A well-crafted monologue allows the antagonist to express their inner thoughts and emotions, revealing the complexities of their character. For example, an antagonist who is struggling with doubt or guilt might deliver a monologue that exposes their vulnerability, making them more human and less of a caricature.

## Balancing the Antagonist's Voice with the Protagonist's

While it's important to give the antagonist a voice, it's also crucial to maintain balance in the narrative. The protagonist should remain the central focus of the story, with the antagonist's perspective serving to enrich and complicate the conflict rather than overshadow the protagonist's journey.

To achieve this balance, consider how the antagonist's voice can complement and contrast with the protagonist's. The antagonist's perspective should provide a counterpoint to the protagonist's, challenging their beliefs and forcing them to grow. At the same time, the protagonist's journey should drive the narrative, with the antagonist's actions serving as obstacles or catalysts for the protagonist's development.

One way to maintain this balance is by ensuring that the antagonist's voice is integrated into the story's broader themes. The antagonist's perspective should highlight the central conflicts and dilemmas of the miniseries, deepening the audience's understanding of the themes being explored. For example, if the miniseries is about the nature of power, the antagonist's pursuit of power and the consequences of their actions can serve as a critical exploration of that theme.

## Humanizing the Antagonist

Humanizing the antagonist is key to giving them a voice that resonates with the audience. This doesn't mean justifying their actions or making them sympathetic, but rather showing that they are a complex, multi-dimensional character with their own fears, desires, and vulnerabilities.

One way to humanize the antagonist is by exploring their relationships with other characters. How do they interact with those close to them? Do they have people they care about or trust? These relationships can reveal different facets of the antagonist's personality and make them more relatable. For example, an antagonist who is ruthless in their pursuit of power might show tenderness or concern for a family member, complicating the audience's perception of them.

Another approach is to give the antagonist moments of vulnerability or doubt. Even the most confident and powerful characters have moments of weakness, and showing these moments can make the antagonist more relatable. For example, an antagonist who questions their own actions or struggles with guilt adds depth to their character and makes their voice more compelling.

## The Antagonist's Resolution

The resolution of the antagonist's arc is a crucial part of giving them a voice. How the antagonist's story ends should be consistent with their character development and the themes of the miniseries. Whether the antagonist is defeated, redeemed, or left in ambiguity, their resolution should provide closure to their journey while also reinforcing the broader narrative.

If the antagonist is defeated, consider how their downfall reflects their flaws or miscalculations. For example, an antagonist who is consumed by pride might be undone by their inability to see their own weaknesses. If the antagonist is redeemed, explore how their transformation impacts the protagonist and the overall story. A redemption arc can be powerful, but it should feel earned and consistent with the antagonist's journey.

In some cases, leaving the antagonist's fate ambiguous can add a layer of complexity to the narrative, allowing the audience to grapple with unresolved questions. This approach can be particularly effective if the miniseries explores themes of morality, justice, or the consequences of power.

Giving the antagonist a voice is essential for creating a nuanced and compelling narrative in your miniseries. By developing the antagonist's motivations and backstory, exploring moral complexity, and integrating their perspective into the story, you can create a multi-dimensional character who adds depth and tension to the narrative. Balancing the antagonist's voice with the protagonist's ensures that the conflict remains engaging and the themes are fully explored.

When done effectively, a well-developed antagonist can elevate your miniseries, making the story more thought-provoking and emotionally resonant. The antagonist's voice not only challenges the protagonist but also invites the audience to consider different perspectives, ultimately creating a richer and more impactful viewing experience.

# World-Building on a Budget

World-building is a crucial aspect of storytelling, especially in a television miniseries where the setting plays a significant role in shaping the narrative and immersing the audience in the story's universe. However, creating believable and immersive settings can be challenging, particularly when working with a limited budget. The key to successful world-building on a budget is creativity, resourcefulness, and a focus on the elements that matter most to the story. In this chapter, we'll explore strategies for creating convincing settings without breaking the bank, from maximizing the use of locations and props to leveraging visual storytelling and practical effects.

## Prioritizing Key Elements of the World

The first step in world-building on a budget is to prioritize the elements of the setting that are most essential to the story. Not every detail needs to be fully realized or shown on screen—focus on the key aspects that will have the most impact on the narrative and the audience's experience. This might include specific locations that are central to the plot, cultural or technological details that define the world, or iconic visual motifs that reinforce the themes of the miniseries.

For example, if your story is set in a dystopian future, the most important elements might be the oppressive architecture, the technology that controls society, and the stark contrast between the ruling class and the oppressed. By focusing on these key elements, you can create a strong sense of place without needing to show every aspect of the world in detail.

## Maximizing the Use of Real Locations

One of the most cost-effective ways to build a believable world is by using real locations that can stand in for the settings in your story. With careful scouting and creative framing, ordinary places can be transformed into extraordinary settings. For instance, an abandoned factory might serve as the headquarters of a rebel group, a dense forest could become an ancient, mystical woodland, or a modern urban area could be reimagined as a futuristic city.

When scouting locations, look for places that have distinctive architectural or natural features that can be emphasized to fit the world you're building. You can enhance these locations with minimal set dressing and visual effects to make them feel more unique and specific to your story. Additionally, consider how different angles, lighting, and time of day can change the appearance of a location, allowing you to use the same place for multiple settings with subtle variations.

## Creative Set Design and Dressing

When building sets on a budget, creativity is key. Focus on creating the illusion of a larger, more complex world with the resources you have available. This can involve using modular set pieces that can be rearranged or redressed to create different environments, or using strategic camera angles to suggest the presence of off-screen elements that aren't actually there.

For example, a few well-chosen pieces of furniture, props, and wall treatments can transform a small space into a variety of different settings. By using depth, perspective, and careful lighting, you can make a limited set feel much larger and more detailed than it actually is. Additionally, layering the set with texture—through the use of fabric, paint, or found objects—can add richness and authenticity to the environment.

## Utilizing Props and Costumes for World-Building

Props and costumes are powerful tools for world-building, as they can convey a great deal of information about the setting, culture, and time period with minimal expense. When working on a budget, focus on a few key props or costume pieces that can serve as focal points and enhance the believability of the world.

For instance, a distinctive piece of technology, a unique weapon, or an ornate piece of jewelry can become iconic elements of your story's world. These items can be designed and created using everyday materials, DIY techniques, or modified existing objects. Similarly, costumes can be assembled from thrifted clothing or repurposed materials, with attention to detail in the design and accessories to create a cohesive look that fits the world.

Props and costumes can also be used to suggest larger world-building elements that aren't explicitly shown on screen. For example, a character's uniform might hint at a complex hierarchy or societal structure, while a worn and patched cloak might suggest a world in decline or a character's long journey.

## Leveraging Visual Storytelling Techniques

Visual storytelling techniques can significantly enhance world-building on a budget by allowing you to imply more than you show. Through the use of lighting, color palettes, and framing, you can create a specific mood or atmosphere that communicates the nature of the world without requiring expensive sets or effects.

For example, a desaturated color palette combined with harsh, directional lighting might evoke a bleak, dystopian environment, while warm, diffused lighting and rich colors could suggest a more idyllic or fantastical setting. The way you frame a shot—whether it's tight and claustrophobic or wide and expansive—can also convey the scale and scope of the world.

Another powerful technique is the use of visual motifs and symbols. Repeated visual elements, such as a particular pattern, symbol, or color, can create a sense of unity and cohesion in the world. These motifs can be used in set design, props, costumes, and even in the behavior of characters to reinforce the world's themes and aesthetic.

## Practical Effects and DIY Solutions

Practical effects can be an effective and budget-friendly way to enhance the world of your miniseries. Instead of relying on expensive CGI, consider using practical effects such as smoke, fog, lighting tricks, and miniatures to create a sense of scale and atmosphere. These effects can be achieved with relatively simple materials and techniques, yet they can have a significant impact on the visual believability of the setting.

For example, a well-placed fan and some debris can create the illusion of a windy, desolate landscape, while a carefully lit model or miniature can stand in for a large, imposing structure. Practical effects can also be combined with simple digital effects in post-production to enhance their impact, such as adding a digital sky or extending the depth of a scene.

DIY solutions can also extend to sound design, which is an often-overlooked aspect of world-building. By creating a rich soundscape that includes ambient noises, environmental sounds, and subtle effects, you can immerse the audience in the world you've created. Simple sound effects can be recorded or sourced from free libraries and layered to suggest a bustling city, a haunted forest, or a futuristic control room.

## Story-Driven World-Building

Ultimately, the most effective world-building is story-driven. Every element of the setting should serve the narrative and enhance the audience's understanding of the characters and plot. When working with a limited budget, it's important to ensure that the world-building choices you make are directly tied to the story you're telling.

Ask yourself: What aspects of the world are most important to the story? What does the audience need to see and understand in order to fully engage with the narrative? By focusing on these questions, you can make strategic decisions about where to allocate your resources and how to maximize the impact of the world-building elements you choose to include.

In some cases, suggesting rather than showing can be just as effective. For instance, instead of depicting a massive battle, you might focus on the aftermath, showing the emotional and physical toll it has taken on the characters. This approach not only saves on production costs but also allows for more intimate, character-driven storytelling.

## Collaborating with Creative Talent

Collaboration is key to successful world-building on a budget. By working closely with your production designer, art director, costume designer, and other creative talent, you can brainstorm innovative solutions and make the most of the resources you have. Encourage your team to think outside the box and explore unconventional materials, techniques, and ideas.

Engaging with local artists, craftspeople, and prop-makers can also provide access to unique, handcrafted items that add authenticity and originality to your world. Often, these collaborations can result in more personalized and detailed elements that enrich the visual storytelling without incurring significant costs.

World-building on a budget is a creative challenge that requires resourcefulness, imagination, and a focus on what truly matters to the story. By prioritizing key elements, maximizing real locations, using creative set design, and leveraging visual storytelling techniques, you can create believable and immersive settings that draw the audience into your miniseries.

Practical effects, DIY solutions, and strategic collaboration with your creative team can further enhance the world-building, allowing you to achieve a rich and detailed environment even with limited resources. Ultimately, the goal is to create a world that serves the narrative, deepens the audience's connection to the story, and leaves a lasting impression, regardless of budget constraints.

With careful planning and a focus on storytelling, you can build a world that feels authentic, engaging, and integral to the success of your miniseries, proving that a powerful narrative doesn't always require a blockbuster budget.

# Exploring Themes through Characters

Exploring themes through characters is a powerful way to create a rich, layered narrative in a television miniseries. Themes are the underlying messages, ideas, or questions that the story seeks to explore, and characters serve as the vehicles through which these themes are brought to life. By allowing your characters to embody, struggle with, or represent different aspects of the theme, you create a more engaging and thought-provoking story that resonates on a deeper level. In this chapter, we'll explore how to effectively develop and convey themes through characters, using their arcs, relationships, and conflicts to illuminate the central ideas of your miniseries.

**Understanding the Connection between Theme and Character**

The first step in exploring themes through characters is to understand the connection between the two. Themes are often abstract concepts—such as love, power, justice, or redemption—that can be difficult to convey directly. Characters, on the other hand, are concrete and relatable; they have emotions, desires, and flaws that the audience can connect with. By grounding the theme in the experiences and choices of your characters, you make it more accessible and impactful for the audience.

For example, if your theme is about the corrupting influence of power, you might explore this theme through a character who begins as an idealistic leader but gradually becomes more ruthless as they gain power. Their journey would illustrate the theme, showing how power can change a person's values and behavior. Similarly, a theme about forgiveness might be explored through a character who struggles to forgive someone who has wronged them, ultimately leading to personal growth or self-destruction.

**Developing Characters to Reflect the Theme**

When developing characters to reflect a theme, consider how their personality, backstory, and motivations align with the central ideas of your story. Each character can represent a different facet of the theme, providing various perspectives and adding depth to the narrative.

**Protagonists and Antagonists:** The protagonist often embodies the theme in a way that reflects their journey or struggle. For example, in a story about redemption, the protagonist might be someone seeking to atone for past mistakes, with their arc centered around finding forgiveness or self-acceptance. The antagonist, on the other hand, might represent the opposite side of the theme, challenging the protagonist's beliefs or embodying the consequences of failing to address the theme's central issue.

**Supporting Characters:** Supporting characters can also play a significant role in exploring the theme. Each supporting character might reflect a different perspective or approach to the theme, creating a richer exploration of the central idea. For instance, in a story about justice, one supporting character might believe in strict adherence to the law, while another advocates for a more compassionate, moral approach. Their interactions with the protagonist can highlight the complexities of the theme and provide the audience with a broader understanding of the issues at play.

**Character Flaws and Strengths:** A character's flaws and strengths can be directly tied to the theme, shaping their actions and decisions throughout the story. For example, in a theme about the dangers of pride, a character's arrogance might lead to their downfall, while another character's humility might allow them to succeed where others fail. By linking character traits to the theme, you create a more cohesive and thematically resonant narrative.

## Using Character Arcs to Explore Themes

Character arcs are one of the most effective ways to explore themes, as they show how a character changes or grows in response to the central ideas of the story. A well-crafted character arc can take the audience on a journey that mirrors the thematic exploration, allowing them to experience the theme's impact through the character's eyes.

**Positive Arcs:** In a positive character arc, the protagonist starts with a flaw or misconception related to the theme and gradually overcomes it. This journey often leads to personal growth and a deeper understanding of the theme. For example, in a theme about love, a character who begins as emotionally closed off might learn to open up and form meaningful relationships, ultimately finding happiness and fulfillment.

**Negative Arcs:** In a negative character arc, the character may start with potential for growth but instead falls deeper into their flaws or misconceptions, leading to a tragic or destructive outcome. This type of arc can be used to explore the darker aspects of a theme. For instance, in a theme about ambition, a character might be consumed by their desire for success, leading them to betray others and ultimately destroy themselves.

**Flat Arcs:** A flat character arc, where the character remains largely unchanged but influences the world around them, can also be used to explore themes. In this case, the character's steadfastness in their beliefs might challenge the views of other characters or highlight the theme's significance. For example, a character who maintains their integrity in the face of corruption can serve as a beacon of hope or a moral compass in a story about ethics.

## Exploring Themes through Character Relationships

Character relationships are a powerful tool for exploring themes, as they allow you to examine how different perspectives on the theme interact and influence each other. The dynamics between characters—whether they are friends, lovers, rivals, or enemies—can bring the theme to life in a way that is both emotionally engaging and intellectually stimulating.

**Conflict and Contrast:** Conflict between characters can be used to highlight different aspects of the theme. For example, in a story about freedom, one character might fight for personal liberty, while another believes in the importance of order and control. Their conflicting views create tension and force both characters to confront the theme from different angles. This contrast can deepen the audience's understanding of the theme and add complexity to the narrative.

**Alliances and Bonds:** Alliances and bonds between characters can also be used to explore themes, particularly when these relationships are tested by the central conflict. For example, in a theme about loyalty, characters might be forced to choose between their loyalty to a friend and their loyalty to a cause. The way these relationships evolve in response to the theme can create powerful emotional moments and drive the narrative forward.

**Mentorship and Influence:** Mentorship and influence are other ways to explore themes through character relationships. A mentor character who embodies a particular aspect of the theme can guide or challenge the protagonist, shaping their understanding of the central idea. For instance, in a theme about wisdom, a wise mentor might teach the protagonist valuable lessons about life, or a misguided mentor might lead them astray, forcing them to find their own path.

## Using Dialogue to Explore Themes

Dialogue is a direct way to explore themes through characters, as it allows them to articulate their views, challenge each other's beliefs, and express the internal conflicts that drive their actions. Through carefully crafted dialogue, you can convey the theme in a way that feels natural and integral to the story.

**Philosophical Debates:** Characters can engage in philosophical debates that delve into the theme, presenting different perspectives and forcing the audience to consider multiple viewpoints. For example, in a theme about justice, characters might argue about what constitutes true justice, whether it's retributive, restorative, or something else entirely. These debates can be woven into the plot, with the outcome of the story reflecting the resolution (or lack thereof) of these philosophical conflicts.

**Subtext and Symbolism:** Dialogue can also explore themes through subtext and symbolism, allowing characters to convey deeper meanings without directly stating them. For example, a character might talk about the weather or a mundane event, but their words carry a symbolic weight that reflects the theme. A conversation about a storm on the horizon might symbolize impending conflict, or a discussion about planting seeds might represent hope and renewal.

**Character Monologues:** Monologues are another effective way to explore themes, as they provide characters with an opportunity to reflect on their experiences and the central ideas of the story. A well-placed monologue can reveal a character's internal struggle with the theme, offering insights into their motivations and the larger questions the story is addressing. For instance, a monologue about the nature of courage might explore a character's fear and doubt, ultimately leading to a revelation about what true bravery means.

### Integrating Theme into Plot and Character Decisions

To fully explore themes through characters, it's important to integrate the theme into the plot and character decisions. The choices that characters make, the challenges they face, and the consequences of their actions should all reflect the theme, creating a narrative that is cohesive and thematically rich.

**Thematic Decisions:** Characters should face decisions that force them to confront the theme directly. These decisions might involve moral dilemmas, personal sacrifices, or moments of self-discovery that reveal their true nature. For example, in a theme about sacrifice, a character might have to choose between their own happiness and the greater good, with their decision reflecting their understanding of the theme.

**Plot Developments:** Plot developments should also be tied to the theme, with key events and conflicts serving to reinforce the central ideas of the story. For instance, in a theme about truth, the plot might involve a series of revelations that challenge the characters' beliefs and force them to reassess what they thought they knew. Each twist and turn in the plot should push the characters deeper into the theme, driving both the narrative and their personal growth.

**Consequences and Resolution:** The consequences of the characters' decisions should reflect the theme, providing a resolution that is thematically satisfying. Whether the story ends on a note of triumph, tragedy, or ambiguity, the resolution should leave the audience with a deeper understanding of the theme and its implications. For example, in a theme about forgiveness, the resolution might show the healing power of forgiveness, or it might reveal the lasting scars of unforgiven wrongs.

Exploring themes through characters is a powerful way to create a miniseries that is both emotionally engaging and intellectually stimulating. By developing characters who embody different aspects of the theme, using their arcs to illustrate the theme's complexities, and integrating the theme into their relationships, dialogue, and decisions, you can create a narrative that resonates on multiple levels.

# The Power of the First Episode: Setting the Tone

The first episode of a television miniseries is crucial—it sets the tone for the entire series, introduces the audience to the world and characters, and establishes the narrative style and themes that will be explored. A powerful first episode grabs the audience's attention and leaves them eager to continue watching, while also laying the groundwork for the story to unfold. In this chapter, we'll discuss the key elements of a successful first episode, how to effectively set the tone, and strategies for making a lasting impression that hooks the audience from the very beginning.

**Establishing the Tone**

The tone of your miniseries is the overall mood or atmosphere that permeates the story. It's a combination of the narrative style, visual aesthetic, pacing, and emotional resonance that defines the series. The first episode is your opportunity to establish this tone, setting expectations for the audience about what kind of story they're about to experience.

**Narrative Style:** The narrative style of the first episode should reflect the broader style of the series. This includes decisions about whether the story will be told in a linear fashion, through flashbacks, or with multiple timelines. The use of voiceover, the choice of point of view, and the narrative pace all contribute to the overall tone. For example, a fast-paced, action-packed opening scene sets a tone of urgency and intensity, while a slow, reflective opening might suggest a more contemplative or psychological story.

**Visual Aesthetic:** The visual style of the first episode is another key element in setting the tone. This includes the use of color palettes, lighting, camera angles, and composition. A dark, moody aesthetic with shadowy lighting might create a sense of suspense or danger, while bright, vibrant colors could indicate a more light-hearted or fantastical tone. The way you visually present the world in the first episode will shape the audience's perception and expectations for the series.

**Music and Sound Design:** Music and sound design play a crucial role in establishing the tone of the first episode. The score, choice of songs, and ambient sounds can all contribute to the mood and emotional impact of the story. For example, a haunting, atmospheric score might create a sense of mystery and tension, while upbeat, energetic music could set a more adventurous or comedic tone. The way sound is used to emphasize certain moments or to build tension can also help to define the series' tone.

**Pacing:** The pacing of the first episode is critical in setting the tone. A rapidly paced opening might convey a sense of urgency or chaos, while a more deliberate, measured pace could suggest a focus on character development or thematic exploration. The rhythm of scenes, the timing of dialogue, and the flow of action all contribute to the pacing, which should align with the overall tone you want to establish.

**Introducing the World and Characters**

The first episode is your chance to introduce the audience to the world of the miniseries and the characters who inhabit it. This includes establishing the setting, the rules of the world, and the main characters' personalities, motivations, and relationships.

**World-Building:** Effective world-building in the first episode involves providing enough detail to make the setting feel real and immersive, without overwhelming the audience with too much information. Focus on the key elements that define the world, such as its geography, culture, technology, or societal structure. Show the world in action through the characters' interactions with their environment, allowing the audience to absorb the setting naturally.

For example, in a dystopian future setting, you might show characters navigating a city controlled by a totalitarian regime, with visual cues like surveillance cameras, propaganda posters, and militarized police. These details convey the oppressive nature of the world without needing extensive exposition.

**Character Introduction:** Introducing your main characters effectively in the first episode is crucial for engaging the audience. The audience should quickly understand who these characters are, what they want, and what challenges they might face. This doesn't mean revealing everything about the characters upfront, but rather providing enough information to make them intriguing and relatable.

Consider starting with a scene that highlights the protagonist's core traits, such as their strengths, flaws, or desires. For example, a protagonist who is a skilled but cynical detective might be introduced solving a case with sharp wit but also displaying signs of burnout or disillusionment. This sets up both the character's capabilities and their internal conflicts, giving the audience a reason to care about their journey.

**Establishing Relationships:** The relationships between characters are another important aspect to introduce in the first episode. These relationships will drive much of the drama and conflict in the series, so it's important to establish their dynamics early on. Whether it's a tense rivalry, a budding romance, or a deep friendship, the way characters interact with each other in the first episode sets the stage for their development throughout the series.

## Introducing the Central Conflict

The central conflict of the miniseries should be introduced in the first episode, providing the driving force for the narrative. This conflict could be external, such as a looming threat or a major goal the protagonist must achieve, or it could be internal, such as a personal struggle or moral dilemma. Ideally, the first episode should end with the audience having a clear understanding of what the protagonist is up against and what's at stake.

**The Inciting Incident:** The inciting incident is the event that sets the main plot in motion. It's the catalyst that disrupts the protagonist's status quo and propels them into the story's central conflict. In the first episode, the inciting incident should be clearly established, creating a sense of urgency or intrigue that compels the audience to keep watching.

For example, in a crime drama, the inciting incident might be the discovery of a body that hints at a larger conspiracy, drawing the protagonist into a dangerous investigation. In a character-driven drama, it might be a life-changing decision or revelation that forces the protagonist to reevaluate their life.

**Foreshadowing and Mystery:** In addition to introducing the central conflict, the first episode can also lay the groundwork for future plot developments through foreshadowing and mystery. Subtle hints or unresolved questions can create a sense of anticipation, encouraging the audience to look for clues and speculate about where the story is heading.

For instance, a brief, enigmatic scene involving a mysterious figure or an unexplained event can plant the seeds for a subplot or twist that will be revealed later in the series. This technique helps to build suspense and keeps the audience engaged by suggesting that there is more to the story than meets the eye.

## Creating a Hook

A strong first episode should have a clear hook—something that grabs the audience's attention and makes them want to continue watching. This hook can take many forms, depending on the type of story you're telling.

**A Powerful Opening Scene:** One of the most effective ways to hook the audience is with a powerful opening scene that immediately draws them into the story. This could be a dramatic action sequence, an emotionally charged moment, or a striking visual tableau that piques curiosity. The opening scene sets the tone and gives the audience a taste of what to expect from the rest of the series.

For example, a suspense thriller might open with a tense, fast-paced chase that ends in a shocking twist, while a fantasy series might begin with a visually stunning scene of a magical ritual or battle. The key is to create an opening that is both captivating and thematically relevant to the story.

**Engaging Characters:** Another effective hook is to introduce characters who are immediately engaging, whether through their charisma, complexity, or the intriguing circumstances they find themselves in. If the audience is drawn to the characters—either because they like them, relate to them, or are curious about them—they are more likely to continue watching to see how their stories unfold.

**A Cliffhanger Ending:** Ending the first episode with a cliffhanger or a surprising twist can also serve as a powerful hook. By leaving the audience with an unresolved question or a heightened sense of anticipation, you create a strong incentive for them to tune in to the next episode. The cliffhanger doesn't have to be dramatic or action-packed; it could be a subtle revelation or a moment of emotional tension that raises the stakes.

## Setting Up the Themes

The first episode is an opportunity to introduce the themes that will be explored throughout the miniseries. While these themes don't need to be fully articulated from the start, there should be hints or elements that suggest the broader ideas and questions the series will address.

**Symbolism and Visual Motifs:** Symbolism and visual motifs can be used to subtly introduce the themes of the series in the first episode. For example, recurring images of broken mirrors or shattered glass might hint at themes of identity or self-perception, while the contrast between light and shadow could symbolize the conflict between good and evil. These motifs can be woven into the setting, costumes, and even the cinematography, creating a cohesive visual language that supports the thematic exploration.

**Character Interactions and Dialogue:** The way characters interact with each other and the dialogue they exchange can also introduce themes. For example, a conversation about justice might foreshadow the ethical dilemmas the characters will face, or a scene where a character struggles with a personal decision might hint at the theme of moral ambiguity. These thematic elements should feel organic to the story, emerging naturally from the characters' actions and relationships.

The first episode of a television miniseries is your opportunity to make a strong impression and set the tone for the entire series. By establishing the narrative style, visual aesthetic, and pacing, you create a clear and cohesive tone that guides the audience's expectations. Introducing the world, characters, and central conflict effectively ensures that the audience is engaged and invested in the story from the beginning. Creating a compelling hook—whether through a powerful opening scene, engaging characters, or a cliffhanger ending—encourages the audience to continue watching, while setting up the themes provides a foundation for deeper exploration throughout the series.

# Writing for a Limited Run: Pacing and Structure

Writing for a limited run, such as a television miniseries, presents unique challenges and opportunities when it comes to pacing and structure. Unlike ongoing series that have the luxury of spreading out storylines over multiple seasons, a limited series must tell a complete, cohesive story within a finite number of episodes. This requires careful planning and precise execution to ensure that the narrative remains engaging, well-paced, and satisfying from start to finish. In this chapter, we'll explore strategies for pacing and structuring a limited-run series, focusing on how to make the most of your episode count and create a compelling, tightly woven narrative.

## Understanding the Constraints of a Limited Run

The first step in writing for a limited run is to understand the constraints and possibilities that come with a set number of episodes. Whether your series has four, six, eight, or ten episodes, each installment must contribute meaningfully to the overall narrative. There's no room for filler or extraneous subplots—every scene, character, and line of dialogue should serve the story.

A limited run also means that you must resolve all major plotlines by the end of the series. This constraint can be freeing, as it allows you to create a more focused and intense story with a clear beginning, middle, and end. However, it also requires careful pacing to ensure that the story doesn't feel rushed or dragged out.

## Planning the Overall Structure

Before diving into the writing process, it's crucial to plan the overall structure of your limited-run series. This involves mapping out the key plot points, character arcs, and thematic developments across the entire series. A well-structured series will have a clear narrative arc that builds steadily toward a climax and resolution.

**Breaking the Story into Acts:** One effective approach is to think of your series as a long-form story divided into acts, much like a play or film. For example, a six-episode series might be structured into three acts:

**Act 1 (Episodes 1-2):** Introduce the world, characters, and central conflict. Set the stakes and establish the tone. The inciting incident occurs, propelling the protagonist into the main plot.

**Act 2 (Episodes 3-4):** Develop the central conflict and deepen character relationships. Introduce obstacles, complications, and subplots. Tensions rise, leading to a major turning point or crisis at the end of Act 2.

**Act 3 (Episodes 5-6):** Resolve the central conflict and subplots. Characters face the consequences of their actions. The climax occurs, followed by the resolution and a satisfying conclusion.

This three-act structure provides a clear framework for pacing the story, ensuring that it progresses logically and steadily builds toward the climax.

**Plotting Key Episodes:** In addition to the overall structure, it's important to identify key episodes that will serve as major turning points in the story. These episodes should be strategically placed to maintain momentum and keep the audience engaged. For example, the midpoint of the series might feature a significant revelation or plot twist, while the penultimate episode often involves the highest stakes or most intense conflict.

## Pacing the Narrative

Pacing is critical in a limited-run series, as you must balance the need to keep the story moving forward with the need to develop characters, themes, and subplots. Here are some strategies for achieving effective pacing:

**Start Strong:** The first episode should immediately engage the audience and set the pace for the rest of the series. Introduce the central conflict and key characters early on, ensuring that the story gets off to a strong start. Avoid unnecessary exposition or slow openings—there's no time to waste in a limited run.

**Build Momentum:** Each episode should build on the last, with the stakes rising steadily as the series progresses. This can be achieved by gradually increasing the intensity of the conflicts, introducing new challenges or complications, and deepening the emotional or psychological stakes for the characters. Avoid lulls in the action or overly slow episodes that could lose the audience's interest.

**Balance Action and Character Development:** While it's important to keep the plot moving, don't neglect character development. Use quieter moments and dialogue scenes to explore characters' motivations, relationships, and internal conflicts. These scenes should be strategically placed to provide breathing room between more intense sequences, allowing the audience to connect with the characters and understand their journeys.

**Use Cliffhangers and Revelations:** Cliffhangers and revelations are effective tools for maintaining pacing in a limited-run series. By ending episodes on a suspenseful note or revealing key information at critical moments, you keep the audience eager to see what happens next. However, be careful not to overuse cliffhangers—each one should feel earned and contribute to the overall narrative.

**Pacing Subplots:** Subplots can add depth and complexity to the story, but they must be carefully paced to avoid distracting from the main plot. Introduce subplots early in the series and ensure they progress alongside the central narrative. As the series approaches its climax, begin resolving subplots in a way that ties them into the main story, providing a sense of cohesion.

## Managing Character Arcs

In a limited-run series, character arcs must be carefully managed to ensure that they feel complete and satisfying by the end. Each character should have a clear trajectory, with their growth or transformation closely tied to the central themes of the series.

**Defining Character Arcs:** Start by defining the arcs for your main characters. What are their goals, fears, and flaws at the beginning of the series? How will they change or grow as a result of the events of the story? Each character's arc should have a clear beginning, middle, and end, with key moments of growth or conflict spaced throughout the series.

**Aligning Arcs with Plot Points:** Ensure that character arcs align with the major plot points of the series. For example, a character might face their greatest challenge or make a pivotal decision at the climax, resulting in a significant transformation. By tying character development to the plot, you create a more cohesive and emotionally resonant narrative.

**Balancing Multiple Arcs:** If your series features multiple protagonists or significant supporting characters, it's important to balance their arcs so that each one feels fully developed. Avoid focusing too heavily on one character at the expense of others—each arc should contribute to the overall story and reflect the series' themes. Consider how different characters' arcs can intersect or contrast with each other, creating additional layers of meaning.

### Structuring the Climax and Resolution

The climax and resolution are the culmination of your series, where all the narrative threads come together and the central conflict is resolved. In a limited-run series, it's essential to ensure that the climax is both impactful and satisfying, providing a fitting conclusion to the story.

**Building to the Climax:** The episodes leading up to the climax should steadily increase tension and stakes, preparing the audience for the final confrontation or resolution. Ensure that all major plotlines and character arcs are converging toward this moment, creating a sense of inevitability and urgency.

**Delivering a Satisfying Climax:** The climax should be the most intense and emotionally charged moment of the series, providing a resolution to the central conflict. Whether it's a dramatic showdown, a shocking twist, or a deeply emotional revelation, the climax should feel like the culmination of everything that has come before. It's important to deliver on the promises made throughout the series, giving the audience a payoff that feels earned and satisfying.

**Resolving Subplots and Themes:** After the climax, the resolution should provide closure for the characters and subplots. This doesn't mean that every question needs to be answered, but the main storylines should be resolved in a way that feels complete. Consider how the resolution can reinforce the themes of the series, leaving the audience with something to reflect on.

**Avoiding a Rushed Ending:** One of the risks of a limited-run series is the temptation to rush the ending in order to tie up all loose ends. To avoid this, plan the resolution carefully and ensure that there is enough time to address all key plot points and character arcs. The final episode should have a sense of pacing that allows the audience to fully absorb the conclusion and its implications.

Writing for a limited run requires careful attention to pacing and structure, as every episode must contribute meaningfully to the overall narrative. By planning the structure of the series, pacing the story effectively, and managing character arcs with precision, you can create a tightly woven and compelling narrative that resonates with the audience.

A limited-run series offers the opportunity to tell a focused, intense story with a clear beginning, middle, and end. When done well, it can provide a powerful and satisfying viewing experience, with each episode building on the last and driving toward a memorable climax and resolution.

By understanding the constraints and possibilities of a limited run, and by using pacing and structure to your advantage, you can craft a miniseries that captivates the audience from start to finish, leaving a lasting impression long after the final credits roll.

# Cinematic Techniques in Television: Enhancing Visual Appeal

Cinematic techniques have long been associated with the grandeur and visual storytelling of feature films, but in recent years, these techniques have increasingly found their way into television, particularly in high-quality miniseries. By incorporating cinematic elements into television production, creators can enhance the visual appeal, emotional impact, and overall storytelling of their series, creating a more immersive and memorable experience for viewers. In this chapter, we'll explore various cinematic techniques that can be applied to television, including camera work, lighting, composition, and sound design, and discuss how these techniques can be used to elevate the visual storytelling of a miniseries.

### The Role of Cinematic Techniques in Television

Cinematic techniques bring a level of artistry and sophistication to television production that can make a miniseries feel more like a series of films than traditional episodic TV. These techniques can be used to create a distinct visual style, evoke specific emotions, and reinforce the themes and narrative of the series. By thinking like a filmmaker and applying cinematic principles to television, you can create a more visually compelling and emotionally resonant story.

### Camera Work: Crafting the Visual Narrative

Camera work is one of the most powerful tools in cinematic storytelling. The way a scene is shot can influence how the audience perceives the story, the characters, and the emotions being conveyed. In television, using cinematic camera techniques can add depth and complexity to the visual narrative.

**Camera Movement:** Camera movement can add dynamism and energy to a scene, guiding the audience's focus and enhancing the storytelling. Techniques such as tracking shots, crane shots, and Steadicam movements can create a sense of fluidity and immersion. For example, a long tracking shot following a character through a crowded street can convey a sense of urgency or chaos, while a slow, deliberate dolly-in can build tension or focus attention on a character's emotional state.

**Framing and Composition:** The way a shot is framed and composed can communicate a great deal about the story and characters. Cinematic framing often involves using the rule of thirds, leading lines, and symmetry to create visually pleasing and meaningful compositions. In television, applying these principles can elevate the visual quality of the series. For instance, placing a character in the center of the frame with a lot of negative space around them can emphasize their isolation or vulnerability, while framing a character in a doorway or window can create a sense of entrapment or transition.

**Close-ups and Extreme Close-ups:** Close-ups are a staple of cinematic storytelling, allowing the audience to connect with a character's emotions on a more intimate level. Extreme close-ups can focus on specific details, such as a character's eyes or hands, to highlight subtle emotional cues or important narrative elements. In a television miniseries, judicious use of close-ups can heighten the emotional impact of key moments and draw the audience deeper into the characters' experiences.

**Wide Shots and Establishing Shots:** Wide shots and establishing shots are essential for setting the scene and providing context for the action. A well-composed wide shot can showcase the scale of a location, the relationships between characters, or the thematic significance of a setting. Establishing shots can be used to introduce new locations or to remind the audience of the broader world in which the story takes place. By incorporating cinematic wide shots and establishing shots into your television series, you can create a more immersive and visually rich world.

## Lighting: Shaping Mood and Atmosphere

Lighting is a fundamental element of cinematic storytelling, as it shapes the mood, atmosphere, and visual style of a scene. In television, using cinematic lighting techniques can enhance the emotional tone of the series and reinforce the narrative themes.

**Naturalistic Lighting:** Naturalistic lighting aims to mimic real-world lighting conditions, creating a sense of realism and immersion. This approach often involves using soft, diffused light to create a natural look, with careful attention to how light interacts with the environment and characters. In a television series, naturalistic lighting can be used to create a grounded, authentic atmosphere that draws the audience into the world of the story.

**High-Contrast Lighting:** High-contrast lighting, also known as chiaroscuro, is characterized by strong contrasts between light and shadow. This technique can be used to create a dramatic, moody atmosphere, often associated with film noir and psychological thrillers. In a television series, high-contrast lighting can be used to heighten tension, suggest moral ambiguity, or emphasize the duality of characters or situations.

**Color Temperature and Gels:** The color temperature of light can significantly impact the mood of a scene. Warm tones (yellows, oranges) create a sense of comfort, intimacy, or nostalgia, while cool tones (blues, greens) evoke feelings of detachment, melancholy, or unease. Using colored gels to tint the light can further enhance the emotional tone of a scene. For example, a blue gel might be used to create a cold, eerie atmosphere in a scene set in a mysterious location, while a warm amber gel could suggest the warmth and safety of a home.

**Practical Lighting:** Practical lighting refers to light sources that are visible within the scene, such as lamps, candles, or streetlights. Using practical lighting in a television series can add realism and depth to the visuals, while also providing opportunities for creative storytelling. For example, a flickering candle can create a sense of foreboding or instability, while a single, harsh overhead light might emphasize the starkness of a character's situation.

## Composition and Visual Storytelling

Composition is the art of arranging visual elements within the frame to tell a story or convey a message. In television, applying cinematic composition techniques can enhance the storytelling and create a more visually engaging experience for the audience.

**Symmetry and Balance:** Symmetry in composition can create a sense of order, stability, or formality, while asymmetry can suggest chaos, imbalance, or tension. Using symmetry intentionally can reinforce themes or character dynamics. For example, a perfectly symmetrical shot might emphasize the rigidity and control of a powerful character, while an off-kilter composition might reflect a character's inner turmoil or the instability of their situation.

**Depth and Layering:** Creating a sense of depth in the frame can add dimensionality and richness to the visual storytelling. This can be achieved through the use of foreground, midground, and background elements, as well as techniques like shallow focus, which isolates a subject against a blurred background. In a television series, depth and layering can be used to draw attention to specific elements within the frame, create visual interest, or suggest complex relationships between characters and their environment.

**Leading Lines and Perspective:** Leading lines are lines within the composition that guide the viewer's eye toward a particular point of interest. These lines can be created by architectural elements, roads, or even the positioning of characters. Using leading lines effectively can direct the audience's focus and create a sense of movement or progression within the frame. Similarly, the use of perspective—such as converging lines or a low-angle shot—can create a sense of scale, power, or vulnerability.

**Negative Space:** Negative space refers to the empty or unoccupied areas within the frame. It can be used to create a sense of isolation, loneliness, or tension, as well as to emphasize the subject by contrasting it with its surroundings. In a television series, negative space can be used to powerful effect, drawing attention to a character's solitude, the emptiness of a setting, or the gravity of a situation.

### Sound Design and Music: Enhancing the Emotional Impact

Sound design and music are critical components of cinematic storytelling, adding layers of emotion and atmosphere that complement the visuals. In television, incorporating cinematic sound design and music can significantly enhance the overall viewing experience.

**Diegetic and Non-Diegetic Sound:** Diegetic sound refers to sounds that originate from within the story's world, such as dialogue, footsteps, or ambient noises. Non-diegetic sound includes elements like the score or voiceover, which are not part of the story's world but are added for dramatic effect. Balancing diegetic and non-diegetic sound in a television series can create a more immersive and emotionally resonant experience. For example, the use of non-diegetic music during a tense moment can heighten the suspense, while the sudden absence of sound can create a jarring, unsettling effect.

**Layering Sound Effects:** Layering sound effects can add depth and realism to a scene, making it feel more alive and dynamic. For example, in a bustling city scene, layering sounds like traffic, distant sirens, footsteps, and snatches of conversation can create a rich soundscape that immerses the audience in the environment. In a more intimate scene, subtle sound effects like the rustling of fabric or the ticking of a clock can add to the mood and tension.

**Thematic Music and Leitmotifs:** Music can be used to reinforce themes, create emotional connections, and enhance character development. Leitmotifs—recurring musical themes associated with specific characters, locations, or ideas—can be a powerful tool for building continuity and emotional resonance throughout a series. For example, a haunting melody that recurs whenever a character's tragic past is mentioned can evoke a strong emotional response from the audience, linking the character's theme to their journey.

**Silence and Negative Space in Sound:** Just as negative space in visuals can be powerful, so can the strategic use of silence in sound design. Silence can create tension, emphasize a dramatic moment, or provide a contrast to the surrounding noise. For example, a moment of silence before a significant revelation can heighten the impact of the reveal, while the sudden absence of sound during a high-energy scene can create a sense of disorientation or shock.

### Creating a Cohesive Visual Language

A cohesive visual language is essential for maintaining consistency and enhancing the storytelling in a television series. This involves establishing a unified style, tone, and aesthetic that carries through every episode, creating a seamless viewing experience.

**Visual Motifs and Themes:** Visual motifs—recurring visual elements or symbols—are powerful tools for reinforcing the themes and emotional undertones of your series. By incorporating specific colors, patterns, or imagery throughout your miniseries, you create a cohesive visual language that ties the narrative together. For example, a recurring motif of shattered glass might symbolize the fragmentation of a character's psyche or the breakdown of relationships, while the consistent use of a particular color palette could reflect the thematic contrasts of hope and despair.

Motifs can also be tied to specific characters, locations, or events, helping to establish connections and highlight parallels or contrasts within the story. For instance, a character who is frequently associated with fire imagery might represent destruction, passion, or transformation. These visual motifs become more impactful when they recur at significant moments, creating a sense of continuity and deepening the audience's understanding of the story.

**Consistency in Style:** To create a cohesive visual language, it's important to maintain consistency in the overall style of the series. This includes the use of lighting, color grading, camera angles, and composition. Consistency in style ensures that the audience remains fully immersed in the world of the story, without being jolted out of the experience by abrupt changes in visual tone.

For example, if your series has a dark, moody aesthetic with high-contrast lighting, this style should be maintained throughout the series, even as the story progresses and the characters evolve. Any shifts in style should be intentional and serve the narrative—such as using a brighter, more vibrant visual approach to signal a character's change in outlook or the resolution of a major conflict.

**Collaboration between Departments:** Achieving a cohesive visual language requires close collaboration between various departments, including the director, cinematographer, production designer, costume designer, and sound designer. Each department contributes to the overall look and feel of the series, and it's important that they work together to ensure that all visual and auditory elements align with the intended tone and themes.

Regular communication and a shared vision among the creative team can help maintain consistency and cohesion. For example, the production designer and costume designer should coordinate on color schemes and textures that complement the lighting and camera work, while the sound designer and composer should collaborate to ensure that the music and sound effects enhance the visual storytelling.

**Evolving the Visual Language:** While consistency is key, it's also important to allow the visual language to evolve in response to the narrative. As the story progresses, the visual style can subtly change to reflect character development, shifts in tone, or the escalation of conflict. For example, a series that begins with a muted, desaturated color palette might gradually introduce more vibrant colors as the protagonist gains hope or confidence.

These changes should be carefully planned and integrated into the overall visual language, ensuring that they feel organic and meaningful rather than jarring. By allowing the visual style to evolve in tandem with the narrative, you create a more dynamic and emotionally engaging experience for the audience.

Incorporating cinematic techniques into television production can significantly enhance the visual appeal and storytelling of a miniseries, elevating it to the level of a cinematic experience. By applying techniques such as dynamic camera work, thoughtful composition, expressive lighting, and immersive sound design, you can create a visually compelling narrative that captivates the audience and deepens their emotional connection to the story.

Cinematic techniques in television are not just about aesthetics—they are tools for storytelling, used to convey themes, evoke emotions, and immerse the audience in the world of the series. By creating a cohesive visual language that aligns with the narrative and evolves with the story, you can craft a miniseries that is not only visually stunning but also rich in meaning and resonance.

When done effectively, these cinematic elements can transform a television miniseries into an unforgettable viewing experience, one that lingers in the minds of the audience long after the final credits roll.

# The Role of Flashbacks and Flashforwards

Flashbacks and flashforwards are powerful narrative tools that can add depth, complexity, and intrigue to a television miniseries. By allowing the audience to see events from the past or future, these techniques can reveal important information about the characters, provide context for the present story, and build suspense or anticipation. When used effectively, flashbacks and flashforwards can enrich the narrative, enhance character development, and create a more dynamic storytelling experience. In this chapter, we'll explore the role of flashbacks and flashforwards in television, how to use them effectively, and potential pitfalls to avoid.

## Understanding the Purpose of Flashbacks and Flashforwards

Flashbacks and flashforwards serve different purposes in storytelling, but both are used to manipulate the narrative timeline to achieve specific effects.

**Flashbacks:** Flashbacks are scenes that take the audience back in time to events that occurred before the current narrative. They are often used to provide backstory, reveal key information about a character's past, or explain the origins of a current conflict or situation. Flashbacks can be particularly effective in deepening the audience's understanding of a character's motivations, fears, and desires by showing how past experiences have shaped them.

For example, a flashback might show a pivotal moment in the protagonist's childhood that explains why they are so driven or why they fear certain situations. This insight helps the audience connect with the character on a deeper level and adds emotional weight to the present-day storyline.

**Flashforwards:** Flashforwards, on the other hand, are scenes that take the audience forward in time to events that will occur after the current narrative. They are often used to create suspense, foreshadow future events, or reveal the eventual outcome of the story. Flashforwards can add a layer of dramatic irony, where the audience knows something the characters do not, heightening tension as the story progresses toward that future event.

For instance, a flashforward might show the protagonist in a dire situation, creating suspense as the audience wonders how they ended up there and whether they will survive. This technique can keep viewers engaged, as they are eager to see how the narrative unfolds to reach the future scenario.

## Using Flashbacks Effectively

When using flashbacks in a television miniseries, it's important to ensure that they are integrated smoothly into the narrative and serve a clear purpose. Here are some strategies for using flashbacks effectively:

**Revealing Character Backstory:** One of the most common uses of flashbacks is to reveal character backstory. A well-timed flashback can provide crucial context for a character's actions, beliefs, or relationships, making their present-day behavior more understandable and relatable. For example, a flashback might show a character's traumatic experience that explains their reluctance to trust others or their drive to succeed at all costs.

**Enhancing Emotional Impact:** Flashbacks can be used to heighten the emotional impact of the story by juxtaposing past and present events. For instance, a flashback to a happier time in a character's life can create a poignant contrast with their current struggles, deepening the audience's empathy. Alternatively, a flashback to a painful memory can intensify the emotions of a present-day conflict, showing how past wounds continue to affect the character.

**Revealing Hidden Information:** Flashbacks can also be used to reveal hidden information that changes the audience's understanding of the story. For example, a flashback might show that a seemingly innocent character was actually involved in a past crime, adding complexity and intrigue to the plot. This type of flashback can be particularly effective in mystery or thriller genres, where uncovering the truth is a central element of the narrative.

**Avoiding Overuse:** While flashbacks can be a powerful tool, it's important to avoid overusing them, as too many flashbacks can disrupt the flow of the narrative and confuse the audience. Flashbacks should be used sparingly and with clear intent, adding value to the story rather than merely filling in gaps. Each flashback should have a specific purpose, whether it's to reveal crucial information, develop a character, or enhance the thematic depth of the story.

## Using Flashforwards Effectively

Flashforwards can create anticipation and suspense, but they must be used carefully to maintain the narrative's momentum and coherence. Here are some strategies for using flashforwards effectively:

**Building Suspense:** Flashforwards are particularly effective at building suspense, especially when they hint at a dramatic or catastrophic event in the future. By showing a glimpse of the outcome, the flashforward creates a sense of urgency as the audience anticipates how the story will reach that point. For example, a flashforward showing the protagonist on the brink of defeat can keep viewers on the edge of their seats, wondering what will lead to that moment and whether they will ultimately overcome it.

**Creating Dramatic Irony:** Flashforwards can also be used to create dramatic irony, where the audience knows something the characters do not. This can add tension to the narrative, as the audience watches the characters make decisions that they know will lead to the flashforward scenario. For instance, a flashforward might reveal that a character's seemingly minor decision has far-reaching consequences, making the audience anxious as they see the character unknowingly head toward disaster.

**Foreshadowing Future Events:** Flashforwards can serve as a form of foreshadowing, providing hints or clues about what will happen later in the story. This can create a sense of inevitability, where the audience knows that certain events are coming, even if they don't know exactly how or when. For example, a flashforward might show a character in a different setting or with a different appearance, suggesting that significant changes are on the horizon.

**Maintaining Narrative Coherence:** One of the challenges of using flashforwards is maintaining narrative coherence. It's important to ensure that the flashforward doesn't confuse the audience or disrupt the flow of the story. Flashforwards should be clearly distinguished from the present-day narrative, whether through visual cues, dialogue, or transitions. Additionally, the timing and placement of flashforwards should be carefully considered to ensure they enhance rather than detract from the storytelling.

## Combining Flashbacks and Flashforwards

In some cases, a miniseries may use both flashbacks and flashforwards to create a more complex and layered narrative. This approach can be particularly effective in stories that deal with themes of memory, fate, or the cyclical nature of events. When combining these techniques, it's important to maintain a balance and ensure that each flashback and flashforward serves a distinct purpose.

**Parallel Storylines:** One way to combine flashbacks and flashforwards is by creating parallel storylines that unfold in different timelines. For example, a miniseries might follow the protagonist in the present while periodically flashing back to their past and forward to their future. These parallel timelines can be used to explore how the past shapes the present and how the present leads to the future, creating a rich and interconnected narrative.

**Revealing Cause and Effect:** Another approach is to use flashbacks and flashforwards to reveal the cause-and-effect relationships between different events. A flashback might show the origins of a conflict, while a flashforward reveals its eventual resolution. This technique can be particularly effective in stories with complex plotlines or multiple twists, as it allows the audience to see how different pieces of the puzzle fit together.

**Creating Symmetry:** Flashbacks and flashforwards can also be used to create a sense of symmetry or thematic resonance within the narrative. For example, a flashback to a character's childhood might be mirrored by a flashforward to their later years, highlighting the cyclical nature of their journey or the enduring impact of certain experiences. This approach can add depth and cohesion to the story, making the narrative feel more complete and unified.

## Avoiding Pitfalls

While flashbacks and flashforwards can be powerful storytelling tools, they can also pose challenges if not used carefully. Here are some potential pitfalls to avoid:

**Confusing the Audience:** One of the main risks of using flashbacks and flashforwards is confusing the audience, especially if the shifts in time are not clearly marked. It's important to use visual cues, dialogue, or transitions to signal when the narrative is moving to a different timeline. Additionally, the timing and placement of these scenes should be carefully considered to ensure that they enhance the story rather than create confusion.

**Disrupting Narrative Flow:** Flashbacks and flashforwards can disrupt the narrative flow if they are overused or poorly integrated into the story. It's important to ensure that these scenes are placed strategically, so they contribute to the pacing and build on the momentum of the narrative. Avoid interrupting key moments or breaking the tension with unnecessary flashbacks or flashforwards.

**Overloading with Information:** Flashbacks and flashforwards can be tempting as a way to convey a lot of information quickly, but it's important not to overload the audience. Each flashback or flashforward should be focused and purposeful, revealing just enough information to move the story forward or deepen the audience's understanding. Avoid using these techniques as a crutch to explain everything—sometimes, it's more effective to let the audience piece together the story on their own.

**Losing Emotional Impact:** If not used carefully, flashbacks and flashforwards can dilute the emotional impact of the present-day narrative. It's important to ensure that these scenes enhance the emotional resonance of the story rather than distract from it. Consider how each flashback or flashforward contributes to the character's journey and the overall themes of the series.

Flashbacks and flashforwards are powerful narrative tools that can add depth, complexity, and intrigue to a television miniseries. By allowing the audience to see events from the past or future, these techniques can reveal important information about characters, provide context for the present story, and build suspense or anticipation.

# Narrative Twists: Surprising the Audience

Narrative twists are a powerful storytelling device that can elevate a television miniseries by surprising the audience and shifting their perception of the story. A well-executed twist can deepen the narrative, reveal hidden truths, and keep viewers on the edge of their seats, eager to see what happens next. However, crafting a successful twist requires careful planning and a deep understanding of your story and characters. In this chapter, we'll explore the role of narrative twists in storytelling, how to design effective twists, and strategies for surprising the audience while maintaining the integrity of the narrative.

**The Role of Narrative Twists**

Narrative twists serve several important functions in a miniseries:

**Revitalizing the Plot:** A twist can inject new energy into the story, especially at a point where the narrative might otherwise begin to lag. By introducing an unexpected development, you can reignite the audience's interest and propel the plot in a new direction.

**Deepening Character Complexity:** Twists can reveal hidden aspects of a character's personality, history, or motivations, adding layers of complexity to their development. For example, a twist might reveal that a seemingly trustworthy character has been hiding a dark secret, forcing the audience to reevaluate their perception of that character.

**Subverting Expectations:** Twists are often used to subvert the audience's expectations, challenging their assumptions about the story and its outcome. By leading the audience down one path only to reveal a different reality, you create a more engaging and unpredictable narrative.

**Enhancing Thematic Depth:** A twist can also reinforce or deepen the themes of the story. For instance, a twist that reveals the true nature of a character's quest might highlight the theme of identity, deception, or the consequences of ambition.

**Designing Effective Twists**

To design an effective twist, it's important to ensure that it feels both surprising and inevitable—surprising enough to catch the audience off guard, yet inevitable in hindsight. Here are some key principles for crafting successful twists:

**Foreshadowing:** A great twist should be foreshadowed subtly throughout the narrative. By planting clues and hints earlier in the story, you create a foundation for the twist that makes it feel earned rather than arbitrary. When the twist is revealed, the audience should be able to look back and recognize the signs that were there all along, even if they didn't notice them at the time.

For example, if a twist reveals that a character has been a traitor all along, you might include small details—such as the character's ambiguous behavior or cryptic remarks—that take on new meaning once the twist is revealed.

**Misdirection:** Misdirection involves leading the audience to focus on one aspect of the story while hiding the true nature of the twist. This technique keeps the audience engaged and allows the twist to have maximum impact. Misdirection can be achieved through dialogue, character actions, or narrative structure.

For instance, you might use a red herring—a seemingly important plot point or character that distracts the audience from the real twist. By directing the audience's attention elsewhere, you make the twist more surprising when it finally occurs.

**Timing:** The timing of a twist is crucial to its effectiveness. A twist should be revealed at a moment when it has the greatest impact on the story and characters. This could be at the midpoint of the series, where it changes the direction of the narrative, or in the final episode, where it provides a shocking resolution.

Consider how the timing of the twist aligns with the pacing of the story. Revealing the twist too early might undermine the buildup, while revealing it too late could make it feel rushed or tacked on. The key is to strike a balance, ensuring that the twist enhances the narrative without disrupting the overall flow.

**Emotional Resonance:** A twist should resonate emotionally with the audience, not just serve as a plot device. The best twists are those that affect the characters in profound ways, forcing them to confront new challenges, reconsider their beliefs, or change their goals. This emotional impact deepens the audience's connection to the story and makes the twist more memorable.

For example, a twist that reveals a character's true parentage might not only change the dynamics between characters but also force the protagonist to question their identity and place in the world. The emotional fallout from the twist should be explored in the episodes that follow, adding depth and complexity to the narrative.

**Types of Narrative Twists**

There are several types of narrative twists, each serving different storytelling purposes. Here are some common types:

**The Identity Twist:** This twist involves revealing that a character is not who they appear to be. It could be that a trusted ally is actually the villain, or that a seemingly minor character has a hidden connection to the main plot. Identity twists are effective because they force the audience to reevaluate everything they thought they knew about the character.

**The Revelation Twist:** A revelation twist uncovers a hidden truth about the story's world, history, or central conflict. This type of twist can dramatically alter the audience's understanding of the narrative and shift the direction of the plot. For example, a revelation twist might reveal that the protagonist's quest has been based on a lie, or that the true enemy is someone they've never suspected.

**The Perspective Twist:** This twist changes the way the audience views the story by shifting the narrative perspective. For example, a flashback might reveal that events were not as they seemed, or a new character's point of view might expose the protagonist's actions in a different light. Perspective twists challenge the audience's assumptions and add complexity to the narrative.

**The Plot Twist:** A plot twist is a sudden, unexpected event that dramatically changes the course of the story. This could be the death of a major character, the betrayal of an ally, or the introduction of a new, unforeseen threat. Plot twists are often used to raise the stakes and keep the audience engaged, but they must be carefully integrated into the story to avoid feeling contrived.

**The Ending Twist:** An ending twist is revealed in the final moments of the series, providing a shocking conclusion that recontextualizes everything that came before. This type of twist can leave a lasting impression on the audience, but it requires careful planning to ensure that it feels satisfying rather than frustrating. A successful ending twist should provide closure while also leaving the audience with something to ponder.

## Balancing Twists with Narrative Integrity

While narrative twists can be exciting and engaging, it's important to balance them with the overall integrity of the story. Here are some strategies for ensuring that twists enhance rather than undermine the narrative:

**Stay True to Character:** Twists should be consistent with the characters' established traits and motivations. A twist that requires a character to act out of character can feel forced or unbelievable. Ensure that the twist aligns with what the audience knows about the character, even if it reveals a hidden side of them.

**Maintain Thematic Cohesion:** Twists should reinforce the themes of the story rather than distract from them. Consider how the twist ties into the central ideas or questions the series is exploring. For example, if your series is about the nature of truth, a twist that reveals hidden lies or deceptions can deepen the thematic exploration.

**Avoid Over-Reliance on Twists:** While twists can be effective, relying too heavily on them can make the story feel gimmicky or undermine the audience's emotional investment. Twists should be used sparingly and purposefully, with the focus remaining on character development and thematic depth.

**Build Toward the Twist:** A twist should feel like a natural culmination of the story, not an abrupt or disconnected event. Build toward the twist by laying the groundwork throughout the series, creating a sense of anticipation and inevitability. This makes the twist more satisfying when it is finally revealed.

Narrative twists are a powerful tool in storytelling, capable of surprising the audience, deepening character development, and enhancing the thematic complexity of a television miniseries. By designing twists that are carefully foreshadowed, timed for maximum impact, and emotionally resonant, you can create a more engaging and unpredictable narrative.

Whether it's an identity twist, a revelation twist, a perspective twist, a plot twist, or an ending twist, each type serves a different purpose in the story. The key is to balance these twists with the overall integrity of the narrative, ensuring that they feel earned and contribute to the story's emotional and thematic richness.

# Character Relationships: Creating Chemistry

Character relationships are at the heart of any compelling television miniseries. They drive the plot, deepen the emotional impact of the story, and provide the audience with characters they can connect with on a personal level. One of the most important aspects of building these relationships is creating chemistry between characters—whether it's a romantic spark, a deep friendship, or a tense rivalry. Chemistry makes relationships feel authentic and engaging, pulling the audience into the characters' world and making them care about the outcomes. In this chapter, we'll explore how to create chemistry between characters, the different types of relationships that can enrich a miniseries, and strategies for developing and sustaining these relationships throughout the narrative.

**Understanding Character Chemistry**

Character chemistry is the intangible quality that makes interactions between characters feel dynamic, compelling, and real. It's what draws the audience in and makes them invested in the relationship, whether they're rooting for a romance, intrigued by a rivalry, or touched by a friendship. Chemistry isn't just about romantic attraction; it can exist in any type of relationship and is crucial for creating believable and emotionally resonant connections.

**Factors Contributing to Chemistry:**

**Character Compatibility:** Chemistry often stems from a sense of compatibility between characters. This doesn't mean they have to be similar—often, contrasting personalities can create the most dynamic relationships—but they do need to have qualities that complement each other or create interesting tension.

**Shared History or Experiences:** Characters who share a history or go through significant experiences together often develop strong chemistry. These shared experiences provide a foundation for the relationship, creating bonds that feel genuine and meaningful.

**Mutual Respect or Admiration:** Even in relationships where there is conflict, mutual respect or admiration can contribute to chemistry. Characters who recognize and value each other's strengths, even if they are adversaries, tend to have more engaging interactions.

**Tension and Conflict:** Chemistry is often heightened by tension and conflict. Whether it's unresolved sexual tension, ideological differences, or personal rivalries, the friction between characters can create sparks that keep the audience engaged.

**Emotional Vulnerability:** Moments of emotional vulnerability can also enhance chemistry by allowing characters to connect on a deeper level. When characters open up to each other, share their fears, or support each other in times of need, it creates a bond that feels authentic and compelling.

**Types of Character Relationships**

Different types of relationships can add depth and variety to a miniseries, each bringing its own form of chemistry. Here are some key types of relationships to consider:

**Romantic Relationships:**

Romantic chemistry is often the most immediately recognizable form of character chemistry. It's built on attraction, emotional connection, and sometimes, a sense of inevitability or destiny. To create compelling romantic relationships, focus on the buildup of tension, the obstacles that keep the characters apart, and the moments of connection that bring them together.

**Examples:** A slow-burning romance where two characters gradually fall in love as they learn to trust each other, or a passionate but conflicted relationship where love and duty are at odds.

**Friendships:**

Friendships provide emotional support, camaraderie, and often, moments of levity in a narrative. Chemistry in friendships is built on shared values, experiences, and a sense of loyalty. True friendships are forged through challenges, mutual respect, and the ability to be oneself without judgment.

**Examples:** A long-standing friendship where two characters know each other better than anyone else, or a new friendship that forms as characters go through a challenging experience together.

**Rivalries:**

Rivalries are fueled by competition, jealousy, or conflicting goals. The chemistry in rivalries comes from the tension and intensity of the interactions, as well as the underlying respect or understanding that often exists between rivals. Rivals can push each other to be better, leading to growth and development, even as they oppose each other.

**Examples:** Two characters vying for the same position of power, or rivals who challenge each other's beliefs or skills, leading to mutual growth.

**Mentor-Mentee Relationships:**

Mentor-mentee relationships are based on guidance, learning, and often, a transfer of wisdom or skills. The chemistry in these relationships comes from the dynamic of authority and respect, as well as the emotional bond that forms as the mentor invests in the mentee's growth and success.

**Examples:** A seasoned veteran teaching a younger character the ropes, or a mentor who sees potential in a character that others overlook, leading to a deep and transformative relationship.

**Family Relationships:**

Family relationships are complex and layered, often involving deep bonds, unresolved conflicts, and a sense of duty or loyalty. Chemistry in family dynamics is built on the history, expectations, and shared experiences that define the relationship, whether it's between parents and children, siblings, or extended family members.

**Examples:** Sibling rivalry that masks deep affection, or a strained parent-child relationship where both parties struggle to understand each other.

**Enemies Turned Allies:**

Relationships that evolve from animosity to alliance can create some of the most interesting chemistry in a narrative. The journey from enemies to allies involves overcoming mistrust, finding common ground, and learning to work together despite past conflicts.

**Examples:** Two characters who must put aside their differences to achieve a common goal, leading to a begrudging respect and eventually, a strong partnership.

## Developing and Sustaining Relationships

Creating chemistry between characters is just the beginning. To keep the audience engaged, it's important to develop and sustain these relationships throughout the miniseries. Here are some strategies for doing so:

### Slow Buildup:

Relationships are more engaging when they develop gradually, allowing the audience to see the characters' feelings and dynamics evolve over time. A slow buildup creates anticipation and allows for moments of tension and release that keep the audience invested.

For example, a romance that begins with subtle glances and unspoken feelings can be far more compelling than one where the characters quickly declare their love.

### Meaningful Interactions:

Every interaction between characters should serve a purpose, whether it's advancing the plot, revealing character traits, or deepening the relationship. Meaningful interactions are those that allow characters to connect, challenge each other, or grow together.

For instance, a conversation where characters share their fears or aspirations can deepen their bond and provide insight into their motivations.

### Conflict and Resolution:

Conflict is essential for sustaining relationships, as it creates opportunities for growth and development. Whether it's a misunderstanding, a difference in values, or an external challenge, conflict forces characters to confront their issues and either come closer or drift apart.

The resolution of conflict is just as important. How characters resolve their differences—whether through compromise, understanding, or change—reveals the strength and depth of their relationship.

### Consistency and Evolution:

Relationships should be consistent with the characters' established traits and motivations, but they should also evolve as the story progresses. Characters might start as friends and become lovers, or rivals might develop mutual respect over time. The key is to ensure that these changes feel organic and earned.

For example, a mentor-mentee relationship might evolve into a deep friendship as the mentee grows more confident and independent.

### Moments of Vulnerability:

Vulnerability is a key ingredient in creating chemistry. When characters show their true selves—whether through moments of fear, doubt, or joy—they allow others to connect with them on a deeper level. These moments of vulnerability can create powerful emotional bonds between characters.

For instance, a character who opens up about a past trauma to a friend can strengthen their relationship, making the connection more meaningful.

**Balancing Dynamics:**

Relationships are dynamic, with ups and downs, moments of closeness and distance. Balancing these dynamics keeps the relationship interesting and believable. Avoiding static relationships—where nothing changes or evolves—ensures that the audience remains engaged with the characters' journey.

For example, a couple might go through periods of tension due to external pressures, but their ability to navigate these challenges together can make their relationship more compelling.

**Avoiding Common Pitfalls**

While creating chemistry and developing relationships is essential, there are some common pitfalls to avoid:

**Forced Relationships:**

Avoid forcing characters into relationships that don't feel natural or earned. If there's no genuine chemistry, the relationship will feel contrived and the audience may not buy into it. Focus on relationships that grow organically from the characters' interactions and shared experiences.

**Overly Predictable Relationships:**

Relationships that follow predictable patterns—such as the stereotypical "will they, won't they" romance—can become stale if not handled with care. Adding unexpected elements, such as external challenges or character growth, can keep the relationship fresh and engaging.

**Lack of Development:**

Relationships that remain static throughout the series can lose their impact. Ensure that relationships evolve in response to the events of the story, with characters growing closer or facing new challenges that test their bond.

**Overemphasizing Romance:**

While romantic relationships are important, they shouldn't overshadow other types of relationships. Friendships, rivalries, and family dynamics can be just as compelling, and a well-rounded narrative will explore a variety of relationships to create a rich emotional landscape.

Creating chemistry between characters is a vital aspect of storytelling in a television miniseries. Whether it's a romantic relationship, a deep friendship, a tense rivalry, or a complex family dynamic, chemistry makes relationships feel real, engaging, and emotionally resonant.

# The Importance of Tone and Style

Tone and style are foundational elements of any television miniseries, shaping how the story is perceived and experienced by the audience. They influence everything from the mood and atmosphere of the narrative to the way characters speak and interact, and even how the visuals are presented. The right tone and style can make a series distinctive, memorable, and emotionally resonant, while inconsistencies or mismatches can detract from the audience's engagement. In this chapter, we'll explore the importance of tone and style in storytelling, how to establish them effectively, and how to maintain consistency throughout a miniseries.

**Understanding Tone and Style**

**Tone** refers to the overall mood or emotional quality of the series. It is the lens through which the story is told, influencing how the audience feels about the events and characters. Tone can be dark and brooding, light and humorous, tense and suspenseful, or anything in between. It's conveyed through various elements, including dialogue, music, pacing, and visual style.

**Style** encompasses the aesthetic and narrative choices that define the series' unique voice. This includes everything from the writing style and dialogue to the cinematography, editing, and set design. Style is what gives a series its distinct identity, setting it apart from other shows and creating a cohesive viewing experience.

Together, tone and style work to create a specific atmosphere and guide the audience's emotional response to the story. They help establish expectations, reinforce themes, and enhance the storytelling by aligning every aspect of the series with the intended emotional and narrative impact.

**Establishing Tone and Style**

Establishing the right tone and style is crucial from the very beginning of the miniseries. The first episode is especially important in setting the stage for what the audience can expect. Here's how to effectively establish tone and style:

**Aligning with the Story and Themes:**

The tone and style of your miniseries should align with the story you're telling and the themes you're exploring. For example, a story about loss and redemption might benefit from a somber, reflective tone and a visual style that emphasizes muted colors and stark compositions. On the other hand, a fast-paced thriller might use a tense, urgent tone with quick cuts, dynamic camera work, and sharp dialogue.

Consider what emotional response you want to evoke in the audience and how the tone and style can support that. For example, a dark, gritty tone might be appropriate for a crime drama exploring moral ambiguity, while a whimsical, light-hearted style might suit a coming-of-age story about self-discovery.

**Consistent Visual Language:**

The visual language of your series—encompassing cinematography, color palette, lighting, and set design—should be consistent with the tone and style you've established. This visual consistency helps immerse the audience in the world of the story and reinforces the emotional impact of each scene.

For example, a series with a dark, moody tone might use low-key lighting, deep shadows, and a desaturated color palette to create an atmosphere of tension and uncertainty. Conversely, a series with a more vibrant, optimistic tone might use bright lighting, warm colors, and open, inviting spaces.

**Writing Style and Dialogue:**

The writing style and dialogue play a key role in establishing tone and style. Whether the dialogue is snappy and witty, poetic and lyrical, or blunt and terse, it should reflect the overall tone of the series. The language used by characters should be consistent with their personalities and the world they inhabit.

For instance, a historical drama might use more formal, period-appropriate language, while a contemporary comedy might favor quick, conversational exchanges with a focus on humor and timing. The writing style should complement the pacing and rhythm of the series, contributing to the overall mood and atmosphere.

**Music and Sound Design:**

Music and sound design are powerful tools for setting the tone and enhancing the style of your series. The score can evoke specific emotions, underline dramatic moments, or provide contrast to the visuals. Sound effects and ambient noise can add depth to the world of the series, making it feel more immersive and real.

For example, a suspenseful thriller might use a minimalist, eerie score with dissonant notes and sudden crescendos to build tension, while a romantic drama might use sweeping, melodic music to underscore emotional scenes. The choice of music and sound should be carefully curated to align with the tone and style you want to convey.

**Pacing and Rhythm:**

Pacing is another crucial aspect of tone and style. The rhythm of scenes, the timing of dialogue, and the flow of action all contribute to the overall feel of the series. A slow, deliberate pace might be used to create a sense of foreboding or introspection, while a fast, dynamic pace might convey urgency and excitement.

Consider how the pacing can enhance the emotional impact of key moments and guide the audience's experience. For example, lingering on a character's expression after a significant revelation can heighten the emotional weight of the moment, while quick cuts during an action sequence can increase the sense of chaos and danger.

**Maintaining Consistency in Tone and Style**

Consistency in tone and style is essential for creating a cohesive narrative that resonates with the audience. Inconsistencies can be jarring and pull the viewer out of the story, so it's important to maintain a steady tone and style throughout the series. Here's how to achieve that:

**Establish Clear Guidelines:**

Before production begins, establish clear guidelines for the tone and style of the series. This includes defining the visual aesthetic, the mood you want to convey, and the narrative voice. Share these guidelines with the entire creative team—writers, directors, cinematographers, production designers, and editors—to ensure everyone is aligned with the vision. These guidelines can serve as a reference point throughout the production process, helping to maintain consistency in every aspect of the series.

**Collaborate Across Departments:**

Collaboration between departments is key to maintaining consistency in tone and style. The director, cinematographer, production designer, and composer should work closely together to ensure that the visuals, sound, and narrative elements all contribute to the same overall tone.

Regular meetings and discussions can help keep everyone on the same page and address any potential inconsistencies before they become an issue. This collaborative approach ensures that the series feels unified, with all elements working together to create the desired effect.

**Be Mindful of Transitions:**

Transitions between scenes, episodes, or even between different plotlines should be handled carefully to maintain a consistent tone. Abrupt shifts in tone or style can be disorienting for the audience, so it's important to consider how transitions can be smoothed out or made more deliberate.

For example, if the series shifts between different timelines or perspectives, consider using visual or auditory cues—such as changes in color grading, music, or editing style—to differentiate them while still maintaining an overall cohesive tone.

**Adapt to Narrative Shifts:**

While consistency is important, it's also essential to adapt the tone and style as the narrative evolves. As the story progresses, the tone may naturally shift in response to character development, plot twists, or thematic exploration. The key is to ensure that these shifts feel organic and are reflected in the overall narrative arc.

For instance, a series that starts with a light-hearted, adventurous tone might gradually darken as the characters face greater challenges and moral dilemmas. These tonal shifts should be mirrored in the visuals, music, and pacing, creating a seamless transition that feels true to the story.

**Avoid Tone and Style Mismatch:**

Be mindful of tone and style mismatches that can undermine the narrative. For example, a comedic scene that is too dark or intense can clash with the overall tone of a light-hearted series, while overly casual dialogue in a serious drama can break the immersion.

Ensure that every scene, line of dialogue, and visual choice aligns with the established tone and style. This doesn't mean that a series can't have moments of contrast—such as a moment of levity in a tense drama—but these moments should be carefully integrated to enhance rather than detract from the narrative.

**Evolving Tone and Style**

While consistency is key, it's also important to allow the tone and style to evolve as the series progresses. This evolution should reflect the development of the story and characters, creating a dynamic and engaging viewing experience.

**Reflecting Character Growth:**

As characters grow and change, the tone and style of the series can evolve to reflect their journey. For example, a character who starts off as naive and optimistic might face harsh realities that darken the tone of the series. This shift should be mirrored in the visuals, music, and dialogue, creating a deeper connection between the character's arc and the overall narrative.

The evolution of tone and style can also signal changes in the story's stakes, themes, or conflicts, keeping the audience engaged and invested in the characters' development.

**Marking Narrative Milestones:**

Significant narrative milestones—such as a major plot twist, a character's turning point, or the climax of the series—can be highlighted through shifts in tone and style. These shifts can underscore the importance of the moment and enhance the emotional impact on the audience.

For instance, a more intense, dramatic tone might be adopted during the climax, with quicker pacing, sharper dialogue, and heightened tension, followed by a more reflective, subdued tone in the resolution.

**Experimenting with Style:**

While maintaining overall consistency, there is room to experiment with style, especially in episodes or scenes that deviate from the main narrative. For example, a flashback or dream sequence might adopt a different visual style to distinguish it from the rest of the series while still fitting within the broader tone. These stylistic experiments can add variety and depth to the series, offering new perspectives or insights while keeping the audience engaged.

Tone and style are critical components of a television miniseries, shaping how the story is told and how it resonates with the audience. By carefully establishing and maintaining a consistent tone and style, you create a cohesive narrative that is both emotionally and visually engaging. Whether your series is dark and gritty, light and whimsical, or somewhere in between, the tone and style should align with the story and themes, creating a unified and immersive experience. By collaborating across departments, being mindful of transitions, and allowing for organic evolution, you can ensure that the tone and style enhance the storytelling and leave a lasting impression on the audience.

# Symbolism and Metaphor: Adding Layers to the Story

Symbolism and metaphor are powerful storytelling tools that can add depth, complexity, and richness to a television miniseries. By embedding symbolic elements and metaphors into the narrative, you can create additional layers of meaning that resonate with the audience on both a conscious and subconscious level. These literary devices allow you to explore themes, character motivations, and the underlying messages of the story in a way that is subtle yet impactful. In this chapter, we'll explore how to effectively use symbolism and metaphor in your miniseries, the different forms they can take, and how they can enhance the overall storytelling experience.

## Understanding Symbolism and Metaphor

**Symbolism** involves the use of symbols—objects, characters, colors, or events—that represent something beyond their literal meaning. A symbol might be used to evoke a particular emotion, suggest a theme, or convey a deeper message. For example, a recurring image of a broken mirror might symbolize shattered identity or the fragmentation of a character's psyche.

**Metaphor** is a figure of speech in which one thing is described as being another, often to draw a comparison or highlight a similarity. Metaphors are used to express abstract ideas in more tangible terms, creating connections between seemingly unrelated elements. For example, describing a character's emotional state as a "storm" can convey feelings of turmoil and chaos.

Both symbolism and metaphor enrich the narrative by adding layers of meaning that go beyond the surface story. They invite the audience to engage with the material on a deeper level, encouraging them to interpret and analyze the elements of the story in new and creative ways.

## The Role of Symbolism in Storytelling

Symbolism plays a crucial role in storytelling, providing visual and thematic cues that enhance the audience's understanding of the narrative. Symbols can be used in various ways to reinforce themes, develop characters, and create a more immersive and thought-provoking experience.

### Reinforcing Themes:

Symbols are often used to reinforce the central themes of a story. By repeating certain symbols throughout the narrative, you can emphasize key ideas and create a sense of unity and cohesion. For example, if your miniseries explores the theme of time and its effects, you might use clocks, hourglasses, or the changing seasons as recurring symbols to underscore this theme. The use of symbolism allows you to communicate complex ideas in a visual and accessible way, making the themes of your series more resonant and memorable for the audience.

### Developing Characters:

Symbols can also be used to develop characters by representing their inner thoughts, desires, or conflicts. For example, a character who frequently interacts with a caged bird might symbolize their feelings of entrapment or longing for freedom. Alternatively, a character who wears a particular piece of jewelry might be tied to a past event or relationship, with the object serving as a symbol of their emotional state. By associating characters with specific symbols, you can create a deeper connection between their actions and their underlying motivations, giving the audience insight into their internal world.

**Creating Atmosphere:**

Symbolism can contribute to the overall atmosphere of a miniseries by evoking certain moods or emotions. For example, the use of dark, foreboding imagery such as storm clouds, shadows, or decaying buildings can create a sense of impending doom or despair. On the other hand, symbols like blooming flowers, sunlight, or clear skies can evoke feelings of hope, renewal, or tranquility.

The consistent use of symbolic imagery helps to establish and maintain the tone of the series, drawing the audience into the emotional landscape of the story.

**Enhancing Subtext:**

Symbols can be used to add subtext to a scene, allowing you to convey additional layers of meaning without explicitly stating them. This subtext can create a richer and more nuanced narrative, where the audience is invited to read between the lines and uncover hidden messages.

For instance, a scene where a character gazes out of a window during a rainstorm might symbolize their feelings of isolation or sadness, even if these emotions are not directly addressed in the dialogue. The symbolism of the rain and the window adds depth to the scene, making it more emotionally resonant.

**The Role of Metaphor in Storytelling**

Metaphors are equally important in storytelling, providing a way to draw connections between different elements of the narrative and express abstract ideas in a more concrete form. Metaphors can be woven into dialogue, narration, and visual imagery to enhance the storytelling and create a more layered experience.

**Clarifying Complex Ideas:**

Metaphors are often used to clarify complex or abstract ideas by comparing them to something more familiar or tangible. For example, describing a character's fear as "a shadow that follows them everywhere" can help the audience understand the pervasive nature of their anxiety. By making abstract concepts more relatable, metaphors can help the audience connect with the story on a deeper level and gain a clearer understanding of the characters' experiences.

**Creating Emotional Impact:**

Metaphors can heighten the emotional impact of a scene by using vivid imagery to convey feelings and states of mind. For example, a character describing their grief as "drowning in an ocean of sorrow" creates a powerful image that resonates with the audience, evoking a sense of overwhelming loss. The use of metaphorical language allows you to evoke strong emotions in the audience, making the story more impactful and memorable.

**Highlighting Character Relationships:**

Metaphors can be used to highlight the dynamics between characters, emphasizing the nature of their relationships. For example, a mentor character might describe their relationship with the protagonist as "planting seeds in a garden," suggesting that their guidance is intended to help the protagonist grow and flourish.

This metaphor not only conveys the mentor's intentions but also adds a layer of meaning to the relationship, inviting the audience to reflect on the characters' interactions in a new light.

**Enriching Dialogue and Narration:**

Incorporating metaphors into dialogue and narration can enrich the storytelling by adding depth and texture to the language. Well-crafted metaphors can make the dialogue more engaging and memorable, while also reinforcing the themes and tone of the series. For example, a character who speaks in metaphors might be seen as wise, poetic, or introspective, adding complexity to their personality. Alternatively, a narrator who uses metaphorical language can guide the audience's interpretation of the story, providing insight into the underlying messages and themes.

**Techniques for Incorporating Symbolism and Metaphor**

To effectively incorporate symbolism and metaphor into your miniseries, it's important to consider how these elements will be integrated into the narrative, visuals, and dialogue. Here are some techniques to help you do so:

**Introduce Symbols Early:**

Introduce key symbols early in the series, allowing them to become recurring motifs that build in significance as the story progresses. By establishing these symbols from the beginning, you create a foundation for their later use, making them more impactful when they reappear.

For example, if a red rose symbolizes love and passion, introducing it in the first episode sets the stage for its continued presence and evolving meaning throughout the series.

**Use Visual Metaphors:**

Visual metaphors are a powerful way to convey abstract ideas and emotions through imagery. These can be created through cinematography, set design, or editing. For example, a character walking down a long, dark tunnel might visually represent their journey through despair or uncertainty.

Visual metaphors can be subtle or overt, depending on the tone and style of the series. The key is to ensure that they enhance the storytelling rather than distract from it.

**Layer Multiple Meanings:**

Symbols and metaphors can be layered with multiple meanings, adding complexity to the narrative. A single symbol might represent different things to different characters, or its meaning might evolve over the course of the series. This layering creates a richer, more nuanced story that invites the audience to explore different interpretations.

For example, a recurring image of a locked door might symbolize secrecy, repression, or missed opportunities, depending on the context in which it appears.

**Balance Subtlety and Clarity:**

While symbolism and metaphor are often most effective when they are subtle, it's important to strike a balance between subtlety and clarity. The audience should be able to grasp the intended meaning without feeling that it's too on-the-nose or, conversely, too obscure to understand.

Consider the context in which the symbol or metaphor is used, and ensure that it aligns with the overall tone and style of the series. Sometimes, a well-placed piece of dialogue or a visual cue can help clarify the meaning without over-explaining.

**Use Metaphor in Dialogue:**

Dialogue is a natural place to incorporate metaphor, allowing characters to express complex ideas and emotions in a more evocative way. Metaphorical language can reveal a character's perspective, worldview, or emotional state, adding depth to their interactions.

For example, a character who describes their life as "a chess game where every move is calculated" reveals something about their strategic, perhaps cynical, approach to relationships and decisions.

**Be Consistent with Symbolism:**

Consistency is key when using symbolism. Repeating symbols throughout the series reinforces their meaning and significance, creating a sense of continuity and cohesion. However, it's also important to ensure that symbols don't become overused or lose their impact.

Use symbols strategically, allowing them to gain meaning over time. When a symbol reappears at a crucial moment, it should resonate with the audience and enhance the emotional or thematic weight of the scene.

**Avoiding Common Pitfalls**

While symbolism and metaphor can greatly enhance a miniseries, there are potential pitfalls to avoid:

**Overloading the Story:**

It's possible to overload a story with too many symbols or metaphors, which can overwhelm the audience and detract from the clarity of the narrative. Focus on a few key symbols or metaphors that are central to the themes and characters, and develop them thoughtfully throughout the series.

Avoid the temptation to include symbolism in every scene—sometimes, simplicity can be more powerful.

**Being Too Obscure:**

While subtlety is important, being too obscure with symbolism and metaphor can confuse the audience or leave them feeling disconnected from the story. Ensure that there are enough contextual clues for the audience to interpret the meaning, even if they don't catch every nuance.

Consider how different viewers might interpret the symbols and metaphors, and provide a balance that allows for multiple interpretations without losing the intended impact.

**Forcing Symbols:**

Symbols and metaphors should arise naturally from the story and characters, rather than feeling forced or contrived. If a symbol or metaphor doesn't fit organically into the narrative, it can come across as heavy-handed or distracting.

Focus on symbols and metaphors that enhance the story rather than ones that simply sound clever or artistic. The best symbols and metaphors are those that feel like an integral part of the narrative.

**Ignoring Cultural Context:**

Be mindful of the cultural context in which symbols and metaphors are used, as their meanings can vary widely depending on cultural background, historical significance, or individual interpretation. What might be a powerful symbol in one culture could have a completely different meaning—or no meaning at all—in another. Research and consider the cultural implications of the symbols and metaphors you choose, ensuring that they resonate appropriately with your intended audience.

Symbolism and metaphor are invaluable tools for adding layers of meaning to a television miniseries. By thoughtfully incorporating these elements into your narrative, you can enrich the storytelling, deepen character development, and explore themes in a more nuanced and impactful way.

Whether through visual symbols, metaphorical language, or recurring motifs, these devices invite the audience to engage with the story on a deeper level, encouraging them to interpret and reflect on the underlying messages.

# Editing the Script: Refining Your Vision

Editing the script is a critical phase in the creation of a television miniseries. It's the process where you refine your vision, tighten the narrative, enhance character development, and ensure that the story flows seamlessly from beginning to end. While writing the initial draft is about getting your ideas down on paper, editing is about shaping those ideas into a cohesive, compelling, and polished narrative. In this chapter, we'll explore the importance of script editing, key strategies for refining your script, and common pitfalls to avoid during the editing process.

**The Importance of Script Editing**

Script editing is essential for several reasons:

**Enhancing Clarity and Coherence:** During the writing process, it's easy to lose sight of the big picture. Editing helps you ensure that the story is clear, coherent, and logically structured. It's an opportunity to make sure that all plot points are connected, that character motivations are clear, and that the narrative flows smoothly.

**Tightening the Narrative:** First drafts often contain extraneous scenes, dialogue, or subplots that don't serve the story. Editing allows you to trim the fat, focusing on what's essential and cutting out what's unnecessary. This results in a tighter, more focused narrative that keeps the audience engaged.

**Strengthening Character Development:** Characters are the heart of any story, and editing gives you the chance to refine their arcs, motivations, and interactions. It's an opportunity to deepen character relationships, ensure consistency in their behavior, and make sure that their development aligns with the overall themes of the series.

**Enhancing Pacing and Timing:** The pacing of a miniseries is crucial for maintaining audience interest. Editing allows you to fine-tune the timing of scenes, ensuring that the narrative moves at the right pace. Whether it's building suspense, delivering emotional moments, or keeping the action flowing, editing helps you control the rhythm of the story.

**Ensuring Consistency in Tone and Style:** Editing is also about making sure that the tone and style of the script are consistent throughout the series. It's important to ensure that the dialogue, visuals, and overall mood align with the vision you've established, creating a cohesive viewing experience.

**Key Strategies for Editing Your Script**

Editing a script is a multi-step process that involves both big-picture revisions and detailed fine-tuning. Here are some key strategies to guide you through the process:

**Take a Break Before Editing:**

After completing your first draft, it's helpful to take a break before diving into the editing process. This distance allows you to return to the script with fresh eyes, making it easier to spot issues and evaluate the narrative more objectively.

**Focus on the Big Picture First:**

Start by focusing on the big-picture elements of the script: plot structure, character arcs, and thematic coherence. Ask yourself whether the story is clear and compelling, whether the characters are well-developed, and whether the themes are effectively communicated. Look for any major structural issues, such as plot holes, inconsistent character motivations, or pacing problems.

**Refine the Structure:**

Ensure that the structure of your script is strong. This includes checking that the narrative has a clear beginning, middle, and end, with well-defined acts or episodes that build toward a satisfying climax. Make sure that each episode serves the overall story and that there is a logical progression from one episode to the next.

Consider whether any scenes or subplots can be combined, shortened, or eliminated to streamline the narrative. Each scene should have a purpose—whether it's advancing the plot, developing a character, or reinforcing a theme.

**Strengthen Character Arcs:**

Revisit your characters and their arcs. Are their motivations clear? Do they grow and change in a believable way throughout the series? Ensure that each character's journey is consistent and aligns with the overall narrative.

Pay attention to character relationships and interactions. Are they authentic and engaging? Do they contribute to the characters' development and the story's themes? Make sure that every character serves a purpose and that their presence in the story is justified.

**Fine-Tune Dialogue:**

Dialogue is a crucial aspect of any script, and editing provides an opportunity to refine it. Focus on making the dialogue sharp, natural, and reflective of each character's voice. Eliminate unnecessary or repetitive lines and ensure that the dialogue drives the story forward.

Look for opportunities to reveal character traits, relationships, and themes through dialogue. Ensure that the dialogue is consistent with the tone and style of the series.

**Enhance Pacing and Timing:**

Pacing is key to keeping the audience engaged, and editing allows you to fine-tune the timing of scenes and events. Consider whether the narrative flows smoothly and whether the timing of key moments—such as reveals, emotional beats, or action sequences—is effective.

Pay attention to the rhythm of the script. Are there any sections that drag or feel rushed? Adjust the pacing as needed to maintain a balanced and engaging narrative.

**Maintain Consistency:**

Consistency is essential for creating a cohesive story. Check for consistency in tone, style, character behavior, and plot details. Ensure that the tone remains steady throughout the series, and that any shifts in tone are intentional and well-executed.

Look for continuity errors or inconsistencies in the story, such as character actions that don't align with their established traits or plot points that contradict earlier events. Correct these issues to ensure a seamless narrative.

**Pay Attention to Subtext and Themes:**

Revisit the subtext and themes of your series. Are they effectively woven into the narrative? Are there opportunities to reinforce these themes through dialogue, symbolism, or character interactions? Ensure that the themes are clear without being overly explicit, allowing the audience to engage with the story on a deeper level.

Consider whether the script contains any unnecessary exposition or on-the-nose dialogue that could be revised to create a more subtle and nuanced storytelling experience.

**Seek Feedback:**

Once you've completed your own round of edits, it's helpful to seek feedback from trusted sources—whether it's fellow writers, directors, or producers. Fresh perspectives can help identify issues you might have missed and provide valuable insights into how the script can be improved.

Be open to constructive criticism and willing to make changes based on feedback. However, also trust your own instincts and vision for the series—editing is about refining your story, not compromising your creative vision.

**Polish and Proofread:**

After addressing the major revisions, it's time to focus on the finer details. This includes polishing the language, tightening the dialogue, and ensuring that the script is free of grammatical errors, typos, and formatting issues.

Proofreading is crucial, as even minor errors can distract from the quality of the script. Take the time to carefully review each page, and consider having someone else proofread the script as well.

**Common Pitfalls to Avoid**

Editing a script can be challenging, and there are some common pitfalls to be aware of:

**Over-Editing:**

It's possible to over-edit a script, resulting in a narrative that feels overly polished or lacking in spontaneity. While it's important to refine the story, be careful not to lose the original spark or energy that made the first draft compelling. Sometimes, leaving in a bit of roughness or imperfection can add authenticity to the dialogue or character interactions.

**Losing Sight of the Big Picture:**

During the editing process, it's easy to get bogged down in the details and lose sight of the big picture. Remember to periodically step back and assess the overall narrative, ensuring that the story remains cohesive and true to your original vision.

**Cutting Too Much:**

While tightening the script is important, be careful not to cut too much, especially if it means losing important character development, thematic elements, or subtext. Make sure that any cuts are justified and that the story still has the depth and richness needed to engage the audience.

**Ignoring Feedback:**

It's important to consider feedback from others, as fresh perspectives can help identify blind spots or areas for improvement. However, it's equally important to balance feedback with your own vision. Avoid making changes solely to please others—stay true to the story you want to tell.

**Rushing the Process:**

Editing takes time, and it's important not to rush the process. Give yourself the time needed to thoroughly review and revise the script, ensuring that every aspect is polished and well-considered. A well-edited script is worth the extra effort.

Editing the script is a vital step in refining your vision for a television miniseries. It's a process that requires both big-picture thinking and meticulous attention to detail, allowing you to shape the narrative, enhance character development, and ensure consistency in tone and style.

# Casting the Characters: Finding the Right Fit

Casting the right actors for your television miniseries is a crucial step in bringing your story to life. The actors you choose will embody the characters, convey their emotions, and establish the chemistry that drives the narrative forward. Finding the right fit involves more than just selecting talented performers—it's about ensuring that the actors resonate with the characters they'll portray, have the ability to bring depth and nuance to their roles, and can work well with the rest of the cast. In this chapter, we'll explore the importance of casting, how to approach the casting process, and tips for finding the perfect actors for your miniseries.

**The Importance of Casting**

Casting is a vital part of the production process because:

**Bringing Characters to Life:** The actors you choose will be the face of your story. Their performances will define the characters, making them relatable, memorable, and believable. A well-cast actor can bring nuances to a role that may not have been fully realized on the page, adding layers of depth and emotion to the character.

**Establishing Chemistry:** Chemistry between actors is essential, especially in a miniseries where relationships drive much of the plot. Whether it's a romantic connection, a deep friendship, or a tense rivalry, the actors must be able to create authentic and engaging interactions that draw the audience in.

**Enhancing the Narrative:** The right casting can elevate the entire narrative. A great actor can take a well-written character and make them unforgettable, adding charisma, vulnerability, or intensity that enriches the story. Conversely, a poor casting choice can weaken the impact of key scenes and undermine the believability of the characters.

**Contributing to the Series' Tone and Style:** The actors' performances contribute to the overall tone and style of the series. Their delivery, physicality, and chemistry help set the mood and reinforce the themes of the story. Casting actors who align with the tone and style you've established ensures a cohesive viewing experience.

## Approaching the Casting Process

Casting is both an art and a science, requiring a balance of intuition, collaboration, and practical considerations. Here's how to approach the casting process:

### Define the Characters Clearly:

Before casting begins, it's essential to have a clear understanding of each character. This includes their personality traits, physical appearance, backstory, motivations, and relationships with other characters. A detailed character breakdown can guide the casting process, helping you identify the key qualities you're looking for in an actor. Consider how the character's traits should be reflected in their physical appearance, voice, and mannerisms. While it's important to be open to different interpretations, having a clear vision will help you make more informed casting decisions.

### Collaborate with a Casting Director:

Working with an experienced casting director can be invaluable. Casting directors have a deep understanding of the industry, a wide network of actors, and the expertise to identify potential candidates who might not be immediately obvious. They can provide valuable insights, suggest actors you may not have considered, and help manage auditions and callbacks. Collaboration between the director, producers, and casting director is key to ensuring that everyone is aligned with the vision for the series and the characters.

### Consider Chemistry Between Actors:

Chemistry reads or screen tests can be an important part of the casting process, especially for roles where relationships are central to the narrative. These tests allow you to see how actors interact with each other and whether they can create the necessary connection on screen. It's important to consider both the individual performances and how well the actors work together as an ensemble. Strong chemistry between key characters can make a significant difference in the believability and emotional impact of the series.

### Look Beyond the Script:

While it's important to find actors who match the character descriptions, it's also worth considering those who bring something unexpected to the role. An actor who offers a fresh interpretation or unique energy can add a new dimension to the character that wasn't originally envisioned. Be open to surprises in the casting process. Sometimes, an actor who doesn't fit the initial vision for a character can bring something extraordinary to the role, elevating the entire project.

### Assess Range and Versatility:

Consider the range and versatility of the actors you're casting. In a miniseries, characters often undergo significant development or face complex emotional challenges. The ability to convey a wide range of emotions and adapt to different situations is crucial. During auditions, look for moments where the actor demonstrates depth, subtlety, or the ability to shift between emotions. This versatility will be important as the character evolves throughout the series.

### Prioritize Fit Over Fame:

While casting well-known actors can bring attention to your series, it's more important to prioritize fit over fame. The right actor for the role is one who can fully embody the character, regardless of their level of fame or previous work. Consider how each actor's strengths align with the needs of the character and the story. A lesser-known actor who perfectly fits the role can deliver a performance that resonates deeply with the audience and makes the character unforgettable.

**Diversity and Representation:**

Ensure that your casting process considers diversity and representation. This includes casting actors from different backgrounds, cultures, and identities that reflect the world of your story. Authentic representation can enrich the narrative and make it more relatable to a broader audience.

Avoid typecasting or relying on stereotypes. Instead, focus on casting actors who can bring authenticity and depth to their roles, regardless of their background.

**Trust the Process:**

Casting can be a lengthy and sometimes challenging process, but it's important to trust it. Take the time needed to find the right actors for each role, and don't rush the decision-making process. The effort you put into casting will pay off in the long run when you see the characters come to life on screen.

**Tips for Successful Auditions**

Auditions are a key part of the casting process, and it's important to create an environment where actors can perform at their best. Here are some tips for conducting successful auditions:

**Provide Clear Direction:**

Before the audition, give actors clear instructions about the scenes they'll be performing, the context of the character, and any specific qualities you're looking for. This helps the actors prepare and gives you a better sense of their ability to interpret and adapt to direction.

**Create a Comfortable Environment:**

Auditions can be nerve-wracking for actors, so it's important to create a comfortable and supportive environment. Encourage actors to ask questions, and be open to different interpretations of the character. A positive atmosphere allows actors to give their best performance.

**Focus on Performance Over Perfection:**

During auditions, focus on the actor's performance and their ability to connect with the character, rather than on delivering a perfect line reading. Look for authenticity, emotional depth, and the ability to bring the character to life, even if there are small imperfections in the delivery.

**Consider the Whole Package:**

Assess the actor's physical presence, voice, and energy, as well as their interpretation of the character. Think about how they'll look and sound on screen, and whether they have the qualities that will make the character memorable and compelling.

**Test for Range:**

If possible, ask actors to perform a range of scenes that showcase different aspects of the character—emotional, comedic, dramatic, or action-oriented. This helps you assess their versatility and ability to handle the various demands of the role.

**Take Notes and Review:**

Take detailed notes during auditions, and if possible, record the performances for later review. This allows you to compare actors, revisit strong performances, and make more informed decisions after the auditions are complete.

**Be Open to Discovery:**

Sometimes, an actor will bring something unexpected to the role that opens up new possibilities for the character or the story. Be open to these discoveries, and consider how they might enhance the series.

**Finalizing the Casting**

Once auditions are complete and you've reviewed all the performances, it's time to finalize the casting decisions:

**Review Chemistry and Ensemble Fit:**

Consider the overall chemistry and fit of the cast as an ensemble. Think about how the actors will work together and whether they can create the dynamics needed for the story. A strong ensemble can elevate the series and make the relationships between characters more believable and engaging.

**Trust Your Instincts:**

While it's important to consider all factors, ultimately, trust your instincts when making casting decisions. If an actor feels right for the role and brings the character to life in a way that resonates with you, that's a strong indication they're the right fit.

**Communicate Clearly:**

Once you've made your decisions, communicate clearly with the actors and their representatives. Be professional and respectful, whether you're offering a role or notifying someone that they weren't selected. Maintaining positive relationships in the industry is important for future collaborations.

**Prepare for Rehearsals:**

After casting is finalized, begin preparing for rehearsals. Rehearsals are an opportunity to build chemistry, explore character dynamics, and refine performances before shooting begins. Use this time to ensure that the actors are comfortable with their roles and ready to deliver their best performances.

Casting the characters in your television miniseries is one of the most important steps in the production process. The right actors will bring your characters to life, create chemistry that drives the narrative, and contribute to the overall tone and style of the series.

By approaching the casting process with a clear vision, an open mind, and a focus on finding the best fit for each role, you can assemble a cast that elevates your story and resonates with the audience.

# Directorial Choices: Translating Script to Screen

Directorial choices play a pivotal role in translating a script into a compelling visual experience for the audience. As a director, your vision will shape how the story is told, from the performances of the actors to the look and feel of each scene. It's your job to bring the written word to life, making creative decisions that enhance the narrative, engage the audience, and stay true to the tone and style of the miniseries. In this chapter, we'll explore the key directorial choices that influence the translation of a script to screen, including working with actors, visual storytelling, pacing, and the overall creative vision.

## Understanding the Director's Role

The director is the creative leader of the production, responsible for interpreting the script and guiding the cast and crew in bringing that vision to life. The director's role encompasses a wide range of responsibilities, including:

**Interpreting the Script:** The director must thoroughly understand the script, including its themes, characters, and narrative structure. This understanding informs all creative decisions, ensuring that the final product aligns with the original vision while also taking advantage of the unique possibilities of the visual medium.

**Guiding Performances:** Directors work closely with actors to develop their characters and deliver performances that resonate with the audience. This involves coaching actors on their delivery, body language, and emotional expression, as well as helping them understand their characters' motivations and arcs.

**Shaping the Visual Style:** The director collaborates with the cinematographer, production designer, and other key crew members to establish the visual style of the series. This includes decisions about camera angles, lighting, color schemes, set design, and more.

**Controlling Pacing and Rhythm:** The director is responsible for the pacing and rhythm of the series, ensuring that each scene flows smoothly and maintains the audience's engagement. This involves making decisions about the timing of scenes, transitions, and the overall tempo of the narrative.

**Maintaining Cohesion:** Throughout the production process, the director ensures that all elements of the series—performances, visuals, sound, and editing—work together to create a cohesive and unified whole. This requires clear communication, collaboration, and a strong creative vision.

## Key Directorial Choices

The following are key directorial choices that influence how a script is translated to screen:

## Visual Storytelling

**Camera Work:** Camera angles, movements, and framing are essential tools for visual storytelling. As a director, you'll need to decide how to use the camera to enhance the narrative and convey the emotions of each scene.

**Angles and Framing:** The choice of camera angles can dramatically affect how a scene is perceived. A low-angle shot might make a character appear powerful or intimidating, while a high-angle shot can make them seem vulnerable or insignificant. The framing of a shot can also create visual emphasis, drawing attention to specific details or symbols within the scene.

**Camera Movement:** Movement adds dynamism to a scene. A tracking shot that follows a character can create a sense of urgency or tension, while a slow zoom can heighten emotional intensity. The movement of the camera should always serve the narrative, guiding the audience's focus and enhancing the mood of the scene.

**Shot Composition:** The composition of each shot should be carefully considered to support the themes and emotions of the story. This includes the placement of characters within the frame, the use of negative space, and the arrangement of elements in the background and foreground. Composition can also be used to create symmetry, balance, or contrast, depending on the desired effect.

**Lighting and Color:** Lighting and color are powerful tools for setting the tone and atmosphere of a scene. The director works closely with the cinematographer to determine how lighting will be used to create mood, emphasize certain elements, and guide the audience's emotional response.

**Lighting Choices:** The quality, direction, and color of light can drastically change the look and feel of a scene. Soft, diffused lighting might be used for a tender or romantic scene, while harsh, directional lighting can create a sense of tension or danger. Low-key lighting with strong contrasts between light and shadow can add drama and mystery.

**Color Palette:** The color palette of the series should align with the overall tone and themes. Warm tones can evoke feelings of comfort, nostalgia, or intimacy, while cool tones might suggest detachment, melancholy, or foreboding. The director and production designer will collaborate to ensure that the color scheme is consistent and reinforces the narrative.

**Set Design and Locations:** The design of the sets and the choice of locations contribute significantly to the visual storytelling. The director must work with the production designer to ensure that the environments reflect the story world and enhance the narrative.

**Set Design:** The design of the sets should reflect the characters, themes, and mood of the series. A cluttered, chaotic set might symbolize a character's inner turmoil, while a minimalist, orderly environment could represent control or detachment. Details like props, textures, and furnishings should be chosen carefully to support the story.

**Location Choices:** The choice of filming locations can add authenticity and richness to the series. Whether you're shooting in a real location or building sets, the environment should feel like an integral part of the story. Consider how the location interacts with the characters and the plot, and whether it enhances the visual style of the series.

**Working with Actors**

**Character Development:** The director plays a key role in helping actors develop their characters. This involves discussing the character's backstory, motivations, and relationships, as well as exploring how these elements influence the character's actions and emotions.

**Character Motivation:** Understanding a character's motivation is crucial for delivering a believable performance. The director should work with the actors to explore what drives their characters and how these motivations evolve throughout the series.

**Emotional Range:** The director helps actors access and express the full range of emotions required for their roles. This may involve rehearsing different emotional beats, experimenting with various line readings, or exploring physical expressions of emotion.

**Performance Style:** The style of performance should align with the overall tone of the series. For example, a naturalistic drama might require subtle, restrained performances, while a more stylized or heightened narrative could call for more exaggerated or theatrical acting.

**Consistency in Performance:** It's important for the director to maintain consistency in the actors' performances throughout the series. This involves ensuring that the characters' behavior, speech patterns, and emotional responses are consistent from scene to scene, even as they evolve over the course of the story.

**Guiding Improvisation:** While some directors prefer strict adherence to the script, others may encourage improvisation to discover new facets of the characters or add spontaneity to the dialogue. If improvisation is used, it should still align with the character's motivations and the overall narrative.

**Building Chemistry:** The director is responsible for fostering chemistry between actors, especially in scenes where relationships are central to the plot. This involves creating a collaborative environment where actors feel comfortable exploring their characters' dynamics and experimenting with different approaches.

**Rehearsals:** Rehearsals are an important tool for building chemistry and refining performances. They provide a space for actors to connect with each other, try out different interpretations of their roles, and receive feedback from the director.

**Blocking and Movement:** The director also guides the physical interactions between characters, known as blocking. Effective blocking can enhance the emotional impact of a scene and highlight the relationships between characters. Movement should feel natural and contribute to the storytelling.

## Pacing and Rhythm

**Scene Timing:** The timing of each scene is crucial for maintaining the pacing of the series. The director must decide how long to linger on key moments, how quickly to cut between scenes, and how to build or release tension through pacing.

**Building Tension:** For scenes that require tension, the director might use slower pacing, longer takes, and deliberate pauses to create a sense of unease or anticipation. Conversely, rapid cuts and quick pacing can convey urgency or chaos.

**Pacing Variations:** A well-paced series will vary its pacing to keep the audience engaged. The director should consider the ebb and flow of the narrative, balancing fast-paced action scenes with slower, more introspective moments. This variation helps to sustain interest and allows for emotional peaks and valleys.

**Episode Structure:** Each episode of a miniseries should have its own internal rhythm, with a clear beginning, middle, and end. The director must ensure that the pacing within an episode feels natural and that the transitions between scenes are smooth and coherent.

**Cliffhangers and Resolutions:** In a serialized format, the director may use pacing to build to a cliffhanger or resolution at the end of an episode. The timing of these moments is key to maintaining audience interest and encouraging viewers to continue watching.

### Sound and Music

**Sound Design:** Sound is an essential part of the storytelling process, adding layers of meaning and emotion to the visuals. The director collaborates with the sound designer to create a soundscape that enhances the mood and atmosphere of the series.

**Diegetic vs. Non-Diegetic Sound:** The director must decide when to use diegetic sound (sound that originates from within the story world) and non-diegetic sound (sound that comes from outside the story world, such as a musical score). Each type of sound serves a different purpose in the narrative.

**Sound Effects:** Sound effects can be used to heighten tension, emphasize actions, or create a sense of realism. The director should consider how sound effects will complement the visuals and contribute to the overall tone of the series.

**Music Score:** The musical score is a powerful tool for evoking emotions and reinforcing the themes of the series. The director works with the composer to determine the tone and style of the music, as well as where and how it will be used within the series.

**Theme Music:** The choice of theme music can set the tone for the entire series. The director must consider how the theme music will introduce the series and prepare the audience for the story that follows.

**Scoring Key Moments:** The director should identify key moments in the narrative where music can enhance the emotional impact, such as during a climactic scene, a character's turning point, or a dramatic revelation. The music should align with the pacing and rhythm of the scene, adding to the overall effect.

### Maintaining the Creative Vision

The director's ultimate responsibility is to maintain a clear and consistent creative vision throughout the production process. This involves making decisions that align with the tone, style, and themes of the series, as well as ensuring that all elements of the production work together harmoniously.

**Collaborating with the Crew:** Effective collaboration with the crew is essential for realizing the director's vision. This includes working closely with the cinematographer, production designer, editor, sound designer, and other key departments to ensure that every aspect of the production supports the narrative.

**Communicating Clearly:** Clear communication is key to translating the director's vision into reality. The director must articulate their ideas and expectations to the cast and crew, providing guidance and feedback throughout the production.

**Adapting to Challenges:** The director must also be adaptable, as unexpected challenges are inevitable in any production. Whether it's adjusting to unforeseen technical issues, changes in the script, or the need for improvisation, the director must be able to make quick decisions that keep the production on track while maintaining the integrity of the story.

**Balancing Vision with Practicality:** While it's important to stay true to the creative vision, the director must also balance this with practical considerations, such as budget constraints, time limitations, and logistical challenges. Finding creative solutions to these challenges is part of the director's role.

Directorial choices are at the heart of translating a script into a compelling television miniseries. From guiding performances to shaping the visual style, controlling pacing, and collaborating on sound and music, the director's decisions influence every aspect of the production.

# Music and Sound: Setting the Emotional Tone

Music and sound are integral components of storytelling in a television miniseries, setting the emotional tone and enhancing the narrative in ways that visuals alone cannot achieve. They have the power to evoke emotions, create atmosphere, and reinforce themes, making them essential tools in the director's arsenal. In this chapter, we'll explore how to effectively use music and sound to set the emotional tone of your miniseries, including the role of the score, sound design, and the strategic use of silence. We'll also discuss how these elements can be integrated into the storytelling process to create a more immersive and emotionally resonant experience for the audience.

**The Role of Music in Storytelling**

Music is one of the most powerful tools for evoking emotion and setting the tone of a scene. It can heighten the impact of key moments, underscore character emotions, and guide the audience's response to the narrative. Here's how music can be used effectively in a miniseries:

**Establishing the Series' Identity:**

The main theme or opening music of a series plays a crucial role in establishing its identity and setting the tone for what's to come. A memorable theme can instantly evoke the atmosphere of the series and become synonymous with its story and characters.

Consider how the theme music reflects the overall tone of the series—whether it's epic and sweeping, dark and foreboding, or light and whimsical. The choice of instrumentation, tempo, and melody should all contribute to the desired emotional effect.

**Underscoring Emotional Moments:**

Music can amplify the emotional impact of a scene, whether it's a moment of joy, sadness, tension, or triumph. The right musical cue can intensify the audience's connection to the characters and the story, making the experience more immersive and affecting.

For example, a soft, melodic piano piece might underscore a tender moment between characters, while a tense, dissonant string section could heighten the suspense in a thriller. The music should align with the emotions of the scene, enhancing rather than overpowering the narrative.

**Reinforcing Themes:**

Music can also reinforce the themes of the series, creating a deeper connection between the story and the audience. By using recurring musical motifs or leitmotifs—melodic themes associated with specific characters, locations, or ideas—you can subtly remind the audience of key themes throughout the series.

For instance, a character might have a specific musical motif that plays whenever they appear on screen, symbolizing their journey or inner conflict. As the character evolves, the motif can change, reflecting their growth or transformation.

**Creating Atmosphere:**

The atmosphere of a scene is heavily influenced by the music that accompanies it. Whether it's a bustling city, a quiet forest, or a haunted house, the music can help transport the audience to the setting and enhance the mood of the scene. Ambient music or soundscapes can create a sense of place, while more dynamic scores can drive the narrative forward. For example, a fast-paced action scene might be accompanied by a high-energy score with driving percussion, while a mysterious, eerie setting might feature a more subdued, atmospheric soundtrack.

**Pacing and Rhythm:**

Music can influence the pacing and rhythm of a scene, guiding the audience's emotional journey and helping to build or release tension. The tempo of the music can affect how a scene feels—whether it's slow and contemplative or fast and intense.

Consider how music can be used to control the pacing of the narrative. For example, a gradual crescendo might build anticipation for a climactic moment, while a sudden drop in volume or a shift to a slower tempo can signal a change in tone or mood.

**The Role of Sound Design in Storytelling**

Sound design is the art of creating and manipulating audio elements to enhance the storytelling experience. This includes everything from sound effects and Foley to dialogue and ambient noise. Effective sound design can add depth and realism to the narrative, making the world of the series feel more immersive and alive.

**Enhancing Realism:**

Sound effects and Foley (the reproduction of everyday sound effects added in post-production) are essential for creating a sense of realism in a scene. These sounds help ground the audience in the story world, making it feel more tangible and authentic.

For example, the sound of footsteps on gravel, the creak of a door, or the rustling of leaves can make a scene feel more immediate and real. By carefully selecting and layering these sounds, you can create a rich audio environment that complements the visuals.

**Creating Emotional Impact:**

Just like music, sound effects can have a significant emotional impact on the audience. A sudden loud noise can startle, a low rumble can create a sense of unease, and a subtle sound in the background can evoke a specific mood or memory.

The choice of sound effects should align with the emotional tone of the scene. For instance, the distant howl of wind in a desolate landscape might evoke feelings of loneliness or despair, while the cheerful chirping of birds could signify peace and contentment.

**Supporting the Narrative:**

Sound design can be used to support and enhance the narrative in various ways. This might include using sound to signal transitions between scenes, highlight important plot points, or create a sense of continuity throughout the series.

For example, a recurring sound effect—such as the ticking of a clock—could symbolize the passage of time or the pressure of an impending deadline. Sound can also be used to foreshadow events or reveal information that isn't immediately apparent in the visuals.

**Creating Tension and Suspense:**

Sound is particularly effective for building tension and suspense. The absence of sound can be just as powerful as the presence of it, with silence often heightening the audience's anticipation and making them more attuned to the slightest noise.

For example, in a suspenseful scene, the sound design might focus on subtle, isolated sounds—such as a creaking floorboard or a distant drip of water—creating an atmosphere of unease and keeping the audience on edge.

**Using Diegetic and Non-Diegetic Sound:**

Diegetic sound originates from within the story world and is heard by the characters (e.g., dialogue, footsteps, music playing on a radio), while non-diegetic sound is added for the audience's benefit and isn't heard by the characters (e.g., the musical score, a voiceover).

The director must decide when to use diegetic versus non-diegetic sound and how each will contribute to the narrative. For example, a character might hear a song on the radio that holds personal significance, serving as a diegetic sound that also reinforces a theme or emotion.

**The Power of Silence**

Silence can be one of the most powerful tools in a director's arsenal, often carrying as much weight as music or sound. The strategic use of silence can create moments of introspection, tension, or emotional release, allowing the audience to fully absorb the impact of a scene.

**Creating Tension:**

Silence can heighten tension by creating an eerie or unsettling atmosphere. When used effectively, silence can make the audience hyper-aware of every small sound, building anticipation and making the eventual payoff more impactful.

For example, a scene where a character cautiously explores a dark, empty house might be punctuated by silence, with every creak and whisper amplified by the lack of background noise.

**Highlighting Emotional Moments:**

Silence can also be used to underscore moments of deep emotion, giving the audience space to connect with the characters' feelings. In a dramatic scene, the absence of music or sound effects can focus the audience's attention on the actors' performances and the raw emotion of the moment.

For instance, a scene depicting a character's grief or loss might be accompanied by silence, allowing the weight of the emotion to resonate more strongly with the audience.

**Providing Contrast:**

Silence can be used to create contrast within the narrative, making loud or chaotic scenes feel even more intense by comparison. Alternating between sound and silence can create a dynamic rhythm in the storytelling, drawing the audience's attention to key moments.

For example, a sudden drop into silence after a loud explosion or a heated argument can create a powerful emotional shift, emphasizing the impact of the event.

**Enhancing Realism:**

In certain situations, silence can enhance the realism of a scene, reflecting the natural ebb and flow of sound in the real world. This can make a scene feel more grounded and authentic, particularly in quiet, contemplative moments.

For instance, a scene of a character sitting alone in a room, lost in thought, might be accompanied by silence or very minimal sound, reflecting the stillness of the moment.

**Integrating Music and Sound into the Storytelling Process**

The integration of music and sound should be a collaborative and thoughtful process, involving close communication between the director, composer, sound designer, and editor. Here's how to effectively integrate these elements into your miniseries:

**Collaborate Early in the Process:**

Engage the composer and sound designer early in the production process, allowing them to become familiar with the script, characters, and themes. This collaboration will help ensure that the music and sound design align with the overall vision for the series.

Discuss the tone, style, and emotional goals for each scene, providing references or examples to convey your ideas. The more information you can provide, the better equipped your collaborators will be to create music and sound that enhances the narrative.

**Use Music and Sound as Storytelling Tools:**

Consider how music and sound can be used to reinforce themes, highlight character development, and guide the audience's emotional journey. For example, a recurring musical motif might symbolize a character's struggle with an internal conflict, subtly reminding the audience of this theme throughout the series. Similarly, sound design can be used to reflect a character's mental state, such as using distorted or dissonant sounds during moments of anxiety or confusion.

Explore how music and sound can enhance the narrative arc of the series. As the story progresses, the evolution of the musical score and sound design can reflect changes in the characters and the plot. For instance, a character who starts as hopeful but becomes disillusioned might be accompanied by music that shifts from light and melodic to darker and more fragmented as their journey unfolds.

**Integrate Music and Sound with Visuals:**

Music and sound should work in harmony with the visuals to create a cohesive and immersive experience. Consider how the two elements can complement each other, such as syncing musical cues with visual actions or using sound effects to draw attention to specific details in the frame.

Pay attention to the timing of music and sound within each scene. The placement of a musical cue or sound effect can dramatically alter the impact of a moment. For example, delaying the onset of music until after a significant reveal can heighten the surprise and emotional weight of the scene. Similarly, a well-timed sound effect can add emphasis to a visual detail that might otherwise go unnoticed.

Experiment with the interplay between sound and silence to create contrast and build tension. Silence can be used to set up a moment of sudden action or revelation, making the ensuing sound all the more powerful. This technique can be particularly effective in scenes that require suspense or emotional intensity.

**Tailor Music and Sound to Each Character:**

Consider how music and sound can be personalized to reflect the unique traits and journeys of the characters. This might involve assigning specific musical motifs or themes to individual characters, which can evolve along with their development.

For example, a protagonist might have a theme that is initially simple and tentative, but grows in complexity and confidence as they overcome challenges. Conversely, an antagonist's theme might be dark and foreboding, gradually becoming more intense as they close in on their goal.

Sound design can also be character-specific. For instance, a character who is constantly on edge might be accompanied by subtle, jittery sound effects or an ever-present background hum that underscores their anxiety. Tailoring these elements to the characters adds depth to the storytelling and helps the audience connect with their experiences.

**Be Mindful of Genre Conventions:**

Different genres have established conventions for music and sound that can guide your creative choices. Understanding these conventions can help you meet audience expectations while also finding opportunities to subvert or innovate within the genre.

For example, in a horror series, you might use unsettling, dissonant music and sharp, sudden sound effects to create jump scares and build an atmosphere of dread. In contrast, a romantic drama might use sweeping orchestral music and soft, ambient sounds to evoke intimacy and warmth.

While it's important to be aware of these conventions, don't be afraid to experiment and find your own unique approach. Unexpected musical choices or unconventional sound design can make your series stand out and leave a lasting impression on the audience.

**Collaborate During Post-Production:**

The post-production phase is where music and sound are fully integrated into the series. This stage requires close collaboration between the director, composer, sound designer, and editor to ensure that all elements work together seamlessly.

During post-production, review the timing and placement of music and sound effects within each scene, making adjustments as needed to achieve the desired emotional impact. Consider how the music transitions between scenes and episodes, and whether the overall soundscape supports the pacing and flow of the narrative.

Pay attention to the mixing and balancing of audio elements. Dialogue should be clear and intelligible, while music and sound effects should enhance the scene without overpowering it. The goal is to create a cohesive audio experience that draws the audience into the story without distracting from it.

**Embrace Silence and Minimalism:**

Sometimes, less is more. Embracing silence or using a minimalist approach to sound and music can be incredibly effective in creating moments of introspection, tension, or emotional impact. Silence can force the audience to focus more intently on the visuals and the performances, allowing the emotions of the scene to resonate more deeply. Consider when to let a scene breathe without music or sound effects, allowing the natural sounds of the environment or the silence itself to convey meaning. This approach can be particularly powerful in scenes that explore themes of isolation, loss, or contemplation.

Music and sound are indispensable tools for setting the emotional tone and enhancing the storytelling in a television miniseries. When used thoughtfully, they can elevate the narrative, deepen the audience's emotional connection to the characters, and create a more immersive and memorable viewing experience. As a director, it's important to approach music and sound as integral components of the storytelling process, collaborating closely with composers, sound designers, and editors to ensure that these elements align with your creative vision. Whether it's the choice of a sweeping musical score, the subtle use of sound effects, or the strategic deployment of silence, your decisions will shape how the audience experiences the story and feels about the characters and events on screen. By carefully integrating music and sound with the visuals, tailoring them to the characters and themes, and using them to control pacing and atmosphere, you can create a miniseries that resonates emotionally with the audience and leaves a lasting impact long after the final episode has aired.

# Designing the Look: Costumes and Sets

Designing the look of your television miniseries through costumes and sets is a crucial part of the visual storytelling process. The costumes and sets not only define the world of the story but also reflect the characters' personalities, backgrounds, and development. They help establish the time period, setting, and tone, and contribute to the overall atmosphere of the series. In this chapter, we'll explore how to effectively design costumes and sets, the importance of collaboration, and how these elements can enhance the narrative and bring your story to life.

## The Role of Costumes in Storytelling

Costumes are more than just clothing for the characters; they are an extension of the narrative that can reveal insights into a character's personality, social status, emotional state, and evolution throughout the story. Here's how costumes can be used effectively in your miniseries:

### Defining Characters:

Costumes help define who the characters are, providing visual clues about their identity, background, and personality. A character's clothing can reflect their profession, social status, or cultural background, and can also indicate their psychological state or development.

For example, a powerful, wealthy character might wear tailored, luxurious clothing that signifies their status and confidence, while a more vulnerable or conflicted character might wear looser, less refined garments that reflect their uncertainty or struggle.

### Supporting Character Development:

As characters evolve over the course of the series, their costumes can change to reflect their growth, challenges, or changes in status. This visual evolution can help the audience track the character's journey and development.

For instance, a character who starts as timid and unsure might wear muted, conservative clothing at the beginning, but as they gain confidence, their wardrobe could shift to bolder colors and more assertive styles. These changes should align with the narrative arc and help tell the story visually.

### Establishing Time and Place:

Costumes are key to establishing the time period and setting of the series. Whether it's a historical drama, a contemporary story, or a futuristic sci-fi adventure, the costumes should be accurate and appropriate to the world in which the story takes place.

Attention to detail is crucial, especially in period pieces where historical accuracy can enhance the authenticity of the series. Researching the fashion of the era and region you're depicting will ensure that the costumes feel true to the time and place.

### Reflecting Themes:

Costumes can also be used to reflect the themes of the series. For example, a story that explores identity and transformation might use costumes that symbolize these concepts—such as masks, disguises, or changing styles that reflect the character's shifting sense of self.

The color palette of the costumes can also reinforce themes. A series that deals with themes of hope and renewal might use brighter, warmer colors, while a darker, more introspective story might favor muted or monochromatic tones.

**Enhancing Visual Style:**

The costumes should align with the overall visual style of the series, complementing the cinematography, set design, and color grading. This cohesion creates a unified look that enhances the storytelling and makes the series visually distinctive.

For instance, in a stylized or heightened narrative, the costumes might be exaggerated or more theatrical to match the tone, while in a gritty, realistic drama, the costumes would likely be more subdued and practical.

**The Role of Sets in Storytelling**

Sets are the physical environments in which the story takes place, and they play a crucial role in creating the world of the series. The design of the sets can influence the mood, atmosphere, and believability of the narrative. Here's how to effectively design sets for your miniseries:

**Establishing the Setting:**

The sets establish the physical world of the series, whether it's a specific historical period, a contemporary urban environment, or a fantastical world. The design of the sets should be consistent with the time, place, and cultural context of the story.

Consider the details that make the setting feel authentic—such as architecture, furnishings, decor, and props. These elements should be carefully chosen to reflect the world in which the characters live and to make the setting believable and immersive.

**Reflecting Character and Story:**

The design of the sets can reveal important information about the characters and the story. A character's home, workplace, or personal space can provide insights into their personality, lifestyle, and emotional state.

For example, a character's apartment might be cluttered and chaotic, reflecting their disorganized life, or it might be minimalist and immaculate, suggesting a need for control. The way a set is dressed—such as the choice of props, colors, and layout—can add layers to the storytelling.

**Creating Atmosphere:**

Sets are key to creating the atmosphere and mood of the series. The use of lighting, color, and texture within the sets can evoke specific emotions and contribute to the tone of the narrative.

For instance, a dimly lit, shadowy set with dark colors and heavy textures might create a sense of foreboding or mystery, while a bright, airy set with light colors and soft textures might convey warmth and comfort. The atmosphere of the sets should align with the emotional tone of the scenes they're used in.

**Supporting Visual Style:**

The design of the sets should complement the overall visual style of the series. This includes considering how the sets will look on camera, how they interact with the lighting and cinematography, and how they contribute to the visual narrative.

For example, in a series with a heightened, surreal visual style, the sets might be designed with exaggerated proportions, unusual colors, or fantastical elements. In a more realistic series, the sets would likely be designed with a focus on authenticity and detail.

**Facilitating Storytelling:**

Sets can be designed to facilitate the storytelling, providing opportunities for character interactions, action sequences, or plot developments. The layout and structure of the sets should be considered with the blocking and movement of the characters in mind.

For example, a set with multiple levels, doorways, or hidden spaces might be used to create tension or drama in a scene, allowing characters to move through the space in ways that enhance the narrative. The design of the sets should serve the needs of the story and help bring the script to life.

## Collaboration in Design

Effective costume and set design require close collaboration between the director, costume designer, production designer, and other key departments. Here's how to ensure a successful collaboration:

**Establish a Clear Vision:**

The director should communicate a clear vision for the look and feel of the series to the costume and production designers. This includes discussing the tone, themes, and visual style, as well as any specific ideas or inspirations for the costumes and sets.

Providing visual references—such as mood boards, concept art, or examples from other films or series—can help convey the desired look and ensure that everyone is on the same page.

**Encourage Creative Input:**

While the director sets the overall vision, it's important to encourage creative input from the costume and production designers. These professionals bring a wealth of expertise and ideas to the table, and their contributions can enhance the final look of the series.

Collaboration should be a two-way process, with open communication and a willingness to explore different approaches. The best results often come from a collaborative environment where ideas are shared and refined.

**Coordinate with Other Departments:**

The design of the costumes and sets should be coordinated with other departments, such as cinematography, lighting, and makeup. This ensures that all visual elements work together harmoniously and contribute to a cohesive look.

For example, the color palette of the costumes and sets should complement the color grading of the cinematography, and the lighting design should enhance the textures and details of the sets. Regular meetings and discussions between departments can help maintain consistency and avoid conflicts.

**Consider Practicality:**

While aesthetics are important, it's also essential to consider the practicality of the costumes and sets. Costumes should be comfortable and functional for the actors, allowing them to move and perform without restrictions. Sets should be designed with the logistics of filming in mind, providing enough space for camera equipment, lighting, and crew movement.

Practicality also extends to budget and schedule considerations. The design team should work within the constraints of the production, finding creative solutions that achieve the desired look without exceeding the budget or timeline.

## Design Challenges and Solutions

Designing costumes and sets can present various challenges, but with careful planning and creativity, these challenges can be overcome. Here are some common challenges and potential solutions:

### Budget Constraints:

Challenge: Limited budgets can restrict the options for costumes and set design, making it difficult to achieve the desired look.

Solution: Prioritize key elements that are most important for the narrative and allocate the budget accordingly. Consider using existing locations, repurposing costumes, or renting props and set pieces. Creative use of lighting, camera angles, and set dressing can also enhance the appearance of more modest designs.

### Time Period Accuracy:

Challenge: Accurately depicting a specific historical period or setting can require extensive research and attention to detail.

Solution: Work with historical consultants or researchers to ensure accuracy. Focus on the key elements that will be most visible to the audience, such as iconic clothing styles or architectural details, and use these to create an authentic feel. For less visible elements, prioritize the overall atmosphere and mood rather than strict accuracy.

### Balancing Style and Functionality:

Challenge: Designing costumes and sets that are both visually striking and practical for filming can be difficult.

Solution: Collaborate closely with the costume and production designers to find solutions that balance style and functionality. For costumes, consider using lighter or more flexible materials that still achieve the desired look. For sets, ensure that they are designed with sufficient space for filming and that key visual elements are positioned for optimal camera angles.

### Consistency Across Episodes:

Challenge: Maintaining visual consistency across multiple episodes, especially in a serialized format, can be challenging.

Solution: Create detailed design documentation, including color palettes, fabric samples, and set plans, to ensure consistency. Regularly review previous episodes to check for continuity and make adjustments as needed. Collaboration between departments and clear communication are key to maintaining a consistent look throughout the series.

Designing the look of your television miniseries through costumes and sets is a vital part of the storytelling process. These visual elements help define the world of the story, reflect the characters' personalities and development, and contribute to the overall tone and atmosphere of the series.

By carefully considering the role of costumes and sets in the narrative, collaborating with designers and other departments, and overcoming design challenges with creativity and practicality, you can create a visually stunning and cohesive series that enhances the storytelling and engages the audience.

Whether it's the intricate details of a period costume, the atmospheric design of a set, or the subtle use of color and texture, every element of the design contributes to the audience's experience of the story. With thoughtful design, your miniseries can achieve a distinctive and memorable look that resonates long after the final scene.

# Cinematography in Television: Creating Visual Impact

Cinematography plays a critical role in shaping the visual impact of a television miniseries. It's the art of capturing the story through the camera lens, using techniques such as framing, lighting, camera movement, and composition to enhance the narrative, evoke emotions, and create a distinctive visual style. In this chapter, we'll explore the essential elements of cinematography in television, how to work with your cinematographer to achieve your creative vision, and the ways in which cinematography can elevate the storytelling and leave a lasting impression on the audience.

## The Role of Cinematography in Storytelling

Cinematography is more than just capturing images; it's about telling a story visually. Every shot, angle, and movement should serve the narrative and contribute to the emotional experience of the audience. Here's how cinematography impacts storytelling:

### Establishing Tone and Atmosphere:

The cinematography sets the tone and atmosphere of the series from the very first frame. Whether it's a gritty, dark drama or a bright, whimsical comedy, the choice of lighting, color palette, and camera angles can immediately convey the mood and style of the story.

For example, low-key lighting with deep shadows and a desaturated color palette might create a sense of tension and unease in a thriller, while soft, warm lighting with vibrant colors could evoke a sense of nostalgia or warmth in a romantic drama.

### Enhancing Emotional Impact:

Cinematography can amplify the emotional impact of a scene by focusing the audience's attention on key details, expressions, or movements. The use of close-ups, for instance, can draw the audience into a character's emotional state, capturing subtle nuances in their facial expressions that reveal their inner thoughts.

Camera movement and framing can also influence the emotional experience. A slow zoom into a character's face can heighten a moment of realization or vulnerability, while a sudden, jerky handheld shot might convey panic or chaos.

### Supporting Character Development:

The way characters are filmed can reflect their development and relationships. For example, a character who feels isolated might be framed in wide shots that emphasize their solitude within the environment, while a character in a close relationship might be shown in tight, intimate two-shots with another character.

As characters evolve, the cinematography can change to reflect their journey. A character who starts as passive or powerless might be filmed from a high angle, making them appear smaller and more vulnerable. As they grow in confidence, the camera angles might shift to a more level or low angle, symbolizing their newfound strength.

### Creating Visual Symbolism:

Cinematography can be used to create visual symbolism, adding layers of meaning to the story. The use of certain colors, patterns, or recurring visual motifs can symbolize themes, emotions, or character arcs.

For example, a character might be associated with a specific color throughout the series, symbolizing their emotional state or role in the story. The gradual introduction of another color into their scenes might signify a change in their character arc or a new influence in their life.

**Guiding the Audience's Attention:**

Through framing, focus, and composition, cinematography directs the audience's attention to important details or actions within the frame. This guidance helps ensure that the audience sees what you want them to see and understands the significance of each moment.

For instance, selective focus can be used to blur the background and keep the audience's attention on a character in the foreground. Alternatively, a deep focus shot might allow multiple elements in the frame to be in sharp focus, encouraging the audience to take in the entire scene and its complexities.

**Key Cinematography Techniques**

To create visual impact in your miniseries, it's important to understand and utilize key cinematography techniques. Here are some essential techniques to consider:

**Framing and Composition:**

Framing and composition involve the arrangement of elements within the frame. The placement of characters, objects, and background elements can influence the meaning of a scene and the audience's emotional response.

**Rule of Thirds:** One common technique is the rule of thirds, where the frame is divided into nine equal parts by two horizontal and two vertical lines. Placing key elements along these lines or at their intersections can create a balanced and visually pleasing composition.

**Symmetry and Asymmetry:** Symmetrical compositions can create a sense of order and stability, while asymmetrical compositions can introduce tension or dynamism. The choice between symmetry and asymmetry should align with the tone and mood of the scene.

**Leading Lines:** Leading lines, such as roads, hallways, or the edges of buildings, can draw the viewer's eye toward a specific point in the frame, guiding their attention to a key character or action.

**Camera Angles:**

The angle of the camera relative to the subject can influence how the audience perceives a character or scene.

**High Angle:** A high-angle shot, where the camera looks down on the subject, can make a character appear small, weak, or vulnerable. This angle might be used to emphasize a character's powerlessness in a situation.

**Low Angle:** A low-angle shot, where the camera looks up at the subject, can make a character appear powerful, dominant, or imposing. This angle might be used to convey authority or strength.

**Eye Level:** An eye-level shot places the camera at the same height as the subject's eyes, creating a neutral and natural perspective. This angle is often used for dialogue scenes and to convey a sense of equality between characters.

**Camera Movement:**

Camera movement can add energy, tension, or fluidity to a scene, enhancing the storytelling by influencing the pacing and rhythm.

**Dolly and Tracking Shots:** A dolly shot involves moving the camera on a track or wheeled platform, often to follow a character or reveal new information. A tracking shot follows a character or object as they move through the scene, creating a sense of continuous motion and immersion.

**Pan and Tilt:** Panning involves rotating the camera horizontally from a fixed point, while tilting involves rotating it vertically. These movements can be used to follow action, reveal new elements in the scene, or create a sense of scale.

**Steadicam and Handheld:** A Steadicam shot provides smooth, stabilized movement, often used for dynamic scenes where the camera needs to move fluidly through the environment. Handheld shots, on the other hand, introduce slight shake and instability, creating a more raw, immediate, and sometimes chaotic feel.

**Lighting:**

Lighting is a critical element of cinematography, affecting the mood, atmosphere, and visibility of the scene. The quality, direction, and color of light can dramatically change how a scene is perceived.

**High-Key Lighting:** High-key lighting is bright, even, and low-contrast, often used in comedies, musicals, and other light-hearted genres. It creates a clear, vibrant look with minimal shadows.

**Low-Key Lighting:** Low-key lighting is characterized by strong contrasts between light and shadow, often used in dramas, thrillers, and horror. It creates a moody, dramatic atmosphere with deep shadows and highlights.

**Natural Lighting:** Natural lighting involves using available light sources, such as sunlight or streetlights, to create a more realistic and grounded look. This approach is often used in documentaries and realistic dramas.

**Color and Filters:**

The use of color and filters can enhance the emotional tone of a scene, create visual consistency, and contribute to the overall style of the series.

**Color Palette:** The color palette chosen for a series can influence the mood and themes. Warm tones (reds, oranges, yellows) might evoke feelings of warmth, comfort, or passion, while cool tones (blues, greens, purples) might suggest calm, detachment, or melancholy.

**Color Grading:** Color grading in post-production can be used to adjust the colors in a scene, enhancing the visual style and ensuring consistency across the series. For example, a desaturated color palette might be used to create a gritty, dystopian feel, while vibrant colors might be used to emphasize the energy and vitality of a scene.

**Filters:** Filters can be placed on the camera lens to achieve specific effects, such as enhancing colors, reducing glare, or creating a soft, dreamy look. Filters can also be used to simulate different times of day or weather conditions, such as adding a warm tint for a sunset scene or a blue tint for a cold, wintery setting.

**Depth of Field:**

Depth of field refers to the range of distance within a shot that appears in sharp focus. It can be used to isolate a subject from the background or to keep multiple elements in focus simultaneously.

**Shallow Depth of Field:** A shallow depth of field creates a blurred background, drawing attention to the subject in the foreground. This technique is often used in close-ups or to emphasize a specific detail.

**Deep Focus:** Deep focus keeps everything in the frame in sharp focus, allowing the audience to see and interpret all elements of the scene. This technique is often used in scenes with complex compositions or where multiple actions are happening simultaneously.

## Working with a Cinematographer

The cinematographer, or director of photography (DP), is your key collaborator in achieving the visual style of your miniseries. Here's how to work effectively with your cinematographer:

### Communicate Your Vision:

Start by discussing your vision for the series with the cinematographer. Share your ideas about the tone, style, and themes, as well as any specific visual references or inspirations. The more clearly you can communicate your vision, the better your cinematographer will be able to translate it into visual terms.

Use visual references such as photographs, paintings, or clips from other films to illustrate the look and feel you're aiming for. These references can help ensure that you and your cinematographer are on the same page.

### Collaborate on Storyboarding:

Storyboarding is a valuable tool for planning the cinematography of your miniseries. Work with your cinematographer to create storyboards for key scenes, mapping out the camera angles, movements, and compositions you want to achieve.

Storyboarding allows you to visualize the sequence of shots and make decisions about the pacing and rhythm of the scene. It also helps identify potential challenges or opportunities for creative solutions before you start filming.

### Trust Your Cinematographer's Expertise:

While it's important to have a clear vision, it's also essential to trust your cinematographer's expertise. Cinematographers bring a wealth of technical knowledge and creative experience to the table, and their input can elevate your ideas in ways you might not have considered.

Be open to your cinematographer's suggestions about lighting, camera placement, and composition. Collaboration is key to finding the best solutions and achieving the most visually compelling results.

### Adapt to On-Set Conditions:

On-set conditions can sometimes require adjustments to your original plan. Whether it's changes in lighting, weather, or space constraints, flexibility is crucial. Work with your cinematographer to adapt to these challenges while staying true to the overall vision.

For example, if natural light is stronger or weaker than expected, your cinematographer might suggest adjusting the camera settings or changing the angle to make the most of the available light. Embrace these moments as opportunities for creative problem-solving.

### Maintain Visual Consistency:

Throughout the production, work with your cinematographer to ensure visual consistency across all episodes. This includes maintaining the same color palette, lighting style, and camera techniques to create a cohesive look for the series.

Regularly review footage to check for continuity and consistency. If necessary, make adjustments to ensure that the visual style remains uniform and supports the storytelling.

## Cinematography and Genre Considerations

Different genres have distinct visual styles and cinematography conventions that can guide your approach. Here's how to tailor your cinematography to the genre of your miniseries:

### Drama:

In dramas, the focus is often on character development and emotional depth. Cinematography in dramas typically emphasizes naturalistic lighting, close-ups, and intimate framing to draw the audience into the characters' experiences. Consider using a mix of static and handheld shots to create a balance between composed, reflective moments and more spontaneous, dynamic scenes.

### Thriller:

Thrillers rely on tension, suspense, and unpredictability. Cinematography in thrillers often uses high contrast lighting, unusual camera angles, and rapid camera movements to create a sense of unease and anticipation. Experiment with shadows, silhouettes, and off-kilter framing to keep the audience on edge. Handheld shots and quick cuts can heighten the sense of urgency during action sequences.

### Comedy:

Comedies typically use bright, even lighting and straightforward compositions to create a light-hearted, accessible feel. The focus is often on timing and character interactions, so clear, unobtrusive cinematography works well. Wide shots can capture physical comedy and ensemble scenes, while close-ups can emphasize facial expressions and comedic timing.

### Horror:

Horror relies on creating fear and discomfort through visual and auditory cues. Cinematography in horror often uses low-key lighting, extreme close-ups, and slow camera movements to build tension and suspense. Play with shadows, darkness, and confined spaces to evoke fear. Sudden camera movements or changes in focus can create jump scares and shock the audience.

### Science Fiction and Fantasy:

Science fiction and fantasy often involve world-building and imaginative visuals. Cinematography in these genres can be highly stylized, using color grading, special effects, and creative camera work to bring fantastical worlds to life. Wide shots can showcase expansive landscapes and elaborate set designs, while close-ups can highlight intricate costumes or props. Experiment with unusual angles or camera movements to create a sense of wonder or otherworldliness.

Cinematography is a powerful tool for creating visual impact and enhancing the storytelling in a television miniseries. Through careful consideration of framing, lighting, camera movement, and color, you can craft a visually compelling narrative that resonates with the audience and supports the emotional and thematic goals of the series. By working closely with your cinematographer, planning your shots through storyboarding, and adapting to on-set conditions, you can ensure that your creative vision is realized on screen. Whether you're aiming for a gritty, realistic look or a stylized, otherworldly atmosphere, cinematography allows you to tell your story in a way that is visually striking and emotionally engaging.

# Pacing the Series: Managing Peaks and Valleys

Pacing is a crucial element in the success of a television miniseries. It involves controlling the rhythm and flow of the narrative, ensuring that the story progresses at a speed that maintains the audience's interest while allowing key moments to resonate. Effective pacing requires a careful balance of peaks—moments of high tension, drama, or action—and valleys—quieter, more introspective scenes that provide relief and depth. In this chapter, we'll explore the importance of pacing, strategies for managing the peaks and valleys of your series, and how to create a rhythm that keeps the audience engaged from the first episode to the last.

## The Importance of Pacing

Pacing affects how the audience experiences the story. If the pacing is too slow, viewers may lose interest; if it's too fast, they might feel overwhelmed or miss important details. The goal is to find a rhythm that aligns with the story's tone and enhances the emotional impact of the narrative.

### Sustaining Engagement:

One of the primary goals of pacing is to sustain the audience's engagement throughout the series. By varying the pace—alternating between moments of tension and release—you keep the audience invested in the story and eager to see what happens next.

Effective pacing involves knowing when to slow down to let emotional or character-driven moments breathe and when to pick up the pace to build excitement or suspense.

### Building Tension and Release:

Pacing is essential for building tension and orchestrating its release. Peaks are often moments of conflict, climax, or revelation, while valleys provide the necessary contrast, allowing the audience to process what has happened and prepare for the next escalation.

This ebb and flow create a dynamic viewing experience that keeps the audience emotionally engaged. Properly timed peaks and valleys can heighten the impact of key scenes, making them more memorable.

### Developing Characters and Themes:

Pacing also plays a role in character development and thematic exploration. Quieter moments allow for deeper character introspection, relationship development, and the subtle unfolding of themes.

These valleys are crucial for giving the audience time to connect with the characters and understand the underlying messages of the story. Without these moments, the series might feel rushed or superficial.

### Enhancing the Overall Narrative Structure:

The pacing of a series contributes to the overall narrative structure, helping to define the beginning, middle, and end of the story. By carefully managing the peaks and valleys, you can ensure that the narrative arc progresses smoothly, with each episode building on the last.

Good pacing helps maintain the momentum of the series, ensuring that the story doesn't stall or become repetitive.

## Strategies for Managing Peaks and Valleys

Managing the peaks and valleys of your series requires a thoughtful approach to structuring each episode and the series as a whole. Here are some strategies to help you achieve effective pacing:

### Plan the Narrative Arc:

Begin by outlining the overall narrative arc of your series, identifying key plot points, character developments, and thematic moments. Determine where the major peaks—such as climactic events, major revelations, or turning points—will occur, and plan the valleys around them.

Consider how each episode fits into the larger arc. Ideally, each episode should have its own mini-arc, with a build-up, peak, and resolution, while also contributing to the overarching story.

### Vary the Pace Within Episodes:

Within each episode, aim to vary the pace to keep the audience engaged. Mix fast-paced, action-packed scenes with slower, more reflective moments. This variation helps maintain interest and allows the audience to fully experience the emotional highs and lows of the story.

For example, after an intense action sequence, you might follow with a quieter scene that focuses on character development or emotional reflection. This allows the audience to catch their breath and deepens their connection to the characters.

### Use Cliffhangers and Revelations:

Cliffhangers and major revelations are effective tools for creating peaks that drive the narrative forward. Placing a cliffhanger at the end of an episode can build anticipation and encourage viewers to keep watching.

However, it's important to balance these high points with quieter moments. Too many consecutive peaks can lead to fatigue, diminishing their impact. By interspersing cliffhangers and revelations with slower scenes, you create a rhythm that keeps the audience hooked without overwhelming them.

### Develop Character Arcs Gradually:

Character development is often best achieved through gradual pacing, allowing the audience to witness subtle changes over time. Use the valleys to explore characters' motivations, relationships, and internal conflicts, setting the stage for more dramatic developments later on.

Peaks in character arcs, such as moments of realization, confrontation, or transformation, should be spaced out to allow the audience time to process and understand the significance of these events.

### Balance Plot and Character Development:

Striking a balance between plot-driven scenes and character-driven moments is essential for effective pacing. Plot-driven scenes often serve as peaks, pushing the narrative forward, while character-driven scenes can function as valleys, providing depth and context.

Ensure that neither aspect is neglected. A series that is all plot can feel shallow, while one that is all character development may lack momentum. By balancing the two, you create a richer, more engaging story.

**Control the Flow of Information:**

The pacing of a series is also influenced by how and when information is revealed to the audience. Gradually unveiling key details or secrets can build suspense and keep viewers invested in the story.

Avoid dumping too much information at once, as this can overwhelm the audience and disrupt the pacing. Instead, consider staggering the release of information, using peaks to reveal significant details and valleys to explore their implications.

**Align Pacing with Genre Expectations:**

Different genres have different pacing conventions. For example, a thriller might have a faster pace with more frequent peaks, while a drama might focus more on character development and slower pacing.

Consider the expectations of your genre when planning the pacing of your series. While it's important to respect these conventions, don't be afraid to innovate or subvert them in ways that serve your story.

**Use Music and Sound to Influence Pacing:**

Music and sound design can be powerful tools for influencing the pacing of your series. A fast-paced score can heighten tension and speed up the feel of a scene, while a slower, more contemplative score can encourage the audience to slow down and reflect.

Consider how the rhythm and tempo of the music align with the pacing of the narrative. Sound design can also be used to create pauses or silences that allow the audience to absorb key moments.

**Revisit and Revise During Editing:**

Pacing is often fine-tuned during the editing process. As you review the footage, pay close attention to the rhythm of the scenes and the flow of the narrative. This is the stage where you can make adjustments to ensure that the pacing aligns with your creative vision.

Don't be afraid to cut or rearrange scenes to improve the pacing. Sometimes, tightening a sequence or adding a brief pause can make a significant difference in how the story is perceived.

**Creating a Rhythmic Flow**

Pacing isn't just about individual peaks and valleys—it's also about creating a rhythmic flow that carries the audience through the series. Here's how to achieve a rhythmic flow:

**Establish a Baseline Rhythm:**

Determine the baseline rhythm of your series, which is the general pace at which the story unfolds. This rhythm will be influenced by the genre, tone, and overall narrative structure.

Once you've established this baseline, you can introduce variations—faster or slower moments—that create the peaks and valleys. The baseline rhythm serves as the foundation upon which these variations are built.

**Build Momentum Over Time:**

Consider how the pacing evolves over the course of the series. Early episodes might have a more measured pace as characters and the world are introduced, while later episodes might pick up speed as the stakes rise and the plot intensifies.

Building momentum over time creates a sense of progression, leading to a climactic final episode that feels earned and satisfying. Be mindful of how each episode contributes to this overall momentum.

**Use Peaks to Propel the Narrative:**

Peaks should serve as turning points or moments of significant change in the narrative. These moments propel the story forward, leading to new developments or challenges for the characters.

Ensure that each peak has a clear impact on the narrative, setting up subsequent scenes or episodes. Peaks should not feel arbitrary or disconnected; they should be integral to the progression of the story.

**Allow Valleys to Deepen the Story:**

Valleys provide the opportunity to deepen the story, exploring characters, themes, and relationships in greater detail. These moments allow the audience to connect more deeply with the characters and to reflect on the events of the series.

Use valleys to build emotional resonance and to lay the groundwork for future peaks. These quieter moments are essential for creating a well-rounded narrative that engages the audience on multiple levels.

**Maintain Consistency with Flexibility:**

While it's important to maintain a consistent pacing rhythm, be flexible enough to adjust as needed. Some episodes or scenes may require a different pace to achieve the desired emotional or narrative effect.

Consistency should not mean rigidity. Be open to varying the pace when it serves the story, while ensuring that the overall rhythm remains coherent.

Pacing is a vital component of storytelling in a television miniseries, influencing how the audience experiences the narrative and connects with the characters. By carefully managing the peaks and valleys of the series, you can create a dynamic and engaging rhythm that keeps viewers invested from start to finish.

# Maintaining Consistency across Episodes

Maintaining consistency across episodes is essential for creating a cohesive and engaging television miniseries. Consistency ensures that the audience remains immersed in the story, that character development is believable, and that the visual and thematic elements align throughout the series. In this chapter, we'll explore the importance of consistency, strategies for maintaining it across episodes, and how to address challenges that may arise during production.

## The Importance of Consistency

Consistency in a television miniseries is critical for several reasons:

### Continuity in Storytelling:

Consistency in the narrative ensures that the story progresses logically and that plot points connect seamlessly from one episode to the next. Discrepancies in the story can confuse or frustrate the audience, undermining their engagement with the series.

Maintaining narrative continuity involves ensuring that the sequence of events, character actions, and plot developments align with the established story arc.

### Believable Character Development:

Characters should evolve in a way that feels natural and consistent with their established traits and motivations. Sudden, unexplained changes in behavior or personality can break the audience's suspension of disbelief and detract from the emotional impact of the series.

Consistency in character development allows the audience to form a deeper connection with the characters, understanding their growth and challenges throughout the series.

### Visual and Stylistic Cohesion:

A consistent visual style helps create a unified look and feel for the series, enhancing the storytelling and reinforcing the tone. This includes maintaining consistency in cinematography, lighting, color palette, costumes, and set design.

Visual cohesion ensures that the audience remains immersed in the story world, with each episode feeling like part of a larger whole rather than a disjointed piece.

### Thematic Alignment:

Themes should be consistently explored and reinforced throughout the series. Inconsistent treatment of themes can lead to a fragmented narrative, making it difficult for the audience to grasp the underlying messages or connect with the story on a deeper level.

Consistent thematic exploration provides depth and resonance, allowing the audience to engage with the series intellectually and emotionally.

### Strategies for Maintaining Consistency

To ensure consistency across episodes, it's important to take a proactive approach during the planning, production, and post-production stages. Here are some strategies to help maintain consistency:

**Develop a Detailed Series Bible:**

A series bible is a comprehensive document that outlines the key elements of the miniseries, including character profiles, plot summaries, thematic goals, visual style, and any important lore or background information.

This document serves as a reference for everyone involved in the production, ensuring that all creative decisions align with the established vision. It's particularly useful for maintaining consistency when multiple writers, directors, or departments are involved.

**Use Story Arcs and Episode Outlines:**

Break down the overall narrative into story arcs and create detailed outlines for each episode. These outlines should include key plot points, character developments, and thematic elements that need to be addressed in each episode.

By mapping out the story in advance, you can ensure that each episode contributes to the overarching narrative and that there is a logical progression from one episode to the next.

**Implement Continuity Checks:**

Continuity checks are essential for catching discrepancies in the narrative, character development, or visual elements. These checks should be conducted regularly throughout the production process, from scriptwriting to filming and editing.

Assign a continuity supervisor or script supervisor to monitor consistency on set, ensuring that details such as character wardrobe, props, and locations match from scene to scene and episode to episode.

**Maintain Visual Consistency:**

Work closely with the cinematographer, production designer, and costume designer to establish a consistent visual style for the series. This includes decisions about lighting, camera angles, color grading, set design, and costumes. Create visual references or style guides that outline the desired look for the series. These guides can include color palettes, lighting schemes, and sample images that illustrate the overall aesthetic. Ensure that all departments refer to these guides when making creative decisions.

**Ensure Consistent Characterization:**

Character consistency is key to maintaining audience investment in the story. Develop detailed character profiles that outline each character's personality, motivations, backstory, and arc. Share these profiles with the actors and directors to ensure that everyone has a clear understanding of the characters. During production, monitor performances to ensure that characters' behavior and dialogue remain true to their established traits. If a character needs to undergo significant change, ensure that this development is well-motivated and gradual, allowing the audience to understand and accept the transformation.

**Align Themes Across Episodes:**

Identify the core themes of your series and ensure that they are explored consistently throughout each episode. This might involve recurring visual motifs, dialogue that reflects the themes, or plot points that reinforce the central message. Work with the writers and directors to weave these themes into the narrative in subtle, meaningful ways. Regularly revisit the series bible and episode outlines to ensure that thematic elements are being addressed consistently.

**Foster Clear Communication:**

Effective communication is essential for maintaining consistency, especially when multiple teams or directors are working on different episodes. Regular meetings, clear documentation, and open channels of communication can help ensure that everyone is on the same page. Encourage collaboration between departments and create a culture where questions or concerns about consistency can be addressed openly and promptly.

**Use Editing to Ensure Consistency:**

The editing process offers an opportunity to refine and ensure consistency across episodes. As the episodes are edited, pay close attention to the flow of the narrative, the continuity of character arcs, and the visual style. Compare scenes from different episodes to check for any inconsistencies in tone, pacing, or visual elements. If discrepancies are found, make adjustments through editing, reshoots, or color grading to achieve a cohesive look and feel.

**Addressing Challenges in Consistency**

Despite careful planning, challenges in maintaining consistency can arise during production. Here's how to address common issues:

**Handling Script Changes:**

Script changes can sometimes lead to inconsistencies in the narrative or character development. To mitigate this, involve the showrunner, head writer, or series creator in any significant script revisions to ensure that changes align with the overall vision. If a script change affects continuity, communicate the change to all relevant departments, and update the series bible and episode outlines accordingly.

**Managing Multiple Directors:**

When different directors work on different episodes, there's a risk of inconsistency in style or tone. To address this, hold meetings with all directors before production begins to discuss the visual and thematic goals of the series. Provide them with the series bible and style guides to ensure they understand the desired consistency. Encourage directors to collaborate and share their approaches, ensuring that there's a unified vision across episodes. The showrunner or head director should oversee the work of all directors to ensure consistency.

**Adapting to Production Constraints:**

Production constraints such as time, budget, or location changes can sometimes lead to inconsistencies. When these challenges arise, prioritize the elements that are most crucial to the narrative and visual cohesion of the series. Be flexible and creative in finding solutions that maintain consistency while working within the constraints. For example, if a key location is unavailable, consider how set design, lighting, or editing can be used to create a similar look and feel.

**Ensuring Actor Consistency:**

Actors may interpret their characters differently across episodes, especially if they work with different directors. To maintain consistency, the showrunner or head director should provide guidance on the character's development and ensure that key traits and motivations are preserved. Rehearsals and discussions between actors and directors can help align performances, ensuring that the character's journey remains coherent throughout the series. Achieving consistency requires careful planning, clear communication, and collaboration between all departments involved in the production. By developing detailed series bibles, episode outlines, and style guides, and by regularly monitoring continuity during production and editing, you can address potential inconsistencies before they become problematic. Ultimately, consistency enhances the storytelling, allowing the audience to fully immerse themselves in the world of the series and connect with the characters on a deeper level. With thoughtful attention to detail and a commitment to maintaining the integrity of the story, your miniseries can achieve the coherence and impact necessary to leave a lasting impression on viewers.

# Foreshadowing: Planting Seeds for the Future

Foreshadowing is a powerful narrative technique used to hint at future events in your television miniseries, creating anticipation and adding layers of depth to the story. When done effectively, foreshadowing plants subtle clues that prepare the audience for significant developments, making the eventual payoff more satisfying and enhancing the overall coherence of the narrative. In this chapter, we'll explore the importance of foreshadowing, different types of foreshadowing, strategies for planting narrative seeds, and how to ensure that foreshadowing enhances rather than overwhelms your story.

**The Importance of Foreshadowing**

Foreshadowing serves several key purposes in storytelling:

**Building Anticipation:**

Foreshadowing creates a sense of anticipation, keeping the audience engaged as they look for connections between earlier hints and later events. This anticipation can make the story more compelling, as viewers become invested in uncovering how the foreshadowed elements will unfold.

By subtly hinting at future events, you build suspense and curiosity, encouraging the audience to pay closer attention to the details of the story.

**Enhancing Narrative Coherence:**

When events are foreshadowed, they feel more natural and less like sudden twists or coincidences. This coherence makes the story more satisfying, as the audience can see how everything fits together in hindsight. Foreshadowing helps create a well-structured narrative where each event feels like an inevitable part of the story's progression, leading to a more seamless and immersive experience for the audience.

**Deepening Themes and Character Development:**

Foreshadowing can also be used to reinforce themes and character arcs, subtly introducing ideas or motifs that will become more significant as the story progresses. This adds depth to the narrative and allows for more nuanced exploration of the story's underlying messages.

For example, a character's seemingly minor decision early in the series might foreshadow a major turning point later on, reflecting the themes of choice and consequence.

**Rewarding Attentive Viewers:**

Well-executed foreshadowing rewards viewers who pay close attention, offering them a deeper understanding of the story and a sense of satisfaction when they recognize the connections. These viewers may pick up on clues and subtle hints that others might miss, making the viewing experience more engaging.

This can also encourage re-watching, as viewers may want to revisit earlier episodes to spot the foreshadowing after knowing how the story unfolds.

**Types of Foreshadowing**

There are several types of foreshadowing, each with its own role in storytelling. Understanding these types can help you choose the most effective approach for your series:

**Direct Foreshadowing:**

Direct foreshadowing involves explicitly hinting at future events, often through dialogue or narration. While the audience may not fully understand the significance at the time, these hints become clear as the story progresses.

For example, a character might make a seemingly offhand comment like, "I've got a bad feeling about this," which later proves to be prophetic when something goes wrong. Direct foreshadowing creates clear connections between the hint and the eventual event, often making the audience feel a sense of impending doom or inevitability.

**Subtle or Indirect Foreshadowing:**

Subtle foreshadowing is more understated, using imagery, symbols, or small details to hint at future events. The audience may not immediately recognize these hints, but they add depth and cohesion to the narrative when the connections are revealed later.

For example, a recurring visual motif, such as a broken mirror or a shadowy figure, might foreshadow a character's eventual mental breakdown or confrontation with a hidden truth. Indirect foreshadowing requires careful attention to detail and can make the story feel more intricate and layered.

**Symbolic Foreshadowing:**

Symbolic foreshadowing uses symbols, metaphors, or allegorical elements to hint at future developments. These symbols often carry deeper meanings that resonate with the themes or character arcs in the series.

For instance, a withering plant in the background of a scene might symbolize a deteriorating relationship, foreshadowing a breakup or conflict later in the series. Symbolic foreshadowing adds richness to the narrative, allowing viewers to explore the story on a more metaphorical level.

**Prophetic or Dream Foreshadowing:**

Prophetic foreshadowing involves using dreams, visions, or prophecies to hint at future events. These can be literal or symbolic, often providing cryptic glimpses of what's to come.

A character might have a dream that seems bizarre or abstract but later plays out in a more grounded way in the narrative. This type of foreshadowing adds an element of mystery and can create tension as the audience wonders how the prophecy will manifest.

**Red Herring Foreshadowing:**

Red herrings are deliberately misleading clues that suggest one outcome but lead to another. While not technically foreshadowing in the traditional sense, red herrings can be used to create suspense and misdirect the audience.

For example, a character might be shown acting suspiciously, leading the audience to believe they are the villain, only for the true antagonist to be revealed later. Red herrings can make the eventual resolution more surprising and satisfying.

**Strategies for Effective Foreshadowing**

To plant narrative seeds effectively, it's important to integrate foreshadowing into your story in a way that feels natural and enhances the overall narrative. Here are some strategies to help you do this:

**Plan Foreshadowing Early:**

Effective foreshadowing requires planning. Consider the key events, character developments, and themes in your series, and identify opportunities to hint at these elements in earlier episodes.

When writing the script, think about how you can introduce subtle hints or symbols that will pay off later in the story. These hints should feel organic to the narrative, rather than forced or overly obvious.

**Keep It Subtle:**

One of the keys to successful foreshadowing is subtlety. The best foreshadowing doesn't draw attention to itself but instead blends seamlessly into the story, only becoming clear in hindsight.

Avoid making foreshadowing too explicit or heavy-handed, as this can reduce the impact of the eventual reveal. Instead, focus on planting small, seemingly inconsequential details that take on greater significance as the story unfolds.

**Use Dialogue and Character Actions:**

Dialogue and character actions can be effective tools for foreshadowing. A character's offhand remark, choice of words, or unusual behavior can hint at their future actions or the direction of the plot.

For example, a character who constantly checks their watch might be foreshadowing their involvement in a time-sensitive event later in the series. Similarly, a character who avoids talking about a specific subject might be hiding a secret that will be revealed later.

**Integrate Visual Foreshadowing:**

Visual elements can be powerful tools for foreshadowing. Consider how you can use cinematography, set design, and props to plant visual clues about future events.

For instance, a lingering shot of a locked door might foreshadow a future discovery behind that door. Repeating visual motifs, such as a specific color or object, can also subtly hint at connections between different plot points or character arcs.

**Reinforce Themes Through Foreshadowing:**

Use foreshadowing to reinforce the themes of your series. By planting symbolic or thematic elements early on, you can create a narrative that feels cohesive and layered.

For example, if your series explores themes of betrayal and trust, you might foreshadow a character's betrayal through subtle visual cues, such as them frequently standing in the shadows or their reflection being fragmented in a mirror.

**Balance Foreshadowing with Surprises:**

While foreshadowing can enhance the narrative, it's important to balance it with surprises. If everything is foreshadowed too clearly, the story can become predictable.

Consider using foreshadowing to hint at certain events while keeping others hidden. This creates a mix of anticipation and surprise, making the story more engaging and dynamic.

**Pay Attention to Timing:**

The timing of foreshadowing is crucial. Plant your narrative seeds early enough that they have time to take root, but not so early that the audience forgets about them by the time they pay off.

Consider the pacing of your series and how long you want the foreshadowing to build before the reveal. The longer the buildup, the more satisfying the payoff can be—provided the audience has been given enough subtle hints to make the connection.

**Use Foreshadowing in Character Arcs:**

Foreshadowing can be particularly effective in character arcs, hinting at a character's future decisions, growth, or downfall. This can add depth to the character development and make their journey feel more intentional.

For example, a character who initially shows signs of moral flexibility might be foreshadowing a later ethical dilemma or betrayal. Alternatively, a character who repeatedly fails at something might foreshadow a significant victory or redemption at the series' climax.

**Ensuring Foreshadowing Enhances the Story**

While foreshadowing can add richness to your narrative, it's important to ensure that it enhances the story rather than detracting from it. Here's how to strike the right balance:

**Avoid Overloading the Narrative:**

Too much foreshadowing can overwhelm the story, making it feel cluttered or overly complex. Focus on foreshadowing the most significant events or developments, rather than trying to hint at everything.

Select a few key moments or themes to foreshadow and let these elements serve as the foundation for the narrative's progression.

**Ensure Foreshadowing Feels Natural:**

Foreshadowing should feel like a natural part of the story, not an obvious setup for future events. Avoid drawing too much attention to the foreshadowing itself; instead, let it blend into the background, so that when the reveal comes, it feels like a natural progression of the narrative.

Test your foreshadowing with early readers or collaborators to see if they pick up on the hints without feeling like they were telegraphed too blatantly.

**Don't Sacrifice Storytelling for Foreshadowing:**

While foreshadowing can be a powerful tool, it should never come at the expense of good storytelling. The story should always come first, with foreshadowing serving to enhance the narrative, not dictate it.

If a piece of foreshadowing feels forced or disrupts the flow of the story, it's better to remove or adjust it. The goal is to create a cohesive and engaging narrative, not to showcase clever foreshadowing.

**Revisit Foreshadowing During Editing:**

During the editing process, revisit the foreshadowing elements you've included. Check that they are clear enough to be recognized in hindsight, but subtle enough not to give away the plot too early.

Consider how the foreshadowing elements contribute to the overall pacing and whether they align with the series' themes and character arcs. Make adjustments as needed to ensure that the foreshadowing enhances the story rather than detracting from it.

Foreshadowing is a valuable technique for planting narrative seeds that enhance the storytelling in a television miniseries. When used effectively, it creates anticipation, deepens themes, and rewards attentive viewers by making the narrative feel cohesive and well-crafted.

# The Role of the Ensemble Cast

The role of the ensemble cast is crucial in a television miniseries, as it allows for the exploration of multiple storylines, perspectives, and character dynamics. An ensemble cast can add depth and complexity to the narrative, making the story richer and more engaging for the audience. In this chapter, we'll discuss the importance of an ensemble cast, how to develop and balance multiple characters, and strategies for ensuring that each character's arc contributes to the overall narrative.

## The Importance of an Ensemble Cast

An ensemble cast is a group of characters who share the spotlight, rather than focusing solely on a single protagonist. This approach offers several advantages:

### Diverse Perspectives:

An ensemble cast allows the story to be told from multiple perspectives, providing a more nuanced and multifaceted view of the narrative. Different characters bring their own backgrounds, motivations, and experiences to the story, enriching the overall narrative.

By exploring different viewpoints, an ensemble cast can create a more complex and layered story, offering the audience a deeper understanding of the themes and conflicts at play.

### Richer Storylines:

With an ensemble cast, multiple storylines can unfold simultaneously, each contributing to the overarching narrative. This adds depth to the story and keeps the audience engaged as they follow the intersecting journeys of various characters.

The interplay between different storylines can create tension, drama, and intrigue, as the actions of one character may have ripple effects on others. This interconnectedness can make the narrative more dynamic and compelling.

### Stronger Character Dynamics:

Ensemble casts are often defined by the relationships between characters. The interactions, conflicts, and alliances among the characters drive much of the drama and emotional impact of the series.

These character dynamics can be explored in greater depth than in a series focused on a single protagonist. The ensemble format allows for the exploration of complex relationships, such as friendships, rivalries, romances, and family bonds, adding layers to the story.

### Flexibility in Focus:

An ensemble cast offers flexibility in terms of narrative focus. Different episodes or scenes can spotlight different characters, allowing for a more varied and textured storytelling experience.

This flexibility also allows for shifts in tone and pace, as different characters bring their own energy and style to the story. It can help maintain audience interest by providing a range of emotional experiences and thematic explorations.

**Audience Investment:**

With an ensemble cast, viewers are likely to connect with different characters for different reasons, broadening the series' appeal. Some viewers may relate to one character's journey, while others may be drawn to a different storyline.

This diversity of characters can create a more engaged and loyal audience, as viewers become invested in the fates of multiple characters and their interwoven stories.

## Developing and Balancing Multiple Characters

Creating and balancing an ensemble cast requires careful planning and attention to detail. Here's how to develop and manage multiple characters effectively:

**Create Distinctive Characters:**

Each character in the ensemble should be distinctive, with their own personality, background, goals, and challenges. Avoid creating characters who are too similar to one another, as this can lead to redundancy and confusion.

Consider how each character's traits and motivations will contribute to the overall narrative. Diverse characters with unique perspectives can create richer, more engaging storylines and interactions.

**Develop Clear Arcs for Each Character:**

Each member of the ensemble should have a clear character arc that contributes to the overall story. Whether it's a journey of growth, redemption, conflict, or discovery, the arc should be well-defined and meaningful.

Ensure that each character's arc is integrated into the larger narrative, with their actions and decisions having an impact on the story as a whole. This interconnectedness is key to creating a cohesive ensemble story.

**Balance Screen Time:**

Balancing screen time among ensemble characters is essential to ensure that each character's story is developed and that no one feels sidelined. While some characters may naturally have more focus in certain episodes, it's important to distribute attention evenly over the course of the series.

Consider using different episodes to highlight different characters, allowing each one to have moments of prominence while still contributing to the overall narrative. This approach can keep the story dynamic and give each character room to grow.

**Explore Interactions and Relationships:**

The relationships between ensemble characters are often where the most compelling drama and emotional depth can be found. Focus on exploring the dynamics between characters, whether through alliances, conflicts, or evolving friendships.

Consider how these relationships will evolve over the course of the series. Relationships should change and develop in response to the events of the story, reflecting the characters' growth and challenges.

**Weave Storylines Together:**

An effective ensemble story often involves weaving multiple storylines together in a way that feels organic and interconnected. Look for ways to link the characters' arcs, whether through shared goals, conflicts, or themes. This interconnectedness can create a sense of cohesion in the narrative, as the audience sees how different storylines influence and impact one another. It also allows for more complex storytelling, as characters' actions have broader consequences.

**Use Themes to Unite the Ensemble:**

Themes can serve as a unifying thread that ties the ensemble cast together. Even if the characters have different goals or conflicts, shared themes can create a sense of coherence and purpose in the story.

For example, if the series explores themes of justice and morality, each character might grapple with these issues in their own way, creating different perspectives on the same central question. This thematic unity can add depth and resonance to the narrative.

**Allow for Character Growth and Change:**

Ensemble characters should not remain static; they should grow and change in response to the events of the series. This evolution is key to keeping the audience engaged and invested in the characters' journeys. Consider how the events of the series will challenge and transform each character. Allow for unexpected developments, conflicts, or alliances that push the characters out of their comfort zones and force them to confront their flaws and strengths.

**Avoid Overcrowding the Story:**

While an ensemble cast offers many opportunities for rich storytelling, it's important to avoid overcrowding the narrative with too many characters. Each character should have a clear purpose in the story, and there should be enough screen time to fully explore their arcs. If the ensemble becomes too large, it can dilute the impact of the characters and make it difficult for the audience to connect with them. Focus on a core group of characters who can carry the narrative, with supporting characters adding depth and complexity without overwhelming the story.

**The Ensemble Cast in Different Genres**

The role of the ensemble cast can vary depending on the genre of the miniseries. Here's how ensemble casts function in different genres:

**Drama:**

In drama, an ensemble cast allows for the exploration of complex character relationships and emotional depth. Each character may represent different facets of a central theme, such as love, ambition, or betrayal. The interactions between characters drive much of the narrative tension, with conflicts and alliances shaping the story. Ensemble dramas often focus on character development, with each character's arc contributing to the overall emotional impact of the series.

**Comedy:**

In comedy, an ensemble cast can provide a diverse range of comedic styles and situations. Different characters might embody different types of humor—such as physical comedy, sarcasm, or wit—creating a varied and dynamic comedic experience. The ensemble format allows for multiple storylines, each with its own comedic payoff, while the interactions between characters can lead to humorous misunderstandings, conflicts, or collaborations.

**Thriller/Mystery:**

In thrillers and mysteries, an ensemble cast can create suspense by presenting multiple suspects, perspectives, or potential plot twists. Each character might have their own secrets, motives, or backstory, contributing to the tension and intrigue. The ensemble allows for red herrings and misdirection, as the audience tries to piece together the clues from different characters' actions and interactions. This format can also heighten the stakes, as the safety and trustworthiness of the ensemble are constantly in question.

**Science Fiction/Fantasy:**

In science fiction and fantasy, an ensemble cast can represent different facets of a complex world, with each character offering a unique perspective on the story's setting, culture, or technology. This diversity of viewpoints can make the world-building more immersive and rich. The ensemble format allows for the exploration of different storylines within a larger narrative, such as quests, political intrigue, or battles, with each character contributing to the broader mythos of the series.

**Action/Adventure:**

In action and adventure series, an ensemble cast can bring together characters with different skills, backgrounds, or goals, creating a dynamic team that must work together to achieve a common objective. The ensemble format allows for varied action sequences, with each character's unique abilities or personality shaping how they approach challenges. The relationships between characters—whether they are allies, rivals, or reluctant partners—add an additional layer of drama and tension to the action.

**Challenges of Working with an Ensemble Cast**

While ensemble casts offer many storytelling opportunities, they also present challenges. Here's how to address some common issues:

**Balancing Focus:**

One of the biggest challenges with an ensemble cast is balancing the focus between characters. It's important to ensure that each character's story is given enough attention to be meaningful, without overshadowing others. To achieve this balance, consider rotating the focus between characters across different episodes or scenes, while maintaining a clear narrative through line that ties the ensemble together.

**Avoiding Stereotypes:**

With multiple characters, there's a risk of falling into stereotypes or clichés. It's important to ensure that each character is fully developed and multidimensional, avoiding simplistic or reductive portrayals.

Invest time in fleshing out each character's backstory, motivations, and personality. This depth will make the ensemble more relatable and realistic, enhancing the audience's connection to the characters.

**Managing Complexity:**

An ensemble cast can lead to a complex narrative with multiple storylines, which can be challenging to manage. It's important to keep the story coherent and avoid overwhelming the audience with too many plot threads. Focus on the key storylines that drive the narrative, while using secondary plots to add depth and texture. Ensure that all storylines are interconnected and contribute to the overall arc of the series.

**Ensuring Cohesion:**

With multiple characters and storylines, it's crucial to maintain cohesion in the narrative. The ensemble should feel like a unified part of the same story, rather than disparate characters in unrelated plots.

Use themes, recurring motifs, or shared goals to tie the ensemble together. Consider how the actions of one character affect others, creating a sense of interdependence and connection within the group.

The ensemble cast is a powerful storytelling tool in a television miniseries, allowing for the exploration of diverse perspectives, rich storylines, and complex character dynamics. By carefully developing and balancing multiple characters, you can create a narrative that is both deep and engaging, with each character contributing to the overall impact of the series. Whether you're working in drama, comedy, thriller, or any other genre, an ensemble cast offers the opportunity to explore a range of emotions, conflicts, and themes, making the story more dynamic and resonant.

# Rewriting and Polishing: The Final Draft

Rewriting and polishing are critical steps in the writing process, transforming your script from a rough draft into a refined, compelling narrative ready for production. The final draft is where you solidify your story, sharpen your dialogue, and ensure that every scene contributes meaningfully to the overall miniseries. In this chapter, we'll discuss the importance of rewriting, strategies for effective revision, and techniques for polishing your script to achieve a professional, engaging final draft.

## The Importance of Rewriting

Rewriting is essential for several reasons:

### Refining the Narrative:

The first draft is often just a starting point. Rewriting allows you to refine the narrative, tightening the plot, enhancing character arcs, and ensuring that the story flows smoothly from beginning to end. This stage is your opportunity to address any structural issues, fill in gaps, and remove any elements that don't serve the overall story.

### Strengthening Dialogue:

Dialogue is a key element of any script, and rewriting gives you the chance to make it sharper, more natural, and more impactful. This is the time to eliminate clunky or expository lines, and to ensure that each character's voice is distinct and true to their personality. Polishing dialogue also involves checking for subtext, ensuring that what's left unsaid is as powerful as what's spoken.

### Enhancing Pacing and Tension:

Rewriting allows you to fine-tune the pacing of your script, ensuring that the rhythm of the story keeps the audience engaged. This might involve cutting or condensing scenes that drag, or adding new moments of tension or release to balance the narrative. Effective pacing is crucial for maintaining the audience's interest, especially in a miniseries where the story unfolds over several episodes.

### Deepening Character Development:

Characters often evolve during the rewriting process. This is your chance to deepen their development, making their motivations clearer and their arcs more compelling. Rewriting can help you ensure that each character's journey is consistent and that their growth or transformation feels earned and believable.

### Ensuring Thematic Consistency:

Themes may emerge more clearly as you revise your script. Rewriting allows you to reinforce these themes throughout the story, creating a more cohesive and resonant narrative. Look for opportunities to weave thematic elements into the dialogue, character arcs, and visual motifs, ensuring that they are integrated naturally into the story.

### Clarifying Storytelling:

Rewriting is also the time to clarify any confusing or ambiguous elements in the script. This might involve tightening the exposition, reworking complex plot points, or ensuring that key information is delivered effectively. The goal is to make the story as clear and accessible as possible, without losing its complexity or depth.

## Strategies for Effective Rewriting

Rewriting can be a daunting process, but with the right approach, it can also be incredibly rewarding. Here are some strategies to help you rewrite effectively:

### Take a Break Before Revising:

After completing your first draft, take a break before diving into revisions. This break allows you to return to the script with fresh eyes, making it easier to spot issues and identify areas for improvement.

Even a short break can help you gain perspective and approach the script with a more critical and objective mindset.

### Focus on Big Picture Revisions First:

Start by focusing on the big picture—plot structure, character arcs, and thematic elements—before getting into the details of dialogue or scene descriptions. This approach ensures that the foundational elements of your story are solid before you refine the smaller details. Consider whether the overall structure of the script is working. Are the plot points in the right places? Does the story build to a satisfying climax? Are the character arcs fully developed?

### Trim the Fat:

Be ruthless in cutting any scenes, dialogue, or characters that don't serve the story. If a scene doesn't move the plot forward, reveal something important about a character, or contribute to the overall theme, consider cutting it or reworking it to make it more relevant. This trimming process helps tighten the script, improving pacing and ensuring that every element is essential to the narrative.

### Strengthen Character Motivations:

Revisit each character's motivations and ensure that they are clear and consistent throughout the script. Characters should act in ways that align with their goals, desires, and personalities, and their decisions should drive the plot forward. If a character's actions feel inconsistent or unexplained, consider rewriting those moments to clarify their motivations and make their behavior more believable.

### Refine Dialogue for Authenticity and Impact:

Dialogue is often where the voice of the script truly comes alive. During rewrites, focus on making the dialogue sound natural and authentic to each character. Avoid overly expository or on-the-nose dialogue, and look for opportunities to add subtext. Read the dialogue out loud to test its flow and rhythm. Does it sound like something a real person would say? Does it reveal character, advance the plot, or enhance the theme?

### Enhance Emotional Resonance:

Look for opportunities to heighten the emotional impact of key scenes. This might involve deepening a character's reaction to an event, adding a moment of vulnerability or intimacy, or using visual or auditory cues to underscore the emotion. Emotional resonance is key to connecting with the audience, so ensure that your script's most important moments hit the right emotional notes.

### Seek Feedback:

Don't be afraid to share your script with trusted colleagues or friends for feedback. Outside perspectives can provide valuable insights and help you see issues you might have missed. Consider organizing a table read, where actors read the script aloud. This can help you hear how the dialogue flows, identify pacing issues, and assess the overall impact of the story.

**Revise for Visual Storytelling:**

Remember that film and television are visual mediums. During rewrites, consider how you can show rather than tell. Look for opportunities to convey information, emotion, or theme through visual means—such as through a character's actions, the setting, or symbolic imagery—rather than through dialogue or exposition. Consider how camera angles, lighting, and set design might be used to enhance the storytelling. This visual approach can add depth and layers to the narrative, making it more engaging for the audience.

**Ensure Consistency and Continuity:**

As you revise, keep an eye on consistency and continuity. This includes everything from character behavior to timeline and setting details. Inconsistencies can distract the audience and break the immersion, so it's important to address them during the rewriting process. Consider creating a continuity document or using script management software to track key details and ensure consistency across scenes and episodes.

**Polish the Script for Clarity and Style:**

Once the major revisions are complete, focus on polishing the script for clarity and style. This includes refining scene descriptions, tightening dialogue, and ensuring that the script is formatted correctly.

Pay attention to the flow of the script—how scenes transition from one to the next, how tension builds and releases, and how the story maintains momentum. The final draft should read smoothly, with no jarring shifts or confusing moments.

**Techniques for Polishing the Final Draft**

Polishing is the final step before your script is ready for production. Here's how to ensure that your final draft is as strong as possible:

**Proofread for Errors:**

Carefully proofread your script for spelling, grammar, and punctuation errors. Even minor mistakes can detract from the professionalism of your script and distract from the story. Consider using proofreading tools or hiring a professional proof-reader to catch any errors you might have missed.

**Check for Formatting Consistency:**

Ensure that your script is formatted consistently and according to industry standards. This includes proper indentation for dialogue, correct use of scene headings, and consistent font and spacing.

Proper formatting not only makes your script easier to read but also demonstrates professionalism and attention to detail.

**Read the Script Aloud:**

Reading the entire script aloud can help you catch awkward phrasing, pacing issues, and dialogue that doesn't flow naturally. It can also help you assess the overall rhythm of the story and identify any moments that need further refinement.

Pay attention to how the script sounds—does it have a natural cadence? Does the dialogue feel true to the characters? Does the pacing keep the story moving?

**Review Pacing and Structure:**

Review the pacing and structure one last time. Ensure that the story builds logically, that tension increases as the plot progresses, and that the climax and resolution are satisfying.

Check that each act, scene, and beat contributes to the overall narrative arc. The final draft should feel tight, with no unnecessary scenes or filler.

**Ensure Emotional and Thematic Cohesion:**

Revisit the emotional and thematic throughlines of your script. Ensure that the emotions resonate throughout the story and that the themes are woven consistently into the narrative.

The final draft should leave the audience with a clear sense of what the story is about—both on the surface and in its deeper, more thematic layers.

**Double-Check Character Consistency:**

Ensure that your characters remain consistent in their behavior, speech, and development throughout the script. Characters should feel like real, complex individuals, with clear motivations and believable growth.

Revisit character arcs to ensure that each character's journey is complete and satisfying, and that their actions align with their established traits and goals.

**Prepare for Production:**

As you finalize your script, consider any practical aspects of production that might impact the story. This includes thinking about locations, special effects, budget constraints, and the feasibility of certain scenes.

While it's important to maintain your creative vision, being mindful of production realities can help you avoid potential issues later on.

Rewriting and polishing are essential steps in the journey from a rough draft to a final, production-ready script. This process allows you to refine the narrative, sharpen the dialogue, and ensure that every scene serves a purpose in the story. By focusing on big-picture revisions first, then honing in on the details, you can transform your script into a compelling and professional final draft.

The final draft is where your story truly comes to life, with polished dialogue, clear and impactful scenes, and a narrative that flows seamlessly from start to finish. By taking the time to rewrite and polish, you ensure that your miniseries is the best it can be—ready to engage, entertain, and resonate with your audience.

Through careful revision, attention to detail, and a commitment to your creative vision, you can achieve a final draft that is not only polished and professional but also rich in character, theme, and emotion. This is your opportunity to make your story shine, setting the stage for a successful and impactful miniseries.

# Creating the Series Bible: A Guide for Continuity

Creating a series bible is a vital step in the development of a television miniseries. A series bible serves as a comprehensive reference guide that details the key elements of the series, including characters, plot arcs, themes, settings, and stylistic choices. It ensures continuity across episodes, helps maintain consistency in storytelling, and serves as a valuable resource for everyone involved in the production. In this chapter, we'll explore the purpose of a series bible, the essential components it should include, and strategies for creating an effective and detailed guide that supports the production of your miniseries.

### The Purpose of a Series Bible

A series bible is more than just a collection of notes; it's a living document that evolves as the series develops. It serves several key purposes:

### Ensuring Continuity:

Continuity is crucial in a television miniseries, where events, character development, and thematic elements need to be consistent across multiple episodes. A series bible helps maintain this continuity by providing a centralized reference for all aspects of the series.

It ensures that details such as character traits, timelines, and plot points are consistent, preventing discrepancies that could confuse the audience or disrupt the narrative flow.

### Guiding Writers and Directors:

For writers and directors, the series bible is an invaluable tool. It provides detailed information on the story world, character backstories, and plot arcs, helping to guide the creative decisions made throughout the series.

When multiple writers or directors are involved, the series bible ensures that everyone has a shared understanding of the series' vision, tone, and direction, leading to a more cohesive final product.

### Supporting Production Teams:

The series bible is also essential for production teams, including costume designers, set designers, and cinematographers. It outlines the visual style, settings, and important details that need to be reflected in the production design.

By providing a clear vision of the series, the bible helps ensure that all departments work together harmoniously to create a unified look and feel for the show.

### Serving as a Pitch Document:

In the early stages of development, a series bible can also serve as a pitch document to potential networks, studios, or investors. It provides a comprehensive overview of the series, showcasing the depth of planning and the potential for compelling storytelling.

A well-crafted series bible can convey the uniqueness of the series, its marketability, and its potential appeal to viewers, making it an essential tool for securing funding or distribution.

**Essential Components of a Series Bible**

A thorough series bible should cover several key elements to ensure that it serves its purpose effectively. Here are the essential components to include:

**Series Overview:**

**Logline:** Start with a logline—a brief, compelling summary of the series that encapsulates the core premise and main conflict. This should be no more than a sentence or two, designed to grab attention and convey the essence of the series.

**Genre and Tone:** Clearly define the genre of the series (e.g., drama, comedy, thriller) and describe the tone (e.g., dark, light-hearted, suspenseful). This helps set expectations for the storytelling style and audience experience.

**Themes:** Outline the central themes of the series. These are the underlying ideas or messages that the story explores, such as justice, identity, or redemption. Understanding the themes helps guide the narrative and character development throughout the series.

**Plot and Story Arcs:**

**Series Arc:** Provide an overview of the series arc—the overarching story that spans the entire miniseries. This should include the main conflict, key turning points, and how the story will resolve by the end of the series.

**Episode Summaries:** Offer brief summaries of each episode, highlighting the key plot points, character developments, and any significant events. These summaries help track the progression of the story and ensure that each episode contributes to the overall narrative.

**Character Arcs:** Detail the character arcs for each major character. Describe how each character evolves over the course of the series, including their personal challenges, growth, and how their story intersects with the main plot.

**Character Profiles:**

**Main Characters:** Provide detailed profiles for the main characters, including their names, ages, physical descriptions, and key personality traits. Include information about their backstory, motivations, relationships, and goals.

**Supporting Characters:** Include profiles for supporting characters as well, though these can be less detailed. Focus on how these characters contribute to the main story and their relationships with the main characters.

**Character Dynamics:** Describe the relationships and dynamics between characters. This includes friendships, rivalries, romantic interests, and familial ties. Understanding these dynamics is crucial for writing authentic interactions and conflicts.

**Setting and World-Building:**

**Primary Locations:** Detail the primary locations where the series takes place, including descriptions of the settings, their significance to the story, and any relevant historical or cultural background.

**World-Building Elements:** For series set in unique worlds—such as science fiction, fantasy, or historical dramas—provide additional information on the world-building elements. This might include the political landscape, social structures, technology, or magical systems.

**Visual Style:** Describe the visual style of the series, including the color palette, lighting, and overall aesthetic. This section helps guide the production design and cinematography, ensuring that the visual elements align with the story's tone and themes.

**Episode Structure:**

**Format and Length:** Specify the format of the episodes (e.g., hour-long episodes, limited series) and the expected length of each episode. This helps with planning the pacing and structure of the story.

**Recurring Elements:** Identify any recurring elements that will appear in each episode, such as opening sequences, flashbacks, or thematic motifs. Consistency in these elements helps establish the series' identity and tone.

**Thematic and Symbolic Elements:**

**Themes Revisited:** Expand on the themes introduced in the series overview, explaining how they will be explored and developed throughout the series. Consider how different characters and plotlines will reflect these themes.

**Symbolism:** Identify any symbolic elements or motifs that will recur throughout the series. This might include objects, colors, or imagery that carry deeper meanings and reinforce the themes.

**Production Considerations:**

**Budget Considerations:** Provide an overview of the budget considerations, including any high-cost elements such as special effects, complex sets, or location shoots. Understanding these constraints can help guide creative decisions and ensure the series remains feasible to produce.

**Casting Ideas:** While not always necessary, including potential casting ideas for key roles can help convey the intended tone and style of the series. It can also provide a sense of how the characters might be brought to life on screen.

**Evolution and Updates:**

**Updates and Revisions:** As the series develops, the series bible should be updated to reflect any changes in the story, characters, or production plans. Keeping the bible current ensures that everyone involved in the production has access to the latest information.

**Feedback Integration:** Incorporate feedback from writers, directors, and producers into the series bible. This collaborative approach ensures that the bible remains a useful tool throughout the production process.

**Strategies for Creating an Effective Series Bible**

Creating a series bible is a detailed process, but with the right strategies, you can produce a document that effectively supports the development and production of your miniseries. Here's how to approach the creation of your series bible:

**Start with a Clear Vision:**

Before you begin writing the series bible, take the time to clarify your vision for the series. Consider the story you want to tell, the themes you want to explore, and the emotional impact you want to create.

This vision will guide the development of the series bible and ensure that all the elements are aligned with the overall goals of the series.

**Be Comprehensive but Concise:**

While it's important to be thorough, the series bible should also be concise and easy to navigate. Focus on providing the essential information that will guide the production, without overwhelming the reader with unnecessary details.

Use clear headings, bullet points, and summaries to make the document easy to reference. This ensures that it remains a practical tool for the entire production team.

**Collaborate with Key Creatives:**

Involve key creatives, such as writers, directors, and producers, in the creation of the series bible. Their input can help ensure that the document reflects the collective vision of the team and addresses any practical considerations.

Collaboration also helps build a shared understanding of the series, making it easier to maintain consistency and continuity throughout the production process.

**Use Visuals to Enhance the Bible:**

Including visuals, such as concept art, location photos, or character sketches, can make the series bible more engaging and help convey the intended look and feel of the series.

Visuals can also serve as inspiration for the production design and help ensure that the entire team shares a common vision for the series' aesthetic.

**Keep the Audience in Mind:**

As you create the series bible, consider the audience you're writing for—whether it's potential networks, investors, or the production team. Tailor the document to meet their needs and expectations, focusing on the elements that will be most important to them.

For example, if the bible is being used to pitch the series to networks, emphasize the series' marketability, unique selling points, and potential audience appeal.

**Regularly Update the Bible:**

The series bible should be a living document that evolves as the series develops. Regularly update the bible to reflect any changes in the story, characters, or production plans, ensuring that it remains a relevant and useful resource.

Keeping the bible current helps prevent confusion and ensures that all departments have access to the latest information, leading to a smoother production process.

**Review and Revise:**

Before finalizing the series bible, review it carefully to ensure that all the information is accurate, clear, and aligned with the overall vision for the series. Consider seeking feedback from trusted colleagues to identify any areas that need further refinement.

Revisions might involve clarifying character motivations, tightening plot summaries, or refining the description of the series' visual style. The goal is to create a polished, professional document that effectively communicates the series' potential.

Creating a series bible is a crucial step in the development of a television miniseries, serving as a comprehensive guide that ensures continuity, consistency, and clarity throughout the production process. By detailing the key elements of the series—such as plot arcs, character development, themes, and visual style—the series bible provides a valuable reference for everyone involved in the project, from writers and directors to production designers and network executives. A well-crafted series bible not only supports the creative vision of the series but also helps guide practical decisions, ensuring that the story is told in a cohesive and compelling way. Whether used as a pitch document or as a production tool, the series bible is essential for maintaining the integrity of the narrative and bringing the series to life on screen.

# Writing the Series Finale: A Memorable Conclusion

Writing the series finale is one of the most important tasks in creating a television miniseries. The finale is your opportunity to bring the story to a satisfying close, resolving key plot points, delivering emotional payoffs, and leaving a lasting impression on the audience. A well-crafted finale can elevate the entire series, ensuring that viewers remember it fondly and feel that their investment in the story was worthwhile. In this chapter, we'll explore the elements of a memorable series finale, strategies for crafting a satisfying conclusion, and how to ensure that the final episode resonates with your audience.

**The Importance of a Strong Series Finale**

The series finale holds a unique significance in a television miniseries. Here's why it's so crucial:

**Resolving the Story:**

The finale is where all the threads of the narrative come together. It's the moment when lingering questions are answered, conflicts are resolved, and the characters' journeys reach their conclusions. A strong finale ties up the story in a way that feels complete and satisfying.

Viewers who have followed the series expect closure, and the finale is your chance to deliver that. Whether it's a dramatic showdown, a poignant moment of reflection, or a triumphant resolution, the finale should provide a sense of completion.

**Delivering Emotional Payoff:**

Throughout the series, you've built emotional connections between the audience and the characters. The finale is where you deliver the emotional payoffs that make those connections meaningful.

Whether it's joy, sadness, relief, or catharsis, the finale should evoke strong emotions. These emotional moments are what will linger with the audience long after the credits roll.

**Reinforcing Themes:**

The finale is an opportunity to reinforce the central themes of the series. It's the moment when the underlying messages of the story come to the forefront, providing a deeper understanding of what the series has been about.

Whether the theme is about love, justice, redemption, or the human condition, the finale should encapsulate and amplify these ideas, leaving the audience with something to ponder.

**Creating a Lasting Impact:**

The finale is often the episode that sticks with viewers the most. It's the last impression they have of the series, so it's crucial to make it memorable and impactful.

A strong finale can turn a good series into a great one, leaving viewers with a sense of satisfaction and a desire to revisit the series in the future.

## Elements of a Memorable Series Finale

To craft a memorable series finale, several key elements should be considered:

### Closure and Resolution:

The finale should provide closure for the main plot and subplots. This means resolving the central conflict, answering important questions, and bringing the characters' arcs to a natural conclusion.

However, closure doesn't necessarily mean tying up every loose end. Sometimes, leaving a few things open to interpretation can add depth and keep the story alive in the audience's mind.

### Emotional Peaks:

The finale should include emotional peaks—moments of high intensity that resonate with the audience. These can be moments of triumph, defeat, revelation, or reconciliation.

Ensure that these emotional peaks are well-earned and align with the characters' journeys. Forced or unearned emotional moments can feel manipulative and undermine the impact of the finale.

### Satisfying Character Arcs:

The characters' journeys should reach satisfying conclusions in the finale. Whether it's a hero's victory, a villain's downfall, or a character's personal growth, the finale should reflect the evolution of the characters throughout the series.

Consider the promises you've made to the audience regarding the characters' arcs and make sure you deliver on them. A well-crafted character arc can make the finale feel fulfilling and rewarding.

### Thematic Resolution:

The finale should bring the series' themes to a head, offering a final statement or exploration of the ideas that have been woven throughout the story.

This could be a powerful line of dialogue, a symbolic action, or a visual motif that encapsulates the series' message. The thematic resolution helps give the finale—and the series as a whole—a sense of purpose and meaning.

### Memorable Moments:

Aim to include at least one or two standout moments in the finale that will stick with the audience. These could be surprising twists, powerful speeches, or visually striking scenes.

Memorable moments are what make the finale unforgettable, ensuring that it remains vivid in the audience's memory long after they've finished watching the series.

### Pacing and Structure:

The pacing of the finale is crucial. It should build to a crescendo, with the final act delivering the most impactful moments. Avoid rushing through important resolutions or dragging out the conclusion unnecessarily.

Structure the finale to ensure a smooth progression from setup to climax to resolution. Each scene should build on the previous one, leading to a cohesive and satisfying ending.

## Strategies for Crafting a Satisfying Conclusion

Writing the series finale requires careful planning and attention to detail. Here are some strategies to help you craft a satisfying conclusion:

### Revisit the Series Arc:

Before writing the finale, revisit the series arc. Ensure that all major plot points, character developments, and thematic elements have been addressed. The finale should feel like the culmination of everything that has come before.

Consider how the finale will reflect the overall journey of the series. It should feel like a natural conclusion, even if it includes surprising twists or revelations.

### Deliver on Promises:

Throughout the series, you've likely made promises to the audience—whether through foreshadowing, character arcs, or thematic exploration. The finale is where you deliver on those promises.

Ensure that key questions are answered, and that the resolutions feel earned. The audience should feel that their investment in the story has paid off.

### Balance Surprises with Expectations:

A great finale often includes surprises, but these should be balanced with meeting audience expectations. Too many surprises can feel like a betrayal, while too few can make the finale predictable.

Consider including a twist or unexpected development that enhances the story, but make sure it aligns with the logic of the series and the characters' motivations.

### Focus on Character Moments:

While the plot is important, the finale should also focus on character moments. These are the moments that resonate emotionally with the audience and provide a sense of closure for the characters' arcs.

Give each main character a moment to shine in the finale, whether it's through a final act of bravery, a heartfelt conversation, or a significant decision.

### Reinforce the Series' Themes:

Use the finale to reinforce the series' themes, bringing them to the forefront in a way that feels natural and impactful. This could be done through dialogue, imagery, or the resolution of key conflicts.

Thematic consistency helps tie the series together, making the finale feel like the logical conclusion of the story's exploration of its core ideas.

### Consider the Emotional Journey:

The emotional journey of the finale should mirror the emotional journey of the series. Consider the tone you want to end on—whether it's hopeful, bittersweet, triumphant, or reflective.

The emotional tone of the finale should feel true to the series and provide the audience with a satisfying conclusion to the emotional arcs they've been following.

**Avoid Over-complication:**

In an effort to tie up all loose ends, it can be tempting to overcomplicate the finale with too many plot points or resolutions. However, simplicity is often more powerful.

Focus on the core elements that need resolution and avoid introducing new conflicts or subplots that could distract from the main story. The finale should be clear, focused, and impactful.

**Leave a Lasting Impression:**

The final scene or moments of the series are your chance to leave a lasting impression on the audience. Consider what you want the audience to take away from the series and how you can encapsulate that in the closing moments.

Whether it's a powerful visual, a poignant line of dialogue, or a lingering shot, the final moments should resonate with the audience and provide a sense of closure.

**Examples of Memorable Series Finales**

Looking at examples of memorable series finales can provide inspiration for crafting your own. Here are a few iconic finales and what made them stand out:

***Breaking Bad*:**

The finale of *Breaking Bad* masterfully ties up the series' major plot points while delivering emotional payoffs for its central characters. Walter White's final acts are both redemptive and tragic, reflecting the series' themes of power, corruption, and identity.

The episode is tightly paced, with each scene building tension and leading to a cathartic conclusion. The final image of Walter, surrounded by the tools of his empire, is haunting and unforgettable.

***The Sopranos*:**

The ambiguous ending of *The Sopranos* remains one of the most discussed finales in television history. By cutting to black in the middle of a tense scene, the show leaves Tony Soprano's fate unresolved, reflecting the uncertainty and danger that have always surrounded his life.

The finale reinforces the series' themes of existential dread and the inescapability of one's choices. The decision to leave the ending open to interpretation has kept the finale in the public consciousness for years.

***Six Feet Under***

The finale of *Six Feet Under* provides closure for its characters by showing their eventual deaths, fitting for a series centered around mortality. The sequence is emotionally powerful, offering both a sense of finality and a celebration of life.

The finale ties together the show's exploration of life, death, and family, giving viewers a sense of closure that is both poignant and uplifting. The final montage, set to the song "Breathe Me" by Sia, is particularly memorable, encapsulating the essence of the series in a way that resonates deeply with the audience.

### *The Good Place*:

The finale of *The Good Place* balances humor with deep philosophical questions about life, death, and what it means to be good. The show's final episode provides closure for each of the main characters, allowing them to complete their journeys in a way that feels true to their development throughout the series.

The finale is emotionally satisfying and thought-provoking, with each character finding peace and making the choice to move on when they are ready. The final scenes are both heartwarming and bittersweet, leaving the audience with a sense of closure and contemplation.

*Friends*:

The finale of *Friends* is a classic example of how to end a beloved sitcom in a way that satisfies long-time fans. The episode focuses on the characters' decisions to move forward with their lives while maintaining the bonds that made the show so endearing.

The final scene, where the group leaves Monica and Chandler's apartment for the last time, is a touching farewell that emphasizes the importance of friendship and the inevitable changes that come with time. The finale strikes a balance between humor and emotion, leaving fans with a sense of nostalgia and closure.

*Lost*:

The finale of *Lost* is notable for its ambitious attempt to provide closure to a complex and mysterious narrative. While it was divisive among fans, the finale did offer emotional resolution for the characters, focusing on their relationships and personal journeys.

The episode used the concept of the afterlife to reunite the characters, allowing them to find peace after their tumultuous experiences on the island. The finale's emphasis on character-driven resolution, rather than unraveling every mystery, underscored the show's themes of faith, destiny, and human connection.

## Crafting Your Own Memorable Series Finale

Now that we've looked at some iconic finales, let's explore how you can apply these lessons to your own series finale.

### Reflect on the Series' Core Themes:

Before writing the finale, revisit the core themes of your series. Consider how these themes have been explored throughout the episodes and how they can be brought to a meaningful conclusion in the finale.

For example, if your series has been about the consequences of power, the finale might explore the final price the characters pay for their ambitions. If it's about redemption, the finale could focus on whether the characters achieve it and at what cost.

### Pay Off Long-Term Storylines:

The finale is the time to deliver on the long-term storylines that have been building throughout the series. Identify the key plot threads that need resolution and ensure that each one is addressed in a way that feels satisfying to the audience. Consider the expectations you've set up over the course of the series. If a character's fate has been a lingering question, the finale should provide an answer that feels earned, whether it's triumphant, tragic, or somewhere in between.

### Focus on Character-Driven Moments:

While plot resolution is important, the emotional core of your finale will come from character-driven moments. These are the moments that resonate most with the audience, providing closure to the characters' arcs. Think about the key relationships in your series and how they can be honored in the finale. Whether it's a heartfelt goodbye, a long-awaited reconciliation, or a final act of courage, these moments should feel true to the characters and their journeys.

**Consider the Audience's Journey:**

The audience has been on a journey with your characters, and the finale is the culmination of that experience. Consider how you want the audience to feel at the end of the series and craft your finale to evoke those emotions. Whether you want to leave the audience feeling hopeful, introspective, or even challenged, the tone and content of the finale should align with the emotional journey you've guided them through.

**Balance Closure with Ambiguity:**

While it's important to provide closure, leaving a bit of ambiguity can add depth and keep the story alive in the audience's mind. Not every question needs to be answered, and sometimes leaving room for interpretation can make the finale more memorable. However, be mindful of which elements to leave ambiguous. Major plot points or character fates should generally be resolved, while more thematic or symbolic elements might benefit from a more open-ended approach.

**Create a Memorable Final Image:**

The final image or scene of your series is what the audience will take with them. Consider what you want that image to be and how it can encapsulate the entire series. Whether it's a powerful visual, a poignant moment of silence, or a line of dialogue that echoes the series' themes, the final image should leave a lasting impression.

**Test the Finale:**

If possible, gather feedback on your finale from trusted colleagues or even through a table read. Seeing how others react to the finale can help you gauge whether it's hitting the right emotional and narrative notes. Be open to revising the finale if something isn't working. It's better to take the time to get it right than to leave your audience feeling unsatisfied.

Writing the series finale is a challenging but rewarding task. It's your opportunity to bring your story to a close in a way that resonates with your audience, delivers on the promises you've made throughout the series, and leaves a lasting impression. By focusing on closure, emotional payoff, thematic resolution, and memorable moments, you can craft a finale that not only satisfies but elevates the entire series.

The finale is the final chapter of your story, the moment where everything comes together. With thoughtful planning, attention to detail, and a clear understanding of what has made your series special, you can create a finale that is both a conclusion and a celebration of the journey your characters—and your audience—have taken together.

# Adapting Source Material: Challenges and Opportunities

Adapting source material for a television miniseries presents both unique challenges and exciting opportunities. Whether you're working from a novel, a short story, a comic book, or even historical events, the process of adaptation requires careful consideration of how to translate the essence of the original work into a compelling visual narrative. In this chapter, we'll explore the key challenges of adapting source material, the creative opportunities it offers, and strategies for successfully bringing an existing story to life on screen.

## Challenges of Adapting Source Material

Adapting a work from one medium to another is not a straightforward task. Here are some of the main challenges you may encounter:

### Staying True to the Source While Innovating:

One of the biggest challenges in adaptation is balancing faithfulness to the original material with the need to innovate for a new medium. Fans of the source material often have strong attachments to the story, characters, and themes, and may have high expectations for the adaptation. However, what works in a book or comic may not directly translate to the screen. You'll need to make creative decisions about what to keep, what to change, and what to omit, all while staying true to the spirit of the original work.

### Condensing or Expanding the Story:

Source material often needs to be condensed or expanded to fit the format of a television miniseries. A novel might contain too much content for a limited series, requiring cuts or the combination of characters and events. Conversely, a short story might need additional material to fill the required runtime, necessitating the creation of new scenes, subplots, or character development.

The challenge lies in making these adjustments without losing the essence of the story. Key plot points must be preserved, and any new material should feel integrated and necessary rather than like filler.

### Visualizing Internal Narratives:

Many source materials, particularly novels, rely heavily on internal monologues, thoughts, and emotions that are challenging to depict visually. Translating these internal narratives into external actions, dialogue, or visual symbolism requires creativity and sensitivity to the original tone and intent.

The goal is to convey the same depth of character and emotion without relying on the inner voice, which can be difficult to achieve without oversimplifying the character's experience.

### Maintaining Pacing and Structure:

The pacing and structure of a book or other source material often differ significantly from the needs of a television series. What unfolds over several chapters in a novel might need to be condensed into a single episode, or stretched to fit multiple episodes.

Adapting the pacing to suit the episodic structure of television while maintaining the narrative's momentum is a key challenge. You'll need to ensure that each episode is engaging, with its own mini-arcs, while also contributing to the overall story.

**Handling Expectations and Fan Reactions:**

Fans of the source material often have preconceived notions about how the adaptation should look and feel. Meeting or exceeding these expectations can be a challenge, especially when necessary changes are made to fit the new medium.

It's important to manage fan expectations while also making creative choices that serve the adaptation. Striking the right balance between fidelity and originality can be difficult, but it's crucial for creating a successful adaptation.

**Opportunities in Adapting Source Material**

While adaptation comes with challenges, it also offers exciting creative opportunities:

**Expanding the Universe:**

Adapting a story into a miniseries allows you to expand on the original material, exploring characters, settings, and subplots that were only hinted at in the source. This can enrich the narrative and provide new insights for both existing fans and new audiences.

For example, secondary characters in a novel might be given more screen time and development in the series, adding depth and complexity to the story world.

**Updating or Reinterpreting the Story:**

Adaptation offers the opportunity to update or reinterpret the source material for a contemporary audience. This might involve modernizing the setting, addressing current social issues, or reimagining certain characters or events to reflect today's values and sensibilities.

Such updates can make the story more relevant and accessible to modern viewers while still honoring the original work.

**Visual Storytelling:**

One of the most significant opportunities in adaptation is the ability to tell the story visually. This allows you to create a rich, immersive experience that leverages the strengths of the television medium—such as cinematography, production design, special effects, and sound design.

Visual storytelling can bring new dimensions to the source material, highlighting themes, emotions, and details in ways that text alone cannot. Symbolism, visual motifs, and color palettes can all be used to deepen the narrative and create a distinctive aesthetic.

**Exploring Themes in New Ways:**

Adapting source material allows you to explore the original themes in new ways, perhaps by shifting the focus or adding layers of meaning. This can give the story fresh relevance and allow for a deeper exploration of the issues it raises.

For instance, a novel's exploration of identity might be expanded in the adaptation to include a broader range of perspectives or cultural contexts, making the theme more resonant for a diverse audience.

**Engaging with a New Audience:**

Adaptations have the potential to introduce the source material to a new audience who may not be familiar with the original work. This can broaden the reach of the story and create a new fanbase for the material.

Additionally, a successful adaptation can reignite interest in the original source, leading to increased sales or readership, and extending the legacy of the work.

## Strategies for Successful Adaptation

To navigate the challenges and seize the opportunities of adaptation, here are some strategies to consider:

**Identify the Core Elements:**

Start by identifying the core elements of the source material—the essential plot points, characters, themes, and tone that define the story. These are the elements that must be preserved in the adaptation, even if other aspects are changed or omitted.

Understanding what makes the source material unique and compelling will guide your decisions about what to keep, what to adapt, and what to expand.

**Embrace the Medium:**

Television is a different medium from literature, comics, or history, with its own strengths and limitations. Embrace the visual and episodic nature of television by finding ways to translate the essence of the story into a format that works for the screen.

Consider how you can use visual storytelling, sound design, and pacing to enhance the narrative. Look for opportunities to create memorable images or sequences that capture the spirit of the original work.

**Collaborate with the Original Creator:**

If possible, collaborate with the original creator of the source material. Their insights and understanding of the story can be invaluable in guiding the adaptation process.

However, it's also important to establish boundaries and communicate your vision for the adaptation. The goal is to honor the source material while also making it your own, so open and respectful dialogue is key.

**Consider Audience Expectations:**

Be mindful of the expectations of both existing fans and new viewers. While it's important to stay true to the source material, you also need to make creative choices that serve the adaptation and resonate with your audience.

Managing these expectations requires clear communication and a willingness to explain why certain changes were made. Engaging with the fanbase—through social media, interviews, or behind-the-scenes content—can help build support for the adaptation.

**Balance Fidelity with Innovation:**

Strive to balance fidelity to the source material with innovation. The best adaptations often remain true to the essence of the original work while also offering something new—whether it's a fresh perspective, an expanded storyline, or a unique visual style. This balance allows you to respect the source material while also making the adaptation a distinct and original work in its own right.

**Test and Refine:**

As you develop the adaptation, test it with a small group of viewers—ideally a mix of those familiar with the source material and those new to it. Their feedback can help you identify what's working and what needs adjustment.

Be open to revising the adaptation based on this feedback, whether it's pacing, character development, or how closely you've adhered to the source material. The goal is to create an adaptation that resonates with a wide audience while staying true to the original story.

Adapting source material for a television miniseries is a complex but rewarding process. It requires careful consideration of how to translate the essence of the original work into a new medium while embracing the creative opportunities that adaptation offers. By balancing fidelity to the source material with innovation, embracing the strengths of television as a medium, and staying true to the core elements of the story, you can create an adaptation that honors the original work while also standing on its own as a compelling and memorable series.

Successful adaptations resonate with both existing fans and new audiences, offering a fresh take on a beloved story while remaining faithful to what made the original material special. With thoughtful planning, collaboration, and a clear vision, you can navigate the challenges of adaptation and create a series that brings the source material to life in exciting and unexpected ways.

# Original Miniseries vs. Adaptation: Pros and Cons

When deciding between creating an original miniseries or adapting existing source material, there are several factors to consider. Both approaches have their own set of advantages and challenges, and the choice depends on your creative goals, audience expectations, and production resources. In this chapter, we'll explore the pros and cons of both original miniseries and adaptations, helping you weigh your options and make an informed decision for your project.

**Pros of Creating an Original Miniseries**

**Creative Freedom:**

One of the most significant advantages of creating an original miniseries is the creative freedom it offers. You have complete control over the story, characters, setting, and themes, allowing you to craft a narrative that reflects your unique vision and voice.

This freedom also means you're not constrained by pre-existing material or audience expectations, giving you the flexibility to experiment with narrative structure, genre, and tone.

**Ownership of Intellectual Property:**

When you create an original miniseries, you own the intellectual property (IP) rights. This can be financially advantageous, as it allows you to retain control over licensing, merchandising, and potential sequels or spin-offs.

Ownership of IP also means you can fully explore the world you've created, without needing to secure rights from another author or creator.

**Building a New Fanbase:**

An original miniseries offers the opportunity to build a new fanbase from scratch. If your story resonates with viewers, you can create a dedicated following that is loyal to your original creation.

This fresh start allows you to define the series' identity without the pressure of meeting existing fan expectations, and you can grow your audience organically based on the strength of your story.

**Flexibility in Development:**

With an original miniseries, you have the flexibility to develop the story and characters as you go. You're not tied to a pre-existing plot, so you can adapt and refine the narrative based on what's working or what you feel inspired to explore further.

This flexibility also extends to production, where you can adjust pacing, tone, or focus without the need to adhere to a specific source material.

**Opportunity for Innovation:**

Original miniseries often allow for greater innovation, as you're not restricted by the conventions or expectations of a pre-existing work. You can experiment with storytelling techniques, genre blending, or character archetypes in ways that might be more challenging in an adaptation.

This innovative approach can set your series apart in a crowded market, making it more appealing to audiences looking for something new and different.

**Cons of Creating an Original Miniseries**

**Greater Risk:**

Without the built-in audience of an adaptation, original miniseries can be riskier to produce. There's no guarantee that the concept will resonate with viewers, and it may be harder to secure funding or distribution without a proven track record. The success of an original miniseries often hinges on strong marketing and word-of-mouth, which can be challenging to achieve in a competitive landscape.

**Time-Intensive Development:**

Developing an original miniseries from scratch is often more time-consuming than adapting existing material. You'll need to create the world, characters, and plot entirely on your own, which requires significant effort and creative energy. The process of refining and polishing the story to make it production-ready can also take longer, as there are no pre-existing blueprints to guide you.

**Uncertain Audience Reception:**

With an original miniseries, there's always the uncertainty of how audiences will respond. Without the familiarity of a well-known book or franchise, it may be harder to attract viewers initially, and the series may struggle to find its audience. The lack of a built-in fanbase means that the series' success depends heavily on its ability to stand out and appeal to viewers on its own merits.

**Difficulty in Pitching:**

Pitching an original concept to networks or streaming platforms can be more challenging than pitching an adaptation of a popular work. Executives may be more hesitant to greenlight a project without an existing fanbase or proven success in another medium. You'll need to have a clear and compelling pitch that communicates the unique value of your original series and why it's worth investing in.

**Pros of Adapting Source Material**

**Built-In Audience:**

One of the most significant advantages of adapting source material is the built-in audience that comes with it. Fans of the original book, comic, or other media are likely to be interested in the adaptation, providing a ready-made viewer base. This existing fanbase can generate buzz and increase the chances of the series being successful, as viewers are already familiar with and invested in the story.

**Established Story and Characters:**

Adapting existing material gives you a solid foundation to build on, with an established story, characters, and themes. This can make the development process more straightforward, as you're not starting from scratch. The source material provides a clear roadmap, allowing you to focus on how to best translate the story to the screen rather than creating it entirely anew.

**Easier to Pitch:**

Networks and streaming platforms are often more willing to greenlight adaptations of popular works, as they come with a level of built-in security. The success of the source material can make the project more appealing and easier to pitch. The familiarity of the original work can also make it easier to attract talent, as actors, directors, and writers may be excited to work on an adaptation of a beloved story.

**Potential for Expanding the Universe:**

Adaptations offer the opportunity to expand on the source material, exploring characters, settings, or subplots that were only touched upon in the original work. This can provide new content for fans and deepen the story world.

Expanding the universe allows you to add your creative stamp to the adaptation, making it feel fresh and exciting while still honoring the original material.

**Proven Market Appeal:**

If the source material has been successful in its original medium, it's a strong indicator that the story has market appeal. This can give producers and investors more confidence in the project's potential success.

Proven market appeal can also help with marketing and distribution, as it's easier to promote a series based on a popular or critically acclaimed work.

**Cons of Adapting Source Material**

**Creative Constraints:**

One of the biggest challenges of adaptation is the creative constraints it imposes. You need to balance staying true to the original work with making necessary changes to fit the new medium, which can limit your creative freedom. Fans of the source material may have strong opinions about how the adaptation should look and feel, and deviating too much from the original can lead to backlash.

**Risk of Comparison:**

Adaptations are often subject to comparison with the original work. Fans and critics alike will compare the adaptation to the source material, and any perceived shortcomings can lead to disappointment or criticism. The pressure to live up to the expectations set by the original work can be daunting, and even a well-executed adaptation may struggle to satisfy everyone.

**Difficulty in Translating Certain Elements:**

Not all elements of the source material may translate well to the screen. Internal monologues, complex plot structures, or intricate world-building may need to be adapted or altered, which can lead to difficult creative decisions. Certain themes or scenes might need to be reinterpreted or omitted entirely, which can change the tone or impact of the story.

**Legal and Rights Issues:**

Adapting a work requires securing the necessary rights, which can be a complex and time-consuming process. Legal issues may arise, particularly if the rights are held by multiple parties or if there are restrictions on how the material can be used. Additionally, there may be contractual obligations to involve the original creator, which can complicate the adaptation process if creative differences arise.

**Fan Expectations and Backlash:**

Fans of the source material often have high expectations for adaptations, and any changes or deviations can lead to backlash. Managing these expectations is a significant challenge, as it's difficult to please everyone. The risk of fan disappointment can be high, especially if the adaptation fails to capture the essence of the original work or makes significant changes that fans disagree with.

Deciding between creating an original miniseries or adapting source material involves weighing the pros and cons of each approach. Original miniseries offer creative freedom, the opportunity for innovation, and ownership of intellectual property, but they come with greater risk and uncertainty. Adaptations, on the other hand, benefit from a built-in audience, established storylines, and proven market appeal, but they can be creatively constraining and subject to intense scrutiny. Ultimately, the choice depends on your creative goals, the resources available to you, and the story you want to tell.

# Creating a Cohesive Vision: Collaboration with the Director

Creating a cohesive vision for a television miniseries is essential to ensuring that all elements of the production come together harmoniously. Collaboration between the writer and the director is crucial in this process, as both roles bring different perspectives and expertise to the project. The writer provides the story, characters, and themes, while the director interprets and visualizes these elements on screen. In this chapter, we'll explore how to establish a strong collaborative relationship with the director, how to align your visions for the project, and strategies for maintaining creative coherence throughout the production.

## The Importance of a Cohesive Vision

A cohesive vision ensures that every aspect of the miniseries—story, performances, visual style, pacing, and tone—works together to create a unified experience for the audience. Without this cohesion, the series can feel disjointed, with different episodes or scenes lacking consistency in style, tone, or message. A shared vision between the writer and director helps to:

### Maintain Narrative Consistency:

A cohesive vision ensures that the story is told consistently across all episodes. This includes maintaining character development, plot progression, and thematic exploration throughout the series.

### Create a Unified Visual Style:

The visual style of the series should reflect the story's tone and themes. A shared vision helps to ensure that the cinematography, set design, costumes, and overall aesthetic align with the narrative.

### Support Character and Performance Consistency:

Consistency in character portrayal is essential for audience engagement. A cohesive vision guides actors in delivering performances that are true to the characters' development and the overall story arc.

### Enhance Audience Engagement:

When all elements of the miniseries work together seamlessly, it creates a more immersive and compelling experience for the audience. A cohesive vision helps to draw viewers into the story and keep them engaged throughout the series.

## Establishing a Strong Collaborative Relationship

Collaboration between the writer and director is key to achieving a cohesive vision. Here's how to build a strong working relationship:

### Open and Honest Communication:

Effective communication is the foundation of any successful collaboration. From the outset, establish open lines of communication with the director, ensuring that both of you feel comfortable sharing ideas, concerns, and feedback.

Regular meetings or check-ins can help maintain this communication, allowing you to discuss the direction of the project, address any issues that arise, and ensure that you're both on the same page.

**Mutual Respect for Each Other's Roles:**

Recognize and respect the unique expertise that each of you brings to the project. The writer's role is to craft the story, characters, and themes, while the director's role is to interpret and visualize these elements on screen.

Trust in the director's ability to bring your script to life, and be open to their creative input. Similarly, the director should respect the writer's vision and narrative intentions.

**Aligning on the Core Vision:**

Before production begins, take the time to align on the core vision for the miniseries. Discuss the themes, tone, and style you want to achieve, and ensure that you both have a shared understanding of what the series is about.

This alignment should extend to key aspects such as character arcs, visual style, pacing, and thematic exploration. A clear and unified vision will guide all creative decisions throughout the production.

**Collaborative Problem-Solving:**

Challenges and creative differences are inevitable in any collaboration. Approach these situations as opportunities for collaborative problem-solving, rather than conflicts.

When differences arise, focus on finding solutions that serve the story and enhance the overall vision. This might involve compromise, experimentation, or rethinking certain elements, but the goal is always to create the best possible outcome for the series.

**Strategies for Maintaining Creative Coherence**

Maintaining creative coherence throughout the production requires ongoing collaboration and attention to detail. Here are some strategies to ensure that your shared vision is consistently reflected in the final product:

**Use a Series Bible as a Reference Tool:**

A detailed series bible is an invaluable tool for maintaining consistency across the miniseries. It should include information on character backstories, plot arcs, themes, visual style, and more.

Both the writer and director should refer to the series bible regularly to ensure that the creative choices being made align with the established vision. This document can also serve as a reference for other departments, such as costume design, set design, and cinematography.

**Storyboarding Key Scenes:**

Storyboarding is a collaborative process that allows the writer and director to visualize key scenes before they are filmed. This can help ensure that the director's interpretation aligns with the writer's intentions.

Through storyboarding, you can discuss camera angles, shot composition, and pacing, ensuring that the visual storytelling supports the narrative and themes of the script.

**Regular Script Discussions:**

Regular discussions about the script are essential for maintaining coherence. These discussions should cover everything from character motivations and dialogue to scene transitions and pacing.

If changes to the script are necessary, whether due to practical constraints or creative decisions, ensure that both the writer and director agree on how these changes will impact the overall vision.

**On-Set Collaboration:**

While the director typically takes the lead on set, the writer's involvement can be valuable, particularly when it comes to ensuring that the narrative and character arcs remain consistent. On-set collaboration might involve discussing how to handle a specific line of dialogue, how a scene should be blocked, or how to capture the intended emotional tone. This hands-on approach can help ensure that the vision is carried through to the final product.

**Post-Production Involvement:**

The post-production phase, including editing, sound design, and color grading, is crucial for maintaining the series' cohesive vision. While the director often oversees this phase, the writer's input can be valuable, particularly when it comes to ensuring that the narrative flow and thematic elements are preserved. Collaborate with the director and post-production team to ensure that the final cut reflects the shared vision. This might involve reviewing rough cuts, discussing the pacing of scenes, or ensuring that the music and sound design support the story.

**Consistent Feedback and Adjustment:**

Throughout the production process, it's important to provide consistent feedback and be open to adjustments. As the series progresses, new ideas or challenges may arise that require rethinking certain aspects of the vision. By maintaining an open dialogue and being willing to adapt, you can ensure that the final product stays true to the shared vision while also allowing for creative evolution.

**Examples of Successful Writer-Director Collaborations**

Looking at examples of successful writer-director collaborations can provide inspiration for your own project:

***True Detective* (Nic Pizzolatto and Cary Joji Fukunaga):**

The collaboration between writer Nic Pizzolatto and director Cary Joji Fukunaga on the first season of *True Detective* is often cited as a model of creative synergy. Pizzolatto's complex, philosophical script was brought to life through Fukunaga's atmospheric direction, resulting in a series that was both visually stunning and thematically rich. Their collaboration was characterized by a shared commitment to the show's dark, existential themes and a willingness to push creative boundaries, resulting in a cohesive and memorable series.

***Fargo* (Noah Hawley and various directors):**

Noah Hawley's role as both writer and showrunner on *Fargo* allowed him to maintain a consistent vision across multiple seasons, even as different directors were brought in for each episode. By collaborating closely with the directors, Hawley ensured that the show's distinctive tone, style, and narrative complexity were preserved throughout.

The use of a detailed series bible, along with regular script discussions and on-set involvement, helped maintain the show's cohesive vision despite the rotating directors.

***Big Little Lies* (David E. Kelley and Jean-Marc Vallée):**

The collaboration between writer David E. Kelley and director Jean-Marc Vallée on *Big Little Lies* resulted in a series that was both emotionally resonant and visually compelling. Kelley's sharp, character-driven script was complemented by Vallée's intimate, almost documentary-style direction, creating a series that felt both real and heightened. Their collaboration was marked by mutual respect and a shared understanding of the story's themes, leading to a final product that was cohesive and impactful.

Creating a cohesive vision for a television miniseries requires close collaboration between the writer and director. By aligning on the core vision, maintaining open communication, and working together throughout the production process, you can ensure that every aspect of the series—from narrative and character development to visual style and pacing—works together to create a unified and compelling experience for the audience.

# Writing for Different Genres: Tailoring the Approach

Writing for different genres requires a tailored approach that takes into account the specific conventions, expectations, and audience engagement strategies unique to each genre. Whether you're crafting a drama, comedy, thriller, or science fiction series, understanding the nuances of genre writing is key to creating a compelling and successful television miniseries. In this chapter, we'll explore how to adapt your writing style to different genres, including tips for maintaining genre consistency, developing genre-specific characters and plots, and meeting audience expectations.

**Understanding Genre Conventions**

Each genre has its own set of conventions—common themes, narrative structures, character types, and stylistic elements that define the genre and shape audience expectations. Understanding these conventions is the first step in tailoring your writing approach:

**Drama:**

**Conventions:** Drama is characterized by its focus on character development, emotional depth, and complex relationships. It often explores serious, real-life situations and moral dilemmas, with a slower pacing that allows for introspection and character growth.

**Approach:** When writing a drama, focus on creating well-rounded characters with rich backstories and internal conflicts. The plot should be driven by the characters' decisions and emotions, with a strong emphasis on dialogue and subtlety. Themes like love, loss, identity, and family are common, and the tone should be consistent with the gravity of the subject matter.

**Comedy:**

**Conventions:** Comedy relies on humor, often through exaggeration, irony, and situational absurdity. It typically features light-hearted, entertaining plots with a focus on witty dialogue and comedic timing. Comedies can range from slapstick to satire, with varying degrees of social commentary.

**Approach:** In comedy writing, timing and pacing are crucial. Focus on crafting sharp, funny dialogue and situations that naturally lead to humor. Characters in comedies often have exaggerated traits or find themselves in ridiculous scenarios. While the tone is lighter, it's important to maintain consistency in the humor style, whether it's dry wit, physical comedy, or satire.

**Thriller:**

**Conventions:** Thrillers are defined by their fast-paced, suspenseful plots, often involving crime, danger, and high stakes. They aim to keep the audience on the edge of their seat with twists, tension, and unexpected revelations. Common themes include betrayal, justice, and survival.

**Approach:** When writing a thriller, focus on building tension and maintaining a tight, fast-paced narrative. Use cliffhangers, red herrings, and plot twists to keep the audience engaged. Characters in thrillers are often driven by urgent goals or desperate situations, and the tone should be intense and gripping, with a sense of imminent danger.

**Science Fiction:**

**Conventions:** Science fiction explores futuristic, speculative, or technologically advanced settings, often with themes related to human existence, societal structures, and the impact of technology. It frequently involves world-building, where the setting itself becomes a key element of the narrative.

**Approach:** In science fiction writing, focus on creating a believable and immersive world. The plot should be driven by the unique rules and technologies of this world, with characters who reflect the complexities of living in such a setting. Themes might include exploration, ethics, and the nature of humanity. Consistency in the logic of the world and the technology is crucial, as is maintaining a tone that fits the speculative nature of the story.

**Fantasy:**

**Conventions:** Fantasy involves magical or supernatural elements, often set in imaginary worlds with their own rules and mythology. It typically features epic quests, battles between good and evil, and characters like wizards, knights, and mythical creatures. Themes of heroism, destiny, and power are common.

**Approach:** When writing fantasy, world-building is key. Create a detailed and consistent setting with its own history, culture, and magic system. Characters in fantasy often have clear roles (heroes, villains, mentors), and the plot usually revolves around an epic journey or battle. The tone can range from dark and serious to whimsical, depending on the subgenre.

**Horror:**

**Conventions:** Horror is designed to evoke fear, dread, and discomfort in the audience. It often involves supernatural elements, psychological terror, or gruesome events, with a focus on atmosphere, suspense, and shock. Common themes include death, madness, and the unknown.

**Approach:** In horror writing, atmosphere and pacing are essential. Build tension slowly, using foreshadowing, eerie settings, and unsettling imagery. Characters in horror often face their deepest fears or confront the unknown, and their reactions drive the plot. The tone should be consistently dark and ominous, with careful attention to creating a sense of dread.

**Romance:**

**Conventions:** Romance focuses on relationships, particularly the emotional and romantic development between characters. It often involves obstacles to love, misunderstandings, and ultimately, a resolution that brings the characters together. Themes of love, trust, and personal growth are central.

**Approach:** When writing romance, focus on character chemistry and the emotional journey of the protagonists. The plot should revolve around the development of the relationship, with moments of tension, misunderstanding, and resolution. Dialogue is crucial for conveying the characters' feelings, and the tone should be heartfelt and engaging, with a balance of conflict and resolution.

**Mystery:**

**Conventions:** Mystery involves the investigation of a crime or unexplained event, with the plot centered around solving the puzzle. It typically features a detective or amateur sleuth, clues, red herrings, and a final revelation. Themes of truth, justice, and the search for knowledge are common.

**Approach:** In mystery writing, focus on creating a tightly woven plot with carefully placed clues and red herrings. The audience should be able to follow the investigation while remaining unsure of the outcome until the final reveal. Characters in mysteries are often defined by their intellect and observational skills, and the tone can range from dark and brooding to light and witty, depending on the subgenre.

## Tailoring Your Writing Approach to the Genre

Once you understand the conventions of the genre you're writing for, the next step is to tailor your approach to fit those conventions while still bringing your unique voice to the story:

### Embrace Genre Tropes, but Subvert When Necessary:

Each genre has its own tropes—common elements that audiences expect. While it's important to include these tropes to meet audience expectations, consider ways to subvert or twist them to keep the story fresh and engaging.

For example, in a thriller, you might play with the trope of the "unreliable narrator" by revealing the truth in an unexpected way. In a romance, you could challenge the "love at first sight" trope by having the characters initially dislike each other.

### Develop Genre-Specific Characters:

Characters in different genres often have distinct roles or archetypes. For example, a detective in a mystery, a hero in a fantasy, or a comedian in a comedy. Understanding these roles can help you create characters that fit the genre while still feeling unique and fully developed.

Focus on how these characters interact with the plot and themes of the genre. In a drama, character development is key, while in a thriller, characters might be defined by their actions and decisions under pressure.

### Maintain Genre-Consistent Tone and Style:

The tone and style of your writing should align with the genre. A horror series requires a dark, suspenseful tone, while a comedy needs a lighter, more humorous approach. Pay attention to language, pacing, and mood, ensuring they fit the genre's expectations.

Consistency in tone helps immerse the audience in the genre and keeps them engaged with the story. Even when blending genres, maintaining a consistent tone that respects the primary genre is important.

### Focus on Pacing Appropriate to the Genre:

Pacing is crucial in genre writing. A thriller needs fast-paced, tense scenes to keep the audience on edge, while a drama might benefit from slower, more contemplative pacing. Adjust your pacing to suit the genre's needs, ensuring that each scene contributes to the overall momentum of the story.

Consider how the pacing of individual episodes or scenes builds towards key moments, whether it's a climactic battle in a fantasy series or a critical revelation in a mystery.

**Engage the Audience's Emotions and Expectations:**

Different genres evoke different emotional responses from the audience. Understanding these expectations allows you to craft scenes and moments that resonate with viewers. For example, a romance aims to evoke feelings of love and warmth, while horror seeks to instill fear and tension.

Play with these emotions to engage the audience, giving them the experience they're looking for in the genre while adding your own creative twist.

**Consider Blending Genres:**

While writing within a specific genre, consider opportunities to blend elements from other genres to create something unique. For example, a romantic comedy combines the emotional journey of a romance with the humor and lightness of a comedy.

Blending genres can add depth and complexity to your story, but it's important to ensure that the primary genre remains clear and that the tone is consistent.

**Research and Analyze Genre Examples:**

To write effectively in a genre, immerse yourself in it. Watch or read successful examples of the genre you're working in, paying attention to how they handle conventions, pacing, and character development.

Analyze what works and what doesn't, and consider how you can apply these lessons to your own writing. This research can also inspire new ideas and approaches within the genre.

**Examples of Genre-Specific Writing**

Looking at examples of successful genre-specific writing can provide inspiration and guidance for your own work:

*Breaking Bad* (**Drama/Thriller**):

*Breaking Bad* masterfully blends drama and thriller elements, with a focus on character development and intense, suspenseful plot twists. The series maintains a consistent tone of moral ambiguity and tension, with well-crafted characters and a plot that escalates towards a dramatic conclusion.

*The Office* (**Comedy**):

*The Office* is a prime example of a comedy that relies on character-driven humor and situational absurdity. The series uses a mockumentary style to create a unique comedic tone, with characters who are exaggerated but relatable, and situations that are both ridiculous and grounded in everyday life.

*Stranger Things* (**Science Fiction/Horror**):

*Stranger Things* combines science fiction with horror, creating a series that is both nostalgic and innovative. The show effectively uses genre conventions like the supernatural, government conspiracies, and coming-of-age themes, all while maintaining a consistent, eerie tone that keeps the audience engaged.

*Sherlock* (**Mystery/Thriller**):

*Sherlock* modernizes the classic detective genre, blending mystery with thriller elements. The series maintains the intellectual challenge of a mystery while adding high-stakes tension and fast-paced action, all within a contemporary setting.

Writing for different genres requires an understanding of the specific conventions, expectations, and emotional engagement strategies that define each genre. By tailoring your approach to fit these conventions while bringing your own creative voice to the story, you can craft a miniseries that resonates with audiences and stands out in its genre.

Whether you're working within the familiar tropes of a genre or blending elements to create something new, the key is to maintain consistency in tone, character, and pacing. Researching and analyzing successful examples, embracing genre-specific characters and plots, and considering audience expectations will help you create a series that is both true to its genre and uniquely your own.

# Character Backstories: Adding Depth and Complexity

Character backstories are essential for adding depth and complexity to your characters, making them feel like real, multi-dimensional individuals rather than mere plot devices. A well-crafted backstory provides context for a character's motivations, decisions, and personality, giving the audience a deeper understanding of who they are and why they behave the way they do. In this chapter, we'll explore the importance of character backstories, how to create effective and meaningful backstories, and strategies for integrating these backstories into your miniseries without overwhelming the narrative.

## The Importance of Character Backstories

Character backstories serve several key purposes in storytelling:

### Explaining Motivations and Behavior:

A character's past experiences shape their present-day actions and decisions. Understanding a character's backstory allows the audience to see why they are motivated to pursue certain goals, avoid certain situations, or react emotionally to specific triggers. For example, a character who experienced betrayal in the past might struggle with trust issues, which could influence their relationships and decisions throughout the series.

### Adding Emotional Depth:

Backstories provide an emotional foundation for characters, making them more relatable and empathetic. When the audience knows what a character has been through, they are more likely to connect with their struggles, hopes, and fears. This emotional depth enriches the narrative, creating moments of poignancy and resonance that engage the audience on a deeper level.

### Creating Consistent Character Arcs:

A well-developed backstory helps ensure that a character's arc is consistent and believable. As the character grows and changes throughout the series, their past experiences provide a logical basis for their development. Whether a character is on a journey of redemption, revenge, or self-discovery, their backstory serves as the foundation for their transformation.

### Enhancing Storytelling with Subtext:

Backstories can add layers of subtext to a character's interactions and decisions. Even if the backstory isn't explicitly stated, it can influence the way a character speaks, behaves, or reacts, adding complexity to the narrative. This subtext can create richer, more nuanced scenes, where the audience can sense that there's more going on beneath the surface.

### Providing Opportunities for Plot Development:

A character's backstory can also be a source of plot material. Past events, unresolved conflicts, or secrets from a character's history can resurface, driving the plot forward and creating new challenges for the character to face. This integration of backstory and plot can lead to more cohesive storytelling, where a character's past and present are intertwined.

### Creating Effective Character Backstories

To create backstories that add meaningful depth to your characters, consider the following strategies:

**Focus on Key Life Events:**

Identify the key events in a character's past that have had a significant impact on their personality, beliefs, and motivations. These could be formative experiences, such as childhood trauma, a pivotal relationship, a life-changing decision, or a major success or failure. These events should be directly relevant to the character's role in the story and help explain their behavior in the present. For example, a character who lost a loved one might be driven by a need to protect others, or they might struggle with unresolved grief.

**Consider Relationships and Influences:**

Relationships play a crucial role in shaping a character's identity. Consider the important people in your character's past, such as family members, mentors, friends, or rivals, and how these relationships have influenced them. Think about how these relationships have affected the character's worldview, self-esteem, and goals. For instance, a character who grew up with a demanding parent might have a deep-seated need for approval or might rebel against authority figures.

**Reflect on Socio-Cultural Context:**

A character's backstory is also influenced by their socio-cultural background, including factors like their upbringing, education, social class, religion, and cultural environment. These elements can shape their values, beliefs, and how they interact with the world. Consider how the character's background has shaped their identity and their place in the world. For example, a character from a marginalized community might face challenges related to discrimination or identity, which could inform their actions and choices.

**Define Internal and External Conflicts:**

Internal and external conflicts are often rooted in a character's backstory. Internal conflicts might include struggles with self-doubt, guilt, or unresolved trauma, while external conflicts could involve ongoing disputes or challenges that stem from past events. These conflicts can drive the character's actions and create tension in the narrative. For example, a character with a history of betrayal might be torn between their desire for connection and their fear of being hurt again.

**Balance Detail with Relevance:**

While it's important to create a detailed backstory, not every detail needs to be included in the narrative. Focus on the aspects of the backstory that are most relevant to the character's role in the story and their current arc. Avoid overwhelming the audience with too much exposition. Instead, use key details that enhance the character's development and contribute to the plot.

**Allow for Mystery and Discovery:**

Not all aspects of a character's backstory need to be revealed at once. Leaving some details mysterious can create intrigue and allow for gradual discovery throughout the series. This approach can also reflect the way people learn about each other in real life—gradually, through shared experiences and revelations. It can also add to the tension and drama as secrets from the past come to light.

**Integrating Backstories into the Narrative**

Once you've developed your characters' backstories, the next step is to integrate them into the narrative in a way that feels natural and enhances the overall story:

**Use Flashbacks Judiciously:**

Flashbacks can be an effective way to reveal key elements of a character's backstory, but they should be used sparingly and purposefully. A well-placed flashback can provide context for a character's current actions or emotions, but too many flashbacks can disrupt the narrative flow. Consider using flashbacks at moments of high emotional impact or when the past is directly influencing the present. This approach helps maintain the story's momentum while adding depth to the character.

**Reveal Backstory Through Dialogue:**

Dialogue is another way to reveal a character's backstory. Characters might share stories about their past, express fears or regrets, or mention significant people or events that shaped them. However, it's important to avoid "info-dumping"—where characters deliver long, expository monologues about their past. Instead, incorporate backstory into natural conversations, where the revelations feel organic and relevant to the current situation.

**Show Backstory through Actions and Reactions:**

A character's actions and reactions can implicitly reveal their backstory without the need for explicit explanation. For example, a character who flinches at loud noises might have a history of trauma, or a character who avoids commitment might have been hurt in the past. This approach allows the audience to infer the backstory based on the character's behavior, creating a more subtle and nuanced portrayal.

**Weave Backstory into the Plot:**

Integrate elements of the character's backstory into the plot, using it to drive the narrative forward. This might involve unresolved conflicts resurfacing, secrets being revealed, or past relationships affecting the character's current decisions. By tying backstory into the plot, you can create a more cohesive and interconnected story, where the character's past and present are inextricably linked.

**Use Symbolism and Visual Cues:**

Symbolism and visual cues can be powerful tools for hinting at a character's backstory. Objects, locations, or recurring motifs associated with the character can evoke memories or emotions tied to their past. For example, a character might carry a locket that reminds them of a lost loved one, or a specific location might trigger memories of a traumatic event. These visual elements can add layers of meaning to the story without the need for explicit explanation.

**Examples of Effective Character Backstories**

Examining examples of well-crafted character backstories can provide insight into how to develop your own:

*Walter White in Breaking Bad*:

Walter White's backstory as a brilliant but underappreciated chemist who left a successful company for a teaching job is crucial to understanding his motivations. His sense of missed opportunity and unfulfilled potential drives his descent into the criminal underworld. This backstory adds complexity to his character, making his transformation from a mild-mannered teacher to a ruthless drug kingpin both tragic and believable.

*Eowyn in The Lord of the Rings*:

Eowyn's backstory as a noblewoman constrained by societal expectations and longing for a life of valor and freedom informs her actions throughout the story. Her deep-seated desire to prove herself and her fear of being trapped in a life she didn't choose drive her to take bold, sometimes reckless actions. This backstory makes her a richly layered character who defies traditional gender roles in the story.

*Michael Corleone in The Godfather*:

Michael Corleone's backstory as a war hero who initially wants nothing to do with his family's criminal empire is key to understanding his eventual transformation. The trauma of his wartime experiences, combined with the pressure of family loyalty, leads him down a dark path. His backstory adds depth to his character arc, making his evolution into a mafia don both inevitable and tragic.

*June Osborne in The Handmaid's Tale*:

June Osborne's backstory as a mother and a professional woman in a pre-Gilead world is central to her character in *The Handmaid's Tale*. Her memories of her daughter, her husband, and her previous life drive her resistance against the oppressive regime. This backstory adds emotional weight to her struggle, making her fight for freedom deeply personal.

Character backstories are a powerful tool for adding depth, complexity, and emotional resonance to your characters. By carefully crafting meaningful backstories and integrating them into the narrative, you can create characters who feel real and multi-dimensional, engaging the audience on a deeper level.

Whether revealed through flashbacks, dialogue, actions, or visual cues, a well-developed backstory can enrich your storytelling, providing context for character motivations and creating a more immersive and cohesive narrative. As you develop your miniseries, take the time to explore your characters' pasts, using their histories to inform their present and drive the story forward.

# The Role of Exposition: Informing Without Overloading

Exposition is a critical component of storytelling, providing the audience with necessary background information about the world, characters, and events within your miniseries. However, handling exposition effectively requires a delicate balance. Too much exposition can overwhelm the audience, slow down the narrative, and feel unnatural, while too little can leave viewers confused and disconnected. In this chapter, we'll explore the role of exposition, strategies for delivering it in a way that feels natural and engaging, and how to inform your audience without overloading them with information.

**Understanding the Role of Exposition**

Exposition serves several important functions in storytelling:

**Establishing the World:**

Exposition helps set the stage for the story by introducing the audience to the world in which it takes place. This includes the setting, time period, cultural context, and any unique rules or systems that govern this world.

For example, in a fantasy or science fiction series, exposition might explain the rules of magic, the technology available, or the political landscape, helping the audience understand how the world operates.

**Providing Backstory:**

Exposition can offer insight into a character's past, their motivations, and the events that have shaped them. This background information is crucial for understanding why characters behave the way they do and how they relate to the current story.

A character's past might be revealed through dialogue, flashbacks, or even visual cues, providing context that enriches their development and the plot.

**Clarifying Relationships and Stakes:**

Exposition can clarify the relationships between characters and the stakes of the story. By understanding how characters are connected and what's at risk, the audience can more fully engage with the narrative.

For instance, exposition might explain a family feud, a past betrayal, or a looming threat, helping the audience grasp the significance of current events.

**Setting Up the Plot:**

Exposition often lays the groundwork for the plot, introducing key elements that will drive the story forward. This might include explaining a character's goal, a conflict that needs resolution, or a mystery that needs to be solved.

By providing this information early on, exposition helps orient the audience and sets expectations for what's to come.

## Challenges of Exposition

While exposition is necessary, it can also present several challenges:

### Risk of Overloading the Audience:

One of the biggest challenges with exposition is the risk of overloading the audience with too much information at once. This can lead to confusion, disengagement, or a sense of being overwhelmed.

It's important to prioritize the most essential information and deliver it in a way that the audience can easily absorb and retain.

### Maintaining Narrative Flow:

Exposition can disrupt the narrative flow if it's presented in a heavy-handed or clunky manner. Long, expository speeches or sudden info-dumps can feel unnatural and slow down the pacing of the story.

Finding ways to integrate exposition seamlessly into the narrative is crucial for maintaining momentum and keeping the audience engaged.

### Avoiding Expository Dialogue:

Expository dialogue—where characters explain things to each other purely for the audience's benefit—can feel forced and unrealistic. Characters should speak naturally, in a way that reflects their knowledge, personality, and relationship dynamics.Balancing the need to convey information with the need for authentic dialogue is a key challenge in handling exposition.

### Keeping the Audience Interested:

Exposition, if not handled carefully, can come across as boring or tedious. The audience needs to be engaged not only by the information itself but by how it's delivered. Engaging exposition often involves combining it with action, emotion, or intrigue, making the information feel relevant and immediate.

## Strategies for Effective Exposition

To handle exposition effectively, consider the following strategies:

### Show, Don't Tell:

One of the most fundamental rules in storytelling is to show rather than tell. Instead of directly explaining something, find ways to demonstrate it through the characters' actions, interactions, and the environment. For example, rather than telling the audience that a character is afraid of heights, you could show them hesitating at the edge of a cliff or refusing to climb a ladder. This approach makes the exposition more engaging and memorable.

### Use Dialogue Naturally:

When using dialogue for exposition, ensure it feels natural to the characters and situation. Characters should only share information that they would realistically discuss in that context. For instance, rather than having a character deliver a lengthy monologue about their tragic past, you could reveal key details through a conversation with a close friend or during an argument where emotions are running high.

**Integrate Exposition into Action:**

Combine exposition with action to keep the narrative dynamic. Exposition delivered during a moment of conflict, tension, or movement is more likely to hold the audience's attention. For example, as characters prepare for a battle, they might discuss the history of the conflict, providing necessary background while maintaining the scene's energy.

**Use Visual Storytelling:**

Visual cues and symbols can be powerful tools for delivering exposition without words. The setting, costumes, props, and cinematography can all convey information about the world, characters, and plot.

A worn photograph, a character's choice of clothing, or the state of a room can all tell the audience something about the character's past, their personality, or their current emotional state.

**Employ Flashbacks and Memories Sparingly:**

Flashbacks and memories can be effective ways to reveal past events or provide context, but they should be used sparingly and purposefully. A well-timed flashback can add depth to a character or plot point, but too many can disrupt the narrative flow. Ensure that flashbacks are relevant to the current story and that they add something new or significant to the audience's understanding.

**Use Multiple Layers of Exposition:**

Instead of delivering all the necessary information at once, spread exposition across multiple scenes or episodes. This layering approach allows the audience to gradually piece together the world, characters, and plot. By revealing information gradually, you can create a sense of intrigue and encourage the audience to stay engaged as they uncover more about the story.

**Trust the Audience:**

Trust that your audience can pick up on subtle clues and piece together information on their own. You don't need to spell everything out explicitly—sometimes less is more. Allow the audience to infer details based on what they see and hear, which can make the viewing experience more interactive and rewarding.

**Examples of Effective Exposition**

Looking at examples of effective exposition in film and television can provide valuable insights:

*Inception*:

*Inception* is a masterclass in delivering complex exposition. The film introduces a complicated world of dream-sharing technology, yet it does so in a way that feels natural and engaging. Exposition is often integrated into action sequences, such as the training scene where Cobb explains the rules of the dream world to Ariadne while they are inside a dream. This approach keeps the audience engaged and ensures that the necessary information is conveyed without slowing down the narrative.

*The Matrix*:

*The Matrix* uses a combination of dialogue, visual storytelling, and action to deliver exposition. The scene where Morpheus explains the concept of the Matrix to Neo is a prime example. The exposition is presented during a simulated fight, making the information feel immediate and relevant. The audience learns about the rules of the Matrix alongside Neo, which helps build a connection to the character while also keeping the pace brisk.

### *Breaking Bad*:

In *Breaking Bad*, exposition is often revealed through character interactions and visual cues. For example, rather than having a character explain Walter White's financial struggles, the show reveals this through scenes of him working multiple jobs, discussing medical bills with his wife, and struggling to fix his home's water heater. This approach allows the audience to understand his situation without relying on heavy-handed dialogue.

### *Game of Thrones*:

*Game of Thrones* had a vast and complex world to introduce, but it often used character-driven dialogue and visual storytelling to deliver exposition. For example, the show often used scenes of characters walking through a location while discussing its history or politics. These "walk-and-talk" scenes kept the exposition dynamic and allowed the audience to absorb information while also moving the plot forward.

Exposition plays a vital role in storytelling, providing the audience with the information they need to understand the world, characters, and plot. However, handling exposition effectively requires careful consideration of how to deliver this information without overwhelming or boring the audience.

By focusing on showing rather than telling, using natural dialogue, integrating exposition into action, and trusting the audience to pick up on subtle clues, you can inform your viewers while maintaining narrative momentum and engagement. Whether you're introducing a complex world, revealing a character's backstory, or setting up the stakes of your story, effective exposition is key to creating a compelling and immersive miniseries.

# Writing for International Audiences: Cultural Considerations

Writing for international audiences requires a thoughtful approach to cultural considerations, ensuring that your miniseries resonates with viewers from diverse backgrounds while maintaining its authenticity and narrative integrity. As global audiences become increasingly interconnected, it's important to create content that is both universally appealing and culturally sensitive. In this chapter, we'll explore the challenges and opportunities of writing for international audiences, strategies for addressing cultural differences, and tips for making your story accessible and engaging to viewers around the world.

## Understanding the Global Audience

Before diving into specific strategies, it's important to understand what it means to write for a global audience:

### Diverse Cultural Perspectives:

International audiences come from a wide range of cultural, linguistic, and social backgrounds. What resonates with one group may not have the same impact on another, so it's crucial to consider how different cultures might perceive your story, characters, and themes. For example, humor, social norms, and values can vary significantly between cultures. A joke that lands well in one country might be misunderstood or even considered offensive in another.

### Universal Themes and Emotions:

While cultural differences are important, certain themes and emotions are universal and can help bridge cultural gaps. Love, loss, ambition, fear, and hope are experiences that resonate across cultures and can form the emotional core of your story. By grounding your narrative in these universal experiences, you can create a story that appeals to a wide audience, even as you incorporate specific cultural elements.

### Localization and Adaptation:

Writing for international audiences often involves localization, the process of adapting content to fit the cultural context of a specific region. This might include translating dialogue, adjusting cultural references, or modifying certain scenes to better align with local sensibilities. Effective localization respects the original intent of the story while making it more accessible and relatable to viewers in different regions.

## Challenges of Writing for International Audiences

Writing for a global audience presents several challenges that require careful consideration:

### Navigating Cultural Sensitivities:

Cultural sensitivities vary widely, and what is acceptable in one culture might be taboo in another. It's important to be aware of potential cultural differences and avoid content that could be misinterpreted or offensive. This requires research and, if possible, consultation with individuals from the cultures you're representing. Sensitivity readers or cultural consultants can provide valuable insights and help you navigate potential pitfalls.

### Balancing Authenticity with Accessibility:

While authenticity is important, especially when representing specific cultures or communities, it's also crucial to make your story accessible to a broad audience. This balance can be challenging, as certain cultural nuances might not be easily understood by viewers unfamiliar with that culture. Finding ways to explain or contextualize cultural elements without resorting to heavy-handed exposition can help make the story more accessible while maintaining its authenticity.

## Avoiding Stereotypes and Clichés:

Stereotypes and clichés can undermine the quality of your story and alienate international audiences. It's essential to avoid one-dimensional portrayals of cultures, as these can perpetuate harmful misconceptions. Instead, strive for nuanced and complex representations that reflect the diversity and richness of different cultures. Characters should be fully developed individuals, not just representatives of a cultural group.

## Dealing with Language Barriers:

Language is a significant barrier when writing for international audiences. While subtitles and dubbing can help, certain nuances, wordplay, or cultural references may be lost in translation. Consider how dialogue and narrative style might be adapted for different languages and cultures, and work closely with translators to ensure that the essence of your story is preserved.

## Strategies for Writing for International Audiences

To effectively write for a global audience, consider the following strategies:

## Research and Understand the Cultures You're Representing:

Thorough research is essential when writing about cultures that are not your own. This includes understanding the history, traditions, values, and social dynamics of the culture you're depicting.

Whenever possible, engage with people from the culture you're writing about. Their perspectives can provide invaluable insights and help you avoid common pitfalls.

## Focus on Universal Themes with Specific Cultural Contexts:

Ground your story in universal themes that resonate across cultures, such as love, conflict, identity, or survival. Then, layer these themes with specific cultural contexts to add depth and authenticity.

For example, a story about family dynamics can be universally relatable, but the way family relationships are portrayed might differ based on cultural norms and values.

**Incorporate Diverse Perspectives and Voices:**

When writing for international audiences, consider including diverse perspectives and voices within your story. This can involve creating characters from different cultural backgrounds or exploring themes that are relevant to multiple cultures. Collaboration with writers, consultants, or advisors from different cultural backgrounds can also enrich your story, ensuring that it reflects a wider range of experiences and viewpoints.

**Be Mindful of Cultural References and Humor:**

Cultural references, idioms, and humor can be challenging to translate across cultures. When using these elements, consider how they will be perceived by international audiences. If a cultural reference or joke is central to your story, think about how it can be explained or adapted for different audiences without losing its impact. Alternatively, consider using more universal references and humor that can be easily understood by a global audience.

**Use Visual Storytelling to Transcend Language Barriers:**

Visual storytelling is a powerful tool for reaching international audiences, as it can convey meaning and emotion without relying on language. Use strong visuals, symbolism, and non-verbal cues to communicate key aspects of your story. For example, a character's emotions can be conveyed through facial expressions, body language, and visual metaphors, which can be understood by viewers regardless of their language or cultural background.

**Adapt and Localize Thoughtfully:**

When adapting your story for different regions, approach localization thoughtfully. Ensure that the adaptations respect the original intent of the story while making it more relatable to local audiences.

Work closely with translators and cultural consultants to ensure that the localization is accurate and culturally sensitive. This might involve adjusting dialogue, modifying certain scenes, or changing character names to better fit the local context.

**Test Your Content with International Audiences:**

Before finalizing your miniseries, consider testing it with international audiences to gather feedback. This can help you identify any cultural nuances or references that may not be working as intended.

Focus groups or preview screenings in different regions can provide valuable insights, allowing you to make adjustments that enhance the story's appeal and accessibility to a global audience.

**Examples of Successful International Storytelling**

Looking at examples of television series and films that have successfully resonated with international audiences can provide inspiration:

*Narcos*:

*Narcos*, a series that follows the rise of drug cartels in Colombia, successfully blends universal themes of power, corruption, and survival with a specific cultural context. The show incorporates both English and Spanish dialogue, with a strong emphasis on authenticity in its portrayal of Colombian culture and history. The use of subtitles for

Spanish dialogue allows international audiences to engage with the story while maintaining the cultural integrity of the characters and setting.

*Parasite*:

*Parasite*, a South Korean film that gained global acclaim, resonates with international audiences through its exploration of universal themes like class struggle and inequality. While deeply rooted in South Korean culture, the film's commentary on social issues is universally relatable, allowing it to connect with viewers worldwide. The film's success demonstrates how a story with a specific cultural setting can still have broad appeal when it addresses universal human experiences.

*Money Heist* (*La Casa de Papel*):

*Money Heist*, a Spanish series, became a global phenomenon due to its thrilling plot, complex characters, and exploration of themes like resistance and loyalty. The show's success is partly due to its strong narrative structure and emotional depth, which resonate across cultures. The series maintained its cultural specificity while also appealing to a wide audience, demonstrating the potential for international success with well-crafted storytelling.

*The Crown*:

*The Crown*, a British series that chronicles the reign of Queen Elizabeth II, has found success internationally by focusing on the universal themes of power, duty, and personal sacrifice. While the series is steeped in British history and culture, its exploration of human relationships and political intrigue makes it accessible to viewers around the world. The show's attention to detail and historical accuracy, combined with its strong character development, have made it a hit with both British and international audiences.

Writing for international audiences involves navigating cultural differences while crafting a story that resonates universally. By focusing on universal themes, conducting thorough research, and being mindful of cultural sensitivities, you can create a miniseries that appeals to viewers from diverse backgrounds. Successful international storytelling requires a balance between authenticity and accessibility, ensuring that your story is both true to its cultural context and engaging for a global audience. By incorporating diverse perspectives, using visual storytelling, and thoughtfully adapting your content for different regions, you can create a miniseries that not only entertains but also connects with viewers around the world, fostering a deeper understanding and appreciation of different cultures.

# The Role of Technology in Modern Miniseries

Technology has revolutionized the way miniseries are created, distributed, and consumed, playing a pivotal role in shaping modern storytelling. From advancements in special effects and digital editing to the rise of streaming platforms and interactive content, technology has expanded the creative possibilities for filmmakers and transformed the viewing experience for audiences. In this chapter, we'll explore the various ways technology influences the creation of miniseries, the opportunities it offers for innovation, and the challenges it presents for creators.

## Technological Advancements in Production

Technology has significantly impacted the production of miniseries, enabling creators to achieve higher levels of creativity and realism:

### Digital Cinematography:

The transition from film to digital cinematography has revolutionized how miniseries are shot. Digital cameras offer greater flexibility, allowing for easier setup, more experimentation with lighting and angles, and the ability to capture high-quality footage in challenging environments. Digital cinematography also simplifies the editing process, as footage can be reviewed and adjusted in real time. This speeds up production and allows for more dynamic and visually stunning storytelling.

### Visual Effects (VFX) and CGI:

Advances in visual effects (VFX) and computer-generated imagery (CGI) have expanded the scope of what's possible in a miniseries. From creating fantastical worlds and creatures to simulating realistic environments and action sequences, VFX and CGI enable filmmakers to bring their most ambitious ideas to life. For instance, a historical drama can recreate ancient cities with stunning accuracy, or a sci-fi series can depict alien landscapes and advanced technology. These tools allow for more immersive storytelling, captivating audiences with visuals that were once impossible to achieve on a television budget.

### Virtual Production:

Virtual production combines live-action footage with digital environments in real time, using LED screens and motion capture technology. This technique, popularized by series like *The Mandalorian*, allows actors to perform in realistic, digitally rendered settings without the need for extensive location shoots or green screen work. Virtual production offers significant advantages in terms of cost, time, and creative flexibility. Directors can visualize and adjust scenes on the spot, and the seamless integration of physical and digital elements enhances the overall visual quality of the series.

### High-Quality Sound Design:

Sound design has become more sophisticated with advances in audio technology. Surround sound, immersive audio formats like Dolby Atmos, and precise sound editing tools enable creators to craft rich, atmospheric soundscapes that enhance the viewing experience. High-quality sound design is essential for building tension, conveying emotion, and immersing the audience in the story's world. Whether it's the subtle ambiance of a city at night or the thunderous roar of a battle, sound plays a crucial role in storytelling.

**Digital Editing and Color Grading:**

Digital editing software has transformed the post-production process, making it faster and more flexible. Editors can experiment with different cuts, effects, and transitions more easily, refining the narrative to achieve the desired pacing and tone. Color grading, another key aspect of post-production, allows filmmakers to create specific moods and atmospheres by adjusting the color palette of each scene. This can range from the cool, desaturated tones of a dystopian future to the warm, vibrant colors of a romantic drama.

## The Impact of Technology on Distribution

Technology has also transformed how miniseries are distributed and accessed by audiences, leading to new opportunities and challenges:

**The Rise of Streaming Platforms:**

Streaming platforms like Netflix, Amazon Prime, Hulu, and Disney+ have changed the way miniseries are distributed and consumed. These platforms offer global reach, allowing miniseries to be released to international audiences simultaneously. Streaming has also popularized the "binge-watching" phenomenon, where entire miniseries are released at once, encouraging viewers to watch multiple episodes in one sitting. This has influenced how stories are structured, with more emphasis on creating engaging, cliffhanger-driven narratives that keep viewers hooked.

**Global Accessibility and Localization:**

Streaming platforms have made miniseries more accessible to global audiences, with subtitles, dubbing, and localization options available in multiple languages. This allows creators to reach a wider audience and tailor content to different cultural contexts. The ability to distribute content globally has also led to the rise of international co-productions, where creators from different countries collaborate to produce miniseries that appeal to diverse audiences.

**On-Demand Viewing:**

The shift to on-demand viewing has given audiences more control over how and when they watch miniseries. This has led to a more personalized viewing experience, where audiences can watch at their own pace, pause and rewind as needed, and choose the device they prefer. For creators, this means adapting storytelling to suit a more flexible viewing environment, where episodes need to be compelling enough to keep viewers engaged, whether they're watching one episode at a time or the entire series in one go.

**Social Media and Audience Engagement:**

Social media platforms have become integral to the promotion and discussion of miniseries. Creators can use social media to build anticipation, release teasers and trailers, and engage with fans through live Q&A sessions, behind-the-scenes content, and interactive campaigns. Audience engagement through social media also provides valuable feedback, allowing creators to gauge viewer reactions, generate buzz, and create a community around the series. This can influence decisions on future seasons or related content.

**Interactive and Immersive Experiences:**

Advances in technology have also enabled the creation of interactive and immersive storytelling experiences. Some miniseries now include interactive episodes where viewers can make choices that affect the narrative, blurring the line between passive viewing and active participation. Virtual reality (VR) and augmented reality (AR) are also being explored as ways to enhance the viewing experience, allowing audiences to immerse themselves in the story's world in new and innovative ways.

## Challenges of Integrating Technology in Miniseries

While technology offers many opportunities, it also presents challenges that creators need to navigate:

**Balancing Technology with Storytelling:**

With so many technological tools available, there's a risk of focusing too much on visual effects or technical prowess at the expense of the story. It's important to remember that technology should serve the narrative, not overshadow it. Effective use of technology enhances the story, but the core of any miniseries should still be its characters, plot, and themes. Creators must strike a balance between leveraging technology and maintaining narrative integrity.

**Managing Budgets and Resources:**

High-end technology, such as CGI, virtual production, and advanced sound design, can be expensive and resource-intensive. Creators must manage budgets carefully to ensure that these tools are used effectively without overspending. Indie and low-budget productions may need to find creative ways to achieve similar results with fewer resources, such as using practical effects, minimalist settings, or more focused character-driven storytelling.

**Ensuring Global Accessibility:**

While streaming platforms offer global reach, ensuring that content is accessible to diverse audiences requires careful consideration of localization, cultural sensitivity, and language barriers. Creators need to work closely with translators, cultural consultants, and localization teams to ensure that the story resonates with international audiences while preserving its original intent.

**Adapting to Rapid Technological Changes:**

Technology in the entertainment industry is constantly evolving, with new tools and platforms emerging regularly. Creators must stay informed about these changes and be adaptable in how they incorporate new technologies into their work. This can be both exciting and challenging, as it requires continuous learning and a willingness to experiment with new approaches.

**Navigating Intellectual Property and Rights Issues:**

The use of digital assets, VFX, and global distribution can raise complex intellectual property and rights issues. Creators need to be mindful of copyright laws, licensing agreements, and the ethical use of technology. Protecting creative rights while navigating the legal landscape of technology and media distribution is a critical aspect of modern miniseries production.

## Examples of Technology in Modern Miniseries

Several modern miniseries have successfully integrated technology into their production and storytelling:

### *The Mandalorian*:

*The Mandalorian* is a prime example of how virtual production can revolutionize filmmaking. The series uses a ground-breaking technology called "StageCraft," which involves filming actors in front of large LED screens that display real-time digital environments. This allows for seamless integration of live-action and CGI, creating a visually stunning and immersive experience while reducing the need for location shoots.

### *Black Mirror: Bandersnatch*:

*Bandersnatch*, an interactive episode of *Black Mirror*, allows viewers to make decisions that affect the storyline, creating a unique viewing experience that blurs the line between television and video games. This use of interactive technology offers a new way to engage audiences, giving them control over the narrative and exploring the concept of choice in a highly innovative format.

### *The Crown*:

*The Crown* demonstrates the power of digital cinematography and CGI in historical dramas. The series uses CGI to recreate iconic locations, such as Buckingham Palace, with incredible detail, while digital cinematography captures the grandeur and intimacy of the royal family's world. The combination of these technologies enhances the visual storytelling and helps transport viewers to different eras in British history.

### *Stranger Things*:

*Stranger Things* effectively combines practical effects, CGI, and digital sound design to create its nostalgic, supernatural world. The series uses CGI to bring the terrifying creatures of the Upside Down to life, while practical effects and retro sound design contribute to its 1980s aesthetic. The seamless integration of these technologies enhances the show's unique atmosphere and appeal.

Technology plays an integral role in the creation, distribution, and consumption of modern miniseries, offering both opportunities and challenges for creators. From digital cinematography and VFX to streaming platforms and interactive storytelling, technology has expanded the possibilities for filmmakers, enabling them to craft more immersive, visually stunning, and globally accessible content.

However, the key to successful integration of technology lies in balancing it with strong storytelling.

While technology can enhance the viewing experience, the heart of any miniseries remains its characters, narrative, and themes. By leveraging technology thoughtfully and creatively, creators can produce miniseries that captivate audiences and push the boundaries of what's possible in television storytelling. As technology continues to evolve, so too will the ways in which stories are told, offering endless possibilities for innovation in the world of miniseries.

# Creating a Franchise: Expanding Beyond the Miniseries

Creating a franchise from a successful miniseries involves expanding the story, characters, and world beyond the original narrative, turning it into a larger, interconnected universe that can include sequels, spin-offs, merchandise, and more. Franchising allows creators to capitalize on the popularity of the original miniseries and build a long-term, multi-platform narrative that engages audiences in new and diverse ways. In this chapter, we'll explore the steps involved in expanding a miniseries into a franchise, the opportunities it presents, and the challenges that come with maintaining consistency and quality across different mediums.

**The Appeal of Franchising**

Franchising a successful miniseries offers several key benefits:

**Extended Storytelling:**

Franchising allows creators to continue exploring the story world, characters, and themes established in the original miniseries. This can involve sequels that pick up where the miniseries left off, prequels that delve into the backstory, or spin-offs that focus on different characters or aspects of the universe.

Extended storytelling gives fans more content to engage with and can deepen their connection to the world you've created.

**Building a Loyal Fanbase:**

A franchise can help build a loyal, long-term fanbase that is invested in the world and its characters. Fans of the original miniseries are likely to follow the franchise as it expands, creating a community of engaged viewers who support new installments and related content. This fanbase can become a powerful asset, driving word-of-mouth promotion, participating in fan events, and generating excitement for future projects.

**Diversifying Revenue Streams:**

Expanding into a franchise opens up new revenue streams, including merchandise, video games, books, and even theme park attractions. By diversifying the ways in which audiences can engage with the franchise, creators can increase profitability and reduce reliance on a single product. Licensing and merchandising opportunities can be particularly lucrative, allowing the franchise to reach a broader audience and create lasting cultural impact.

**Cross-Media Storytelling:**

Franchising offers the opportunity to explore cross-media storytelling, where the narrative extends beyond television into other formats like film, comics, podcasts, and interactive experiences. Each medium offers a unique way to tell different aspects of the story, enriching the overall narrative and providing fans with a multi-dimensional experience. Cross-media storytelling can attract new audiences who might prefer different formats, expanding the reach of the franchise.

**Cultural Impact and Legacy:**

Successful franchises often leave a lasting cultural impact, influencing other media, inspiring fan creations, and becoming a part of popular culture. A well-developed franchise can have a legacy that extends far beyond its original miniseries, shaping trends and setting standards for future storytelling.

The cultural footprint of a franchise can also create opportunities for reboots, reimaginings, and anniversary celebrations, keeping the franchise relevant for years or even decades.

**Steps to Expanding a Miniseries into a Franchise**

Expanding a miniseries into a successful franchise requires careful planning, creativity, and a long-term vision:

**Assess the Franchise Potential:**

Before expanding, evaluate whether the original miniseries has the potential to become a franchise. Consider the story world, characters, and themes—are they rich enough to sustain multiple stories across different formats? Does the miniseries have a passionate fanbase that would support future installments? Identify the core elements that made the miniseries successful and determine how these can be expanded upon or explored further in new content.

**Develop a Franchise Bible:**

A franchise bible is an essential tool for maintaining consistency and coherence across the franchise. It should include detailed information about the story world, characters, timeline, and key themes, as well as guidelines for tone, style, and visual aesthetics. The franchise bible serves as a reference for all creators involved in the franchise, ensuring that new content aligns with the established canon and maintains the quality and integrity of the original miniseries.

**Identify Opportunities for Expansion:**

Consider the different ways in which the franchise can be expanded. This could include sequels, prequels, spin-offs, or companion series that explore different facets of the story world. Think about which characters, storylines, or themes could be further developed and how they might appeal to different audience segments. Look for opportunities to explore new genres or formats within the franchise. For example, a dark, dramatic miniseries might inspire a lighter spin-off that focuses on secondary characters or a different time period.

**Plan Cross-Media Extensions:**

Cross-media storytelling is a key component of franchising. Identify the most suitable media for expanding the narrative—this could include books, comics, video games, films, podcasts, or interactive experiences. Each medium should be chosen based on its strengths and its ability to tell a particular aspect of the story. For example, a video game might allow players to explore the story world interactively, while a comic book could delve into the backstory of a character in greater detail.

**Build a Collaborative Creative Team:**

Expanding a franchise requires a collaborative effort from a diverse creative team. Bring together writers, directors, producers, and designers who are passionate about the franchise and can contribute fresh ideas while respecting the original vision. Ensure that all team members are familiar with the franchise bible and are committed to maintaining the continuity and quality of the franchise. Open communication and collaboration are key to creating a cohesive and successful franchise.

**Engage with the Fanbase:**

The fanbase is one of the most valuable assets of a franchise. Engage with fans through social media, fan events, and interactive campaigns to build excitement for new content and gather feedback on what they want to see next. Consider creating content that specifically caters to fan interests, such as behind-the-scenes documentaries, exclusive merchandise, or fan art competitions. Building a strong, engaged fan community can help sustain the franchise over the long term.

**Focus on Quality and Consistency:**

One of the biggest challenges in franchising is maintaining the quality and consistency of the content. As the franchise expands, it's essential to ensure that each new installment meets the high standards set by the original miniseries. Avoid diluting the brand by overextending the franchise or producing content that doesn't align with the core values and themes of the original. Quality should always take precedence over quantity.

**Challenges of Creating a Franchise**

While franchising offers many opportunities, it also comes with challenges that creators must navigate:

**Maintaining Creative Integrity:**

Expanding a franchise can sometimes lead to creative dilution if new content strays too far from the original vision or if too many different voices are involved without clear guidance. It's important to maintain the creative integrity of the franchise by adhering to the established canon and staying true to the core themes and tone. Balancing innovation with consistency is key—new content should offer fresh perspectives while still feeling like part of the same universe.

**Avoiding Franchise Fatigue:**

Franchise fatigue occurs when audiences become overwhelmed or disinterested due to an oversaturation of content. To avoid this, it's important to pace the release of new content and ensure that each installment offers something unique and valuable to the audience. Consider spacing out major releases, introducing varied formats, and experimenting with different storytelling techniques to keep the franchise fresh and engaging.

**Managing Audience Expectations:**

As a franchise grows, audience expectations can become increasingly high. Fans may have strong opinions about how the story should unfold or how characters should be portrayed, and meeting these expectations while also pushing the narrative forward can be challenging.

Clear communication with the audience, along with a commitment to delivering high-quality content, can help manage expectations and maintain audience loyalty.

**Navigating Intellectual Property (IP) Rights:**

Expanding a franchise involves complex intellectual property (IP) rights management, particularly when multiple media formats and licensing agreements are involved. It's important to ensure that all IP rights are clearly defined and protected, and that licensing agreements are carefully negotiated to maintain control over the franchise. Working with experienced legal and business advisors can help navigate the complexities of IP management and ensure that the franchise remains secure.

**Ensuring Coherence Across Multiple Platforms:**

As the franchise expands into different media, maintaining coherence across platforms can be challenging. Each medium has its own storytelling conventions and audience expectations, and it's important to ensure that the narrative remains consistent and that key plot points and character developments align across all formats. Regular coordination between creators working on different aspects of the franchise is essential for maintaining narrative coherence and avoiding contradictions or inconsistencies.

**Examples of Successful Franchises**

Several franchises have successfully expanded beyond their original series, offering valuable insights into how to create a successful multi-platform narrative:

*The Walking Dead*:

*The Walking Dead* began as a comic book series before becoming a hugely successful television miniseries. The franchise has since expanded into multiple spin-off series, video games, novels, and even a theme park attraction. Each extension builds on the core themes of survival and human nature, while exploring new characters, locations, and narratives within the same post-apocalyptic world.

*Harry Potter*:

The *Harry Potter* franchise, originally a series of novels, has expanded into films, stage plays, theme parks, and a variety of merchandise. The franchise has maintained its popularity by consistently delivering high-quality content that stays true to the magical world created by J.K. Rowling. The expansion into prequel films (the *Fantastic Beasts* series) and the stage play *Harry Potter and the Cursed Child* has allowed the franchise to explore different aspects of the wizarding world, appealing to both long-time fans and new audiences.

*Star Wars*:

*Star Wars* is one of the most iconic and enduring franchises in pop culture history. Beginning with a single film in 1977, the franchise has expanded into numerous films, animated series, novels, comics, video games, and merchandise. The franchise's ability to reinvent itself while maintaining its core themes of good versus evil, heroism, and hope has allowed it to remain relevant across multiple generations.

*Marvel Cinematic Universe (MCU)*:

The Marvel Cinematic Universe is a prime example of how to build a successful franchise through interconnected storytelling. Starting with *Iron Man* in 2008, the MCU has grown into a vast, multi-platform franchise that includes films, television series, comics, and digital content. Each installment is part of a larger narrative arc, with characters and plotlines crossing over between different formats. The MCU's success lies in its meticulous planning, consistent quality, and ability to keep audiences engaged with new and evolving storylines.

Expanding a miniseries into a franchise offers creators the opportunity to build on their original success, explore new storytelling possibilities, and engage audiences in fresh and exciting ways. However, creating a successful franchise requires careful planning, a commitment to quality, and a deep understanding of the original content's appeal.

By developing a clear franchise vision, maintaining consistency across different formats, and engaging with the fanbase, creators can turn a single miniseries into a lasting cultural phenomenon. As the franchise grows, it's important to balance innovation with fidelity to the original, ensuring that each new installment contributes meaningfully to the overarching narrative. With the right strategy and creative vision, a miniseries can become the foundation for a thriving, multi-platform franchise that captivates audiences for years to come.

# Lessons from Successful Miniseries: Case Studies

Examining successful miniseries through case studies offers valuable insights into what makes a series resonate with audiences and achieve critical acclaim. By analyzing the storytelling techniques, character development, production choices, and marketing strategies of these series, creators can learn lessons that can be applied to their own projects. In this chapter, we'll explore several case studies of successful miniseries, highlighting the key factors that contributed to their success and the lessons that can be drawn from them.

**Case Study 1: *Chernobyl* (2019)**

**Overview:**

*Chernobyl*, a five-part historical drama produced by HBO and Sky, recounts the 1986 Chernobyl nuclear disaster and the efforts to contain its aftermath. The series was praised for its meticulous attention to detail, gripping narrative, and powerful performances.

**Key Factors in Success:**

**Commitment to Historical Accuracy:**

*Chernobyl* was lauded for its commitment to historical accuracy, with meticulous research informing everything from the script to the production design. The series captured the grim reality of the disaster and its impact on the people involved, making the story both compelling and educational.

**Lesson:** When dealing with historical events, accuracy and authenticity are crucial. Audiences appreciate when a series respects the truth of the events it portrays, and attention to detail can add credibility and depth to the narrative.

**Tension and Pacing:**

The series maintained a constant sense of tension and dread, even though the outcome of the disaster was well-known. By focusing on the human stories behind the event and the bureaucratic missteps that exacerbated the disaster, *Chernobyl* created a narrative that was both suspenseful and emotionally resonant.

**Lesson:** Effective pacing and a focus on character-driven tension can keep audiences engaged, even when the outcome of the story is known. Building suspense through character decisions and ethical dilemmas adds depth to the narrative.

**Strong Performances:**

The cast of *Chernobyl*, including Jared Harris, Stellan Skarsgård, and Emily Watson, delivered powerful performances that brought the historical figures to life. The actors' nuanced portrayals added emotional weight to the series, making the tragedy feel personal and immediate.

**Lesson:** Casting and performance are critical to the success of a miniseries. Strong performances can elevate the material, making the story more impactful and memorable for the audience.

**Visual and Audio Realism:**

*Chernobyl* used stark, muted visuals and a haunting sound design to convey the bleakness of the disaster and its aftermath. The use of practical effects and real locations added to the sense of realism, immersing viewers in the world of the series.

**Lesson:** A cohesive visual and audio style can significantly enhance the storytelling. Consistent and immersive design choices help create a believable world that draws the audience into the narrative.

**Case Study 2:** *The Queen's Gambit* (2020)

**Overview:**

*The Queen's Gambit*, a Netflix miniseries based on Walter Tevis's 1983 novel, follows the life of chess prodigy Beth Harmon as she rises through the ranks of the chess world while battling addiction and personal demons. The series was a global hit, praised for its storytelling, character development, and stylish production.

**Key Factors in Success:**

**Character-Driven Storytelling:**

At its core, *The Queen's Gambit* is a character study of Beth Harmon, portrayed by Anya Taylor-Joy. The series delves deeply into her psyche, exploring her genius, vulnerabilities, and personal struggles. The character's complexity and relatability were key to the series' appeal.

**Lesson:** Creating a deeply developed, relatable protagonist can anchor the story and engage viewers. Audiences connect with characters who are multifaceted, flawed, and undergoing significant personal growth.

**Making a Niche Subject Accessible:**

Chess is central to *The Queen's Gambit*, but the series succeeded in making the game accessible and exciting to a broad audience. The series used visual storytelling, dynamic camera work, and clear explanations to make chess matches engaging, even for those unfamiliar with the game.

**Lesson:** Even niche or complex subjects can be made compelling and accessible with the right approach. By focusing on the human drama and using creative techniques to explain the subject, creators can draw in a wider audience.

**Visual Style and Production Design:**

The series was noted for its striking visual style, with vibrant colors, period-accurate costumes, and meticulous production design that captured the 1960s setting. The visual elements were not just decorative but integral to the storytelling, reflecting Beth's inner world and the societal pressures she faced.

**Lesson:** A strong visual identity can enhance the narrative and contribute to character development. Production design, costumes, and cinematography should be carefully considered to support the story's themes and tone.

**Thematic Depth:**

Beyond chess, *The Queen's Gambit* explored themes of addiction, loneliness, and the struggle for identity. These universal themes resonated with viewers, making the series relevant and emotionally impactful.

**Lesson:** Incorporating universal themes that resonate with audiences can add depth to the story and make it more relatable. These themes should be woven into the narrative in a way that enhances character development and emotional engagement.

**Case Study 3:** *Fargo* **(2014–present)**

**Overview:**

*Fargo*, an anthology crime drama series inspired by the Coen brothers' 1996 film of the same name, has been widely praised for its dark humor, complex characters, and unique narrative style. Each season tells a self-contained story set in the same universe, with new characters and plotlines.

**Key Factors in Success:**

**Anthology Format:**

*Fargo* uses an anthology format, with each season featuring a new story and characters while maintaining a consistent tone and style. This approach keeps the series fresh, allowing it to explore different aspects of the crime genre while retaining the essence of the original film.

**Lesson:** An anthology format can allow for creative flexibility while maintaining a cohesive brand. It can attract new viewers with each season while rewarding loyal fans with thematic and stylistic continuity.

**Blending Genres:**

The series successfully blends crime drama with dark comedy, a hallmark of the Coen brothers' work. This mix of genres creates a distinctive tone that sets *Fargo* apart from other crime series, appealing to fans of both genres.

**Lesson:** Blending genres can create a unique and memorable tone that distinguishes a series from others in the same category. It also allows for more dynamic storytelling, where tension and humor can coexist.

**Strong Ensemble Casts:**

Each season of *Fargo* features a strong ensemble cast, often including well-known actors who bring depth and nuance to their roles. The characters are richly developed, with complex motivations and moral ambiguities that drive the narrative.

**Lesson:** Investing in a strong ensemble cast can elevate a series, particularly when the story relies on multiple interconnected characters. Each actor's performance contributes to the overall tone and depth of the series.

**Maintaining a Consistent Aesthetic:**

*Fargo* maintains a consistent aesthetic across all seasons, characterized by its cold, snowy landscapes, quirky characters, and stark, often brutal visual style. This consistency helps tie the different seasons together, creating a recognizable brand.

**Lesson:** A consistent aesthetic is important for establishing a series' identity, especially in an anthology format. This includes visual elements, tone, and narrative style, which should all align to create a cohesive viewing experience.

**Case Study 4: *Big Little Lies* (2017–2019)**

**Overview:**

*Big Little Lies*, a drama miniseries based on the novel by Liane Moriarty, follows the lives of a group of women in a wealthy California community, whose seemingly perfect lives unravel after a mysterious death. The series was praised for its compelling performances, sharp writing, and exploration of complex social issues.

**Key Factors in Success:**

**Strong Female Characters:**

The series is centered around a group of strong, complex female characters, each with their own struggles and secrets. The focus on women's perspectives and experiences was a significant factor in the series' appeal, resonating with a wide audience.

**Lesson:** Developing multi-dimensional characters, particularly those from underrepresented groups, can create powerful, relatable narratives that engage a broad audience.

**Exploration of Social Issues:**

*Big Little Lies* tackled important social issues such as domestic violence, gender roles, and the pressures of societal expectations. These themes were woven into the narrative in a way that felt organic and integral to the characters' development.

**Lesson:** Addressing relevant social issues in a thoughtful and nuanced way can add depth to the narrative and make the series more impactful. These issues should be explored through the lens of character development and plot, rather than feeling tacked on.

**High-Profile Cast and Creative Team:**

The series featured a high-profile cast, including Reese Witherspoon, Nicole Kidman, and Laura Dern, as well as direction from acclaimed filmmaker Jean-Marc Vallée. The involvement of such talent added to the series' prestige and drew in a large audience.

**Lesson:** Attaching well-known talent, both in front of and behind the camera, can elevate a series and attract viewers. However, it's important that the talent is a good fit for the material and contributes meaningfully to the story.

**Cinematic Quality:**

*Big Little Lies* was praised for its cinematic quality, with stunning cinematography, a haunting score, and careful attention to visual detail. The series felt like an extended film, with a polished, high-production value that enhanced the storytelling.

**Lesson:** Investing in high production values and a cinematic approach can make a miniseries stand out in a crowded market. Visual and audio quality are key components of creating an immersive viewing experience.

Analyzing successful miniseries provides valuable lessons for creators looking to develop their own projects. Each of the case studies explored in this chapter demonstrates the importance of character development, thematic depth, visual style, and narrative structure in creating a compelling and memorable series. Whether you're working on a historical drama, a character-driven story, an anthology series, or a socially relevant narrative, the key to success lies in thoughtful planning, attention to detail, and a commitment to storytelling that resonates with audiences. By learning from these successful examples, you can apply similar strategies to your own work, ensuring that your miniseries captures the attention and imagination of viewers.

# The Evolution of the Miniseries Format

The miniseries format has undergone significant evolution since its inception, adapting to changing audience preferences, technological advancements, and the shifting landscape of television and streaming. Originally conceived as a way to tell longer, more complex stories over a limited number of episodes, the miniseries has expanded in scope and influence, becoming a powerful storytelling vehicle in the modern entertainment industry. In this chapter, we'll explore the origins of the miniseries format, its transformation over the decades, and how it has come to be a dominant force in contemporary television.

### The Origins of the Miniseries

### Early Beginnings:

The concept of the miniseries, or "limited series," can be traced back to the early days of television, when serialized storytelling was often limited to daytime soaps and weekly dramas. However, the idea of telling a complete, self-contained story over a set number of episodes gained traction in the 1960s and 1970s. Early examples include *The Forsyte Saga* (1967), a 26-part adaptation of John Galsworthy's novels, and *Roots* (1977), a groundbreaking miniseries that chronicled the history of an African American family from slavery to emancipation.

### The Golden Age of the Miniseries:

The 1970s and 1980s are often referred to as the "Golden Age" of the miniseries, particularly in the United States. Networks began to realize the potential of the format to attract large audiences over a short period, often with high-profile adaptations of popular novels. Miniseries like *Roots*, *Shōgun* (1980), and *The Thorn Birds* (1983) became cultural phenomena, drawing massive viewership and critical acclaim. These productions were characterized by their epic storytelling, star-studded casts, and high production values.

### Decline and Shift to Cable:

By the late 1980s and 1990s, the popularity of the miniseries began to wane on broadcast television, as networks shifted focus to shorter, episodic series that could be syndicated. However, cable networks like HBO recognized the potential of the format and began producing their own miniseries. HBO's *Band of Brothers* (2001) and *Angels in America* (2003) demonstrated that the miniseries could still thrive, particularly with the creative freedom and budgetary support that cable networks could provide. These productions were not just commercial successes but also garnered critical acclaim, setting new standards for the format.

### The Miniseries in the Age of Streaming

### The Rise of Streaming Platforms:

The advent of streaming platforms like Netflix, Amazon Prime, and Hulu in the 2010s revolutionized how audiences consumed television content. These platforms offered greater flexibility, allowing viewers to watch content on-demand and at their own pace. The miniseries format was well-suited to this new era of "binge-watching," where viewers could consume an entire story in one sitting if they chose. Streaming platforms began to invest heavily in original miniseries, recognizing their appeal to a broad audience.

**Blurring the Lines between Film and Television:**

Streaming also blurred the lines between film and television, with many miniseries adopting a more cinematic approach to storytelling. The high production values, star-studded casts, and complex narratives traditionally associated with film became common in miniseries produced by streaming platforms. Series like *The Queen's Gambit* (2020) and *When They See Us* (2019) exemplify this trend, offering viewers the depth and scope of a film while maintaining the episodic structure of a television series.

**The Limited Series as Prestige TV:**

The miniseries, often rebranded as the "limited series," became a hallmark of prestige television, attracting top-tier talent both in front of and behind the camera. These productions often tackled weighty, socially relevant themes, positioning themselves as serious, high-quality entertainment.

Limited series like *Big Little Lies* (2017) and *Chernobyl* (2019) not only garnered critical acclaim but also won numerous awards, further cementing the format's status as a key component of the modern television landscape.

**Anthology Series and the Return to Episodic Storytelling:**

The resurgence of anthology series, where each season tells a self-contained story, can be seen as a natural evolution of the miniseries format. Shows like *Fargo* (2014–present) and *American Horror Story* (2011–present) blend the flexibility of episodic storytelling with the narrative depth of a miniseries.

This approach allows creators to experiment with different genres, tones, and settings, while still delivering a complete, satisfying narrative arc within a single season.

**The Contemporary Miniseries: Innovation and Influence**

**The Power of True Stories:**

One significant trend in modern miniseries is the focus on true stories and historical events. Productions like *Chernobyl*, *When They See Us*, and *The People v. O.J. Simpson: American Crime Story* (2016) have captivated audiences by dramatizing real-life events with a high degree of accuracy and emotional impact. The success of these series highlights the public's appetite for stories that are not only entertaining but also informative and reflective of real-world issues.

**Expanding Global Reach:**

Streaming platforms have also enabled miniseries to reach global audiences more easily than ever before. This has led to a greater diversity of voices and stories in the format, with international productions gaining prominence alongside those from the U.S. Series like *Narcos* (2015–2017), which blends English and Spanish dialogue, and *Delhi Crime* (2019), an Indian production, demonstrate the global appeal of the miniseries format and its ability to resonate with audiences across cultures.

**Experimentation with Structure and Format:**

The flexibility of streaming has encouraged experimentation with the structure and format of miniseries. Creators are no longer bound by the traditional constraints of network television, such as episode length or seasonal schedules. This has led to innovative storytelling approaches, such as non-linear narratives, varying episode lengths, and hybrid formats that blend documentary and drama. For example, *Unorthodox* (2020) uses flashbacks and a fluid timeline to explore the protagonist's past and present in a deeply personal way.


### The Miniseries as a Launchpad for Franchises:

In some cases, successful miniseries have served as launchpads for larger franchises. While the format was once defined by its limited nature, there is now a trend of expanding popular miniseries into multi-season series or creating spin-offs that explore different aspects of the story.

*Big Little Lies* is a prime example, initially conceived as a one-season miniseries, but later extended into a second season due to its popularity.

Similarly, *American Horror Story* has spun off into *American Crime Story* and *American Horror Stories*, each focusing on different narratives within the same framework.

### Challenges and Opportunities in the Modern Miniseries

### Balancing Quality and Quantity:

As the demand for content grows, there is a risk that the rush to produce new miniseries could lead to a decline in quality. Maintaining the high standards that have come to define the format is crucial to preserving its prestige. Creators must balance the pressure to produce content quickly with the need to develop rich, compelling stories that resonate with audiences.

### Navigating Audience Expectations:

With the increasing popularity of the miniseries format, audience expectations have risen. Viewers now expect high production values, complex characters, and thought-provoking themes. Meeting these expectations while keeping the content fresh and innovative is a challenge for creators. Understanding the evolving tastes of the audience and being willing to take creative risks can help creators navigate these expectations successfully.

### Leveraging Technology:

Technological advancements have opened up new possibilities for storytelling in the miniseries format. From high-quality visual effects to interactive storytelling, technology allows creators to push the boundaries of what's possible. Embracing these advancements while staying true to the core elements of good storytelling can lead to ground-breaking work in the miniseries format.

### Addressing Representation and Diversity:

As the miniseries format continues to evolve, there is a growing emphasis on representation and diversity, both in front of and behind the camera. Audiences are increasingly demanding stories that reflect a wider range of experiences and perspectives. Creators have the opportunity to use the miniseries format to tell stories that have been underrepresented in mainstream media, contributing to a more inclusive and diverse television landscape.

The evolution of the miniseries format reflects broader changes in the television industry and audience consumption habits. From its origins as a way to tell epic, self-contained stories over a limited number of episodes, the miniseries has transformed into a versatile and influential format that plays a central role in modern television. Today's miniseries can be found across a wide range of genres, exploring complex themes, experimenting with narrative structures, and reaching global audiences. As streaming platforms continue to redefine how content is produced and consumed, the miniseries format is likely to remain a key vehicle for innovative and impactful storytelling.

By understanding the history and evolution of the miniseries, creators can better appreciate the format's potential and navigate the challenges and opportunities it presents. Whether telling a historical epic, a character-driven drama, or an experimental narrative, the miniseries offers a unique platform for creators to tell compelling stories that resonate with audiences around the world.

# Ethical Storytelling: Responsibility in Media

Ethical storytelling in media is increasingly recognized as a crucial aspect of responsible content creation. As storytellers, filmmakers, and content creators wield significant influence over audiences, the choices they make in how they represent people, events, and cultures can have far-reaching consequences. Ethical storytelling involves being mindful of these responsibilities, ensuring that narratives are crafted with care, respect, and a commitment to truthfulness and fairness. In this chapter, we'll explore the principles of ethical storytelling, the challenges it presents, and how creators can navigate these responsibilities to produce media that is both impactful and respectful.

## The Importance of Ethical Storytelling

### Influence and Impact:

Media has the power to shape perceptions, influence behavior, and reinforce or challenge societal norms. This influence comes with a responsibility to consider how stories might affect audiences and the broader culture. Ethical storytelling acknowledges this power and seeks to use it in ways that contribute positively to society, whether by fostering empathy, promoting understanding, or encouraging critical thinking.

### Representation Matters:

The way people, cultures, and communities are represented in media can have significant implications for how they are perceived in the real world. Stereotypes, biased portrayals, and exclusion can perpetuate harmful narratives and reinforce social inequalities. Ethical storytelling strives to offer fair, accurate, and diverse representations, giving voice to underrepresented groups and challenging harmful stereotypes. This approach not only enriches the narrative but also contributes to a more inclusive media landscape.

### Respect for Real-Life Subjects:

When telling stories based on real events or people, there is an ethical obligation to treat the subjects with respect and dignity. This includes being truthful in representation, avoiding sensationalism, and considering the impact that the story may have on the individuals involved or their communities. Ethical storytelling ensures that the pursuit of a compelling narrative does not come at the expense of the dignity or well-being of those whose stories are being told.

### Audience Responsibility:

Audiences look to media not only for entertainment but also for information and guidance on social and cultural issues. Ethical storytelling recognizes the role of media in shaping public discourse and strives to provide content that encourages informed and thoughtful engagement with the issues at hand. This responsibility includes being transparent about the distinctions between fact and fiction, particularly in genres like docudrama or based-on-true-events storytelling, where the lines can sometimes blur.

## Principles of Ethical Storytelling

### Accuracy and Truthfulness:

One of the foundational principles of ethical storytelling is accuracy. This means representing facts and events as truthfully as possible, especially in non-fiction and historical narratives. Creators should be diligent in their research, ensuring that they are not spreading misinformation or distorting the truth for dramatic effect.

In fiction, while creative liberties are allowed, ethical storytelling involves making it clear to the audience when elements of the story are fictionalized or dramatized, particularly when dealing with real events or people.

### Cultural Sensitivity and Respect:

Cultural sensitivity involves being aware of and respecting the cultural contexts of the stories being told. This includes understanding the significance of cultural symbols, practices, and narratives, and avoiding appropriation or misrepresentation. Ethical storytelling involves consulting with cultural advisors, engaging with the communities being represented, and ensuring that portrayals are respectful and authentic. This is particularly important when telling stories from cultures or communities that are not the creator's own.

### Avoiding Harmful Stereotypes:

Stereotypes can reduce complex individuals and cultures to simplistic, often negative, caricatures. Ethical storytelling works to avoid these harmful stereotypes, instead presenting characters and communities in a nuanced and multifaceted way. This involves challenging existing stereotypes and offering alternative narratives that reflect the diversity and complexity of real-life experiences.

### Consent and Collaboration:

When telling stories that involve real people, especially those from vulnerable or marginalized communities, it's essential to seek their consent and collaborate with them in the storytelling process. This ensures that their voices are heard and that the narrative is aligned with their perspectives. Collaboration also extends to sharing the benefits of the story, whether that's through credit, compensation, or providing a platform for the individuals involved to tell their own stories.

### Ethical Representation of Violence and Trauma:

Depictions of violence and trauma should be handled with care, ensuring that they do not sensationalize or exploit suffering. Ethical storytelling involves considering the impact that these depictions may have on both the subjects of the story and the audience. This principle includes avoiding gratuitous violence, providing context for traumatic events, and considering the potential for re-traumatization among viewers who may have experienced similar situations.

### Transparency and Accountability:

Ethical storytellers are transparent about their intentions, methods, and the limitations of their work. This includes acknowledging any biases, potential conflicts of interest, or creative liberties taken in the storytelling process. Accountability involves being open to feedback and criticism, especially from the communities represented in the story. It also means being willing to make corrections or amends if the story inadvertently causes harm or perpetuates falsehoods.

## Challenges in Ethical Storytelling

### Balancing Truth and Creativity:

One of the biggest challenges in ethical storytelling is balancing the need for accurate representation with the creative demands of storytelling. This is particularly true in dramatizations of real events, where the desire to create a compelling narrative can sometimes lead to distortions or omissions. Creators must navigate this tension carefully, ensuring that their creative choices do not compromise the integrity of the story or mislead the audience.

### Navigating Complex Cultural Contexts:

Telling stories from cultures or communities different from one's own can be fraught with challenges. Misunderstandings, misinterpretations, and unintentional cultural insensitivity are risks that storytellers must be aware of and work to mitigate. Engaging with cultural consultants and being open to learning and adapting throughout the creative process are essential strategies for navigating these complexities.

### Representation and Power Dynamics:

The power dynamics involved in storytelling, especially when telling stories about marginalized or vulnerable communities, can be challenging to navigate. There is always a risk of reinforcing existing power imbalances or exploiting the stories of others for personal gain. Ethical storytelling requires a conscious effort to share power, whether through collaboration, giving credit, or ensuring that the community being represented has a voice in how the story is told.

### Audience Expectations and Market Pressures:

There is often pressure from audiences, networks, or producers to sensationalize or simplify stories to make them more marketable. This can lead to ethical compromises, such as exaggerating events, focusing on shock value, or perpetuating stereotypes to attract attention. Ethical storytellers must find ways to balance these pressures with their commitment to responsible storytelling, even if it means making difficult decisions about content or presentation.

### Addressing Missteps and Making Amends:

No storyteller is perfect, and there may be times when a well-intentioned story misses the mark or causes unintended harm. Ethical storytelling involves being willing to address these missteps, listen to criticism, and take steps to make amends. This could involve issuing public apologies, making corrections in future editions or releases, or engaging in dialogue with affected communities to understand their concerns and learn from the experience.

## Examples of Ethical Storytelling

### *When They See Us* (2019):

Ava DuVernay's miniseries *When They See Us* tells the story of the Central Park Five, five Black and Latino teenagers wrongfully convicted of a brutal crime they didn't commit. DuVernay worked closely with the men to ensure their experiences were portrayed accurately and respectfully. The series is a powerful example of ethical storytelling, highlighting systemic racism and injustice while giving a voice to those who were silenced. The collaboration with the real-life subjects ensured that their perspectives were central to the narrative.

*13th* (2016):

Also directed by Ava DuVernay, *13th* is a documentary that explores the intersection of race, justice, and mass incarceration in the United States. The film uses historical analysis and personal testimony to build a compelling argument against the exploitation of Black Americans through the criminal justice system.

The ethical approach to storytelling in *13th* is evident in its thorough research, respectful presentation of subjects, and commitment to shedding light on systemic issues that are often overlooked or misunderstood.

*The Act of Killing* (2012):

*The Act of Killing* is a documentary that challenges traditional storytelling methods by allowing former Indonesian death squad leaders to reenact their crimes in the style of their favorite movie genres. The film exposes the brutal reality of the Indonesian genocide and the impunity enjoyed by its perpetrators.

While the film's unconventional approach sparked debate about its ethical implications, it also serves as a powerful example of how storytelling can confront difficult truths and force audiences to grapple with uncomfortable realities.

*Unorthodox* (2020):

*Unorthodox* is a miniseries that tells the story of a young woman who leaves her ultra-Orthodox Jewish community in Brooklyn to pursue a new life in Berlin. The creators worked closely with consultants from the Hasidic community to ensure an accurate and sensitive portrayal of its customs and beliefs.

The series demonstrates ethical storytelling by presenting a nuanced view of a traditionally private community, avoiding stereotypes and allowing the protagonist's personal journey to unfold in a way that respects the complexity of her cultural background.

Ethical storytelling is an essential aspect of responsible media creation, requiring a commitment to accuracy, respect, and a deeper understanding of the impact that stories can have on individuals and society. As creators, the choices made in how to represent people, cultures, and events carry significant weight, with the potential to influence perceptions, reinforce or challenge stereotypes, and contribute to the broader cultural conversation.

By adhering to the principles of ethical storytelling—accuracy, cultural sensitivity, respect for subjects, and transparency—creators can produce media that not only entertains but also enriches, educates, and empowers audiences. The challenges of ethical storytelling are real, but they are also opportunities to engage in thoughtful, responsible, and impactful storytelling that resonates deeply and contributes positively to the world.

As the media landscape continues to evolve, the importance of ethical storytelling will only grow, making it an essential consideration for anyone involved in the creation and dissemination of stories. Whether working in fiction, non-fiction, or somewhere in between, creators have the responsibility—and the power—to tell stories that reflect the complexity of the human experience and foster a more just and empathetic society.

# Balancing Art and Commerce in Television

Balancing art and commerce in television is a delicate yet essential task that creators, producers, and networks must navigate. While the creative process is driven by artistic vision, storytelling, and a desire to push boundaries, the commercial realities of the television industry—such as funding, viewership ratings, and profitability—cannot be ignored. Achieving a balance between these often competing demands is crucial for the success of any television project, whether it's a high-concept miniseries, a long-running drama, or a light-hearted sitcom. In this chapter, we'll explore the challenges of balancing art and commerce in television, strategies for finding harmony between the two, and examples of shows that have successfully managed this balance.

**The Tension Between Art and Commerce**

**Creative Vision vs. Marketability:**

Creators often have a strong artistic vision for their projects, driven by a desire to tell unique, challenging, or unconventional stories. However, networks and producers are concerned with the marketability of these projects, which involves considerations such as audience appeal, advertising potential, and profitability. This tension can lead to compromises, where creators might be asked to adjust their vision to align with commercial expectations. Finding a way to maintain the integrity of the original vision while making the project commercially viable is a key challenge.

**The Role of Ratings and Advertisers:**

In traditional television, ratings play a significant role in determining the success of a show. Higher ratings attract more advertisers, which in turn generates more revenue for the network. This can create pressure to produce content that appeals to a broad audience, sometimes at the expense of artistic innovation or niche storytelling. Advertisers also have influence over content, as they may be reluctant to associate their brands with shows that are too controversial, edgy, or unconventional. This can lead to self-censorship or creative compromises to avoid alienating sponsors.

**Budget Constraints and Production Values:**

Budget constraints are a practical consideration that affects the creative process. High production values, special effects, and top-tier talent all come with a cost, and securing funding for ambitious projects can be challenging. Creators must find ways to maximize their resources, often making tough decisions about where to allocate budget and how to deliver high-quality content within financial limitations.

**The Impact of Streaming and Subscription Models:**

The rise of streaming platforms has shifted the dynamics of art and commerce in television. Subscription-based models like Netflix, Amazon Prime, and HBO Max are less reliant on traditional advertising and ratings, allowing for greater creative freedom and experimentation. However, these platforms are still driven by subscriber growth and retention, leading to a focus on content that can attract and keep viewers engaged. This can sometimes result in the prioritization of binge-worthy content or shows with viral potential over more niche or experimental projects.

## Strategies for Balancing Art and Commerce

### Understanding the Audience:

One of the most effective ways to balance art and commerce is to deeply understand the target audience. Knowing who the show is for, what they want, and what will resonate with them allows creators to craft content that meets both artistic and commercial goals. Audience research, test screenings, and social media engagement can provide valuable insights into viewer preferences, helping creators tailor their projects without compromising their artistic vision.

### Strategic Compromises:

Compromise is often necessary in balancing art and commerce, but it doesn't have to mean sacrificing artistic integrity. Strategic compromises involve making adjustments that enhance the show's marketability while preserving its core creative elements. For example, adjusting a show's tone or pacing to make it more accessible, incorporating elements that appeal to a broader audience, or finding creative solutions to budget constraints can help strike the right balance.

### Building Relationships with Networks and Producers:

Strong relationships with networks, producers, and executives are crucial for navigating the balance between art and commerce. Open communication, mutual respect, and a willingness to collaborate can lead to a better understanding of both creative and commercial goals. Building trust with decision-makers can also provide creators with more leeway to pursue their vision, as networks and producers may be more willing to take risks on projects that they believe in.

### Leveraging the Power of Niche Markets:

In the age of streaming and digital platforms, niche markets have become increasingly important. Shows that cater to specific, passionate audiences can succeed commercially even if they don't appeal to a broad demographic. By identifying and targeting a dedicated niche audience, creators can maintain artistic integrity while still achieving commercial success. Streaming platforms, in particular, have been instrumental in supporting niche content that might not have thrived on traditional television.

### Innovative Funding Models:

Crowdfunding, co-productions, and partnerships with non-traditional sponsors are some of the innovative funding models that can help balance art and commerce. These models provide alternative sources of funding that may come with fewer creative restrictions. Crowdfunding, for example, allows creators to raise money directly from their audience, ensuring that the people who care most about the project have a stake in its success. Co-productions can also spread the financial risk across multiple partners, allowing for more ambitious projects.

### Emphasizing Quality Over Quantity:

Focusing on quality rather than quantity can help bridge the gap between art and commerce. A well-crafted, high-quality show is more likely to attract viewers, generate buzz, and achieve long-term success, even if it doesn't immediately appeal to the broadest possible audience. Investing in strong writing, compelling characters, and high production values can set a show apart in a crowded market, making it more attractive to both viewers and advertisers.

## Case Studies of Successful Balance

### *Breaking Bad* (2008–2013):

*Breaking Bad* is a prime example of a show that balanced art and commerce successfully. The series began with a relatively modest budget and niche appeal, but its combination of compelling storytelling, complex characters, and innovative direction allowed it to grow into a cultural phenomenon. The show's creator, Vince Gilligan, maintained his artistic vision while making strategic adjustments to appeal to a broader audience, such as increasing the intensity and stakes of the narrative as the series progressed.

### *Stranger Things* (2016–present):

*Stranger Things*, produced by Netflix, masterfully blends 1980s nostalgia with a unique, genre-bending story that appeals to both mainstream audiences and niche fans of horror and science fiction. The show's creators, the Duffer Brothers, managed to craft a series that is both artistically distinct and commercially successful. Netflix's subscription model allowed the Duffer Brothers to take creative risks, such as incorporating a wide range of influences and references, while also benefiting from Netflix's ability to market the show to a global audience.

### *The Crown* (2016–present):

*The Crown* combines high production values, historical accuracy, and strong performances to create a series that is both artistically ambitious and commercially viable. The show's appeal lies in its ability to delve into the personal and political lives of the British royal family, attracting a wide audience across different demographics. By investing heavily in production quality and focusing on a story with broad international interest, *The Crown* has achieved critical acclaim and commercial success, exemplifying the balance between art and commerce.

### *Fleabag* (2016–2019):

*Fleabag*, created by and starring Phoebe Waller-Bridge, is a critically acclaimed show that started as a one-woman play. Its raw, innovative approach to storytelling and character development made it a hit with both critics and audiences, despite its unconventional format. The show's success can be attributed to Waller-Bridge's unique voice, combined with Amazon's willingness to support a project that didn't fit traditional commercial molds. *Fleabag* demonstrates how a show with a strong, distinct creative vision can find commercial success through the right platform.

## Challenges in Balancing Art and Commerce

### Risk of Creative Compromise:

The need to meet commercial demands can sometimes lead to creative compromise, where the original vision of the show is diluted or altered to fit market expectations. This can result in a loss of authenticity, which may alienate the intended audience. Creators must navigate these pressures carefully, finding ways to protect their vision while still making necessary adjustments for commercial viability.

### Pressure for Immediate Success:

The television industry often places a premium on immediate success, with shows needing to perform well from the start to secure continued investment. This pressure can lead to conservative choices in storytelling, avoiding risks that might take longer to pay off. Streaming platforms have mitigated this to some extent, but the pressure for immediate viewership and positive reception remains a challenge.

**Balancing Long-Term Storytelling with Short-Term Gains:**

Television shows are often evaluated on their ability to generate quick returns, which can conflict with the need for long-term storytelling. Shows that require time to develop complex plots and characters may struggle to maintain support if they don't deliver immediate results. Finding a way to build a compelling long-term narrative while also delivering short-term payoffs is key to balancing art and commerce.

**Navigating Changing Viewer Preferences:**

Viewer preferences are constantly evolving, influenced by trends, technology, and cultural shifts. What is commercially viable today may not be tomorrow, and creators must stay attuned to these changes without losing sight of their artistic goals. This requires adaptability and a willingness to experiment with new formats, genres, and storytelling techniques to stay relevant in a competitive market.

Balancing art and commerce in television is a complex and ongoing challenge, but it is one that can be navigated successfully with the right strategies. By understanding the audience, making strategic compromises, building strong relationships with networks and producers, and leveraging innovative funding models, creators can achieve a balance that allows them to stay true to their artistic vision while also meeting commercial objectives.

Successful shows like *Breaking Bad*, *Stranger Things*, and *The Crown* demonstrate that it is possible to create content that is both artistically ambitious and commercially successful. These examples highlight the importance of quality, innovation, and a deep understanding of the audience in achieving this balance.

Ultimately, the key to balancing art and commerce lies in recognizing that both elements are essential to the success of a television project. While the creative vision drives the storytelling, commercial considerations ensure that the project reaches the right audience and has the resources it needs to thrive.

# Dealing with Creative Blocks: Finding Inspiration

Creative blocks are a common challenge for anyone involved in the creative process, whether you're a writer, director, producer, or artist. These blocks can be frustrating and disheartening, leading to self-doubt and a feeling of being stuck. However, they are also a natural part of the creative journey. Finding ways to overcome these blocks and rediscover inspiration is essential for maintaining momentum and continuing to produce meaningful work. In this chapter, we'll explore the nature of creative blocks, strategies for overcoming them, and techniques for finding inspiration when creativity seems elusive.

**Understanding Creative Blocks**

**The Nature of Creative Blocks:**

Creative blocks can manifest in various ways, including a lack of ideas, difficulty focusing, or a feeling that everything you create is subpar. These blocks can be caused by a range of factors, such as burnout, stress, fear of failure, or external pressures. It's important to recognize that creative blocks are a normal part of the creative process. Everyone experiences them at some point, and they don't mean that you've lost your creativity or talent.

**Common Causes of Creative Blocks:**

**Perfectionism:** The desire to create something flawless can lead to self-imposed pressure that stifles creativity. Fear of making mistakes or producing something imperfect can prevent you from starting or finishing a project.

**Burnout:** Extended periods of intense work without adequate rest can lead to burnout, making it difficult to find motivation or inspiration. Burnout can leave you feeling mentally and emotionally drained, with little energy for creative pursuits.

**Fear of Failure:** The fear that your work won't be good enough or won't be well-received can be paralyzing. This fear can prevent you from taking risks or exploring new ideas, leading to a creative block.

**External Pressures:** Deadlines, expectations from others, and financial pressures can create stress and anxiety, making it hard to focus on the creative process. The pressure to produce on demand can sometimes hinder your ability to think freely and creatively.

**Strategies for Overcoming Creative Blocks**

**Change Your Environment:**

Sometimes, a change of scenery can do wonders for your creativity. If you've been working in the same space for a long time, consider moving to a different location—whether it's a different room, a café, a park, or even just rearranging your workspace. A new environment can stimulate your senses and provide a fresh perspective, helping to break the monotony and spark new ideas.

**Take Breaks and Rest:**

Creative work requires mental energy, and if you're feeling drained, it might be time to take a break. Step away from your project and give yourself permission to rest. This could involve taking a walk, doing something unrelated to your work, or simply allowing yourself to relax. Rest and downtime are crucial for replenishing your creative energy. Often, stepping away from a problem allows your subconscious mind to continue working on it, leading to breakthroughs when you return.

**Engage in Different Creative Activities:**

Sometimes, working on a different type of creative project can help unblock your primary one. If you're stuck on writing, try painting, drawing, playing music, or doing something hands-on like cooking or gardening. Engaging in different creative activities can help shift your mindset, reduce pressure, and stimulate different parts of your brain, leading to renewed inspiration.

**Set Small, Manageable Goals:**

When faced with a large or daunting project, it can be helpful to break it down into smaller, more manageable tasks. Set small, achievable goals that allow you to make progress without feeling overwhelmed. By focusing on completing one small task at a time, you can build momentum and gradually overcome the block. Each small success can boost your confidence and motivate you to keep going.

**Embrace Imperfection:**

Let go of the need for perfection and allow yourself to create without judgment. Remind yourself that the first draft doesn't have to be perfect—it just needs to exist. You can always revise and refine your work later. Embracing imperfection means being willing to make mistakes, experiment, and explore new ideas without fear. This mindset can free you from self-imposed restrictions and open up new creative possibilities.

**Reconnect with Your Purpose:**

When you're feeling blocked, it can be helpful to reconnect with the underlying purpose or passion that drives your creative work. Reflect on why you started the project in the first place, what you hope to achieve, and what excites you about the process. Reconnecting with your purpose can reignite your motivation and help you push through the block. It can also remind you that the creative journey is as important as the final product.

**Collaborate with Others:**

Collaboration can be a powerful way to overcome creative blocks. Working with others allows you to share ideas, gain new perspectives, and draw inspiration from different sources.

Whether it's brainstorming with a colleague, getting feedback from a friend, or working on a group project, collaboration can help you break out of your own mental patterns and discover new directions for your work.

**Limit Distractions:**

Creative blocks can sometimes be exacerbated by distractions, whether they're external (like social media or noisy environments) or internal (like stress or anxiety). Try to create a focused, distraction-free environment where you can work uninterrupted. Techniques such as time blocking, meditation, or setting specific hours for creative work can help you stay focused and reduce the likelihood of falling into a block.

**Techniques for Finding Inspiration**

**Seek Out New Experiences:**

Inspiration often comes from experiencing something new. This could be traveling to a new place, trying a new activity, meeting new people, or even just changing your routine. New experiences can expose you to different ideas, cultures, and perspectives, providing fresh material for your creative work. They can also shake up your thinking and help you see your project in a new light.

**Consume Different Forms of Art:**

Engaging with other forms of art—whether it's reading books, watching films, visiting museums, or listening to music—can be a great way to find inspiration. Different forms of art can stimulate your imagination and offer new insights or approaches to your own work. Don't limit yourself to art that's directly related to your field. Sometimes, the most unexpected sources of inspiration can lead to breakthroughs in your creative process.

**Keep a Creative Journal:**

Maintaining a creative journal can be an effective way to capture ideas, thoughts, and inspirations as they come to you. This journal can be a space for free writing, sketching, brainstorming, or collecting quotes and images that resonate with you. Regularly reviewing your journal can help you identify patterns, themes, or ideas that you can explore further in your work. It can also serve as a valuable resource when you're feeling stuck or uninspired.

**Engage in Mindfulness Practices:**

Mindfulness practices, such as meditation, deep breathing, or yoga, can help clear mental clutter and create space for new ideas. These practices encourage you to focus on the present moment, reducing stress and allowing your mind to relax and open up to inspiration. Mindfulness can also help you become more aware of your thoughts and emotions, making it easier to identify and address the root causes of your creative block.

**Revisit Past Work:**

Sometimes, revisiting your past work can help you find inspiration. Look back at previous projects, ideas, or sketches that you may have set aside. You might find a concept that you want to explore further or an unfinished project that sparks new ideas. Revisiting past work can also remind you of your creative growth and achievements, boosting your confidence and helping you move forward.

**Take a "Creative Field Trip":**

A "creative field trip" involves visiting a place that inspires you, such as an art gallery, a natural setting, a library, or a cultural event. Immersing yourself in a different environment can help you see things from a new perspective and spark fresh ideas. The goal of a creative field trip is to step outside of your usual routine and allow yourself to be inspired by the sights, sounds, and experiences of a different place.

**Set Constraints or Challenges:**

Paradoxically, setting constraints or challenges can sometimes stimulate creativity. Limiting yourself to a specific format, time frame, or theme can force you to think more creatively and find innovative solutions within those boundaries. For example, you might challenge yourself to write a story in 500 words, create a piece of art using only one color, or develop a concept based on a single word. Constraints can push you to think outside the box and come up with ideas you might not have considered otherwise.

**Connect with Your Creative Community:**

Engaging with a community of like-minded creatives can be a great source of inspiration. Whether it's through workshops, online forums, social media groups, or local meetups, connecting with others who share your passion can provide support, encouragement, and fresh ideas. Sharing your work with others and seeing what they're creating can also reignite your own creative spark and help you overcome blocks.

Creative blocks are a natural part of the creative process, but they don't have to be insurmountable. By understanding the nature of these blocks and employing strategies to overcome them, you can keep moving forward in your creative journey. Whether it's changing your environment, taking a break, embracing imperfection, or seeking new sources of inspiration, there are many ways to reignite your creativity and find your way back to the flow of ideas.

# Future Trends in Miniseries Writing

The landscape of television and streaming is continuously evolving, and with it, the art of miniseries writing. As audiences' viewing habits change and technology advances, the miniseries format is poised to adapt and innovate in exciting ways. In this chapter, we'll explore some of the future trends in miniseries writing, focusing on how these trends may shape storytelling, production, and audience engagement in the coming years.

**Interactive Storytelling and Audience Participation**

**The Rise of Interactive Content:**

One of the most exciting trends in miniseries writing is the integration of interactive elements that allow audiences to influence the direction of the story. Building on the success of projects like *Black Mirror: Bandersnatch*, where viewers made choices that impacted the plot, future miniseries may offer even more immersive experiences. Writers will need to think about creating branching narratives that can accommodate multiple story paths while ensuring that each version of the story is satisfying and coherent.

**Challenges and Opportunities:**

Interactive storytelling presents unique challenges, such as maintaining narrative cohesion across different branches and ensuring that all potential storylines are engaging. However, it also offers opportunities for deeper audience engagement and personalized viewing experiences. Writers may collaborate more closely with technology specialists to develop these experiences, using tools like artificial intelligence and real-time data to dynamically adapt stories based on viewer preferences.

## Hybrid Formats and Cross-Genre Storytelling

### Blurring Genre Boundaries:

Future miniseries are likely to continue blurring the lines between genres, combining elements of drama, science fiction, horror, comedy, and more to create unique, hybrid stories. This trend reflects the increasing sophistication of audiences who enjoy complex narratives that defy traditional genre classifications. Writers may find themselves experimenting with genre conventions in new ways, creating miniseries that are both genre-defying and deeply resonant.

### Hybrid Formats:

Another trend is the combination of different media formats within a single miniseries. For example, a miniseries might blend traditional scripted drama with documentary-style interviews, animated sequences, or even augmented reality components. These hybrid formats allow for more innovative storytelling approaches, where different styles and techniques can be used to enhance the narrative and engage viewers on multiple levels.

## Globalization and Multilingual Storytelling

### Expanding Global Reach:

With the rise of streaming platforms that serve a global audience, future miniseries will increasingly reflect a more international perspective. This includes the use of multiple languages, settings in diverse cultural contexts, and stories that resonate with audiences around the world. Writers will need to consider how to craft stories that are both locally authentic and globally appealing, possibly collaborating with international writers or consultants to ensure cultural accuracy and relevance.

### Multilingual Narratives:

Multilingual storytelling, where characters speak different languages within the same miniseries, is becoming more common and accepted by global audiences. This approach not only adds authenticity but also broadens the appeal of the miniseries to non-English-speaking viewers. Writers will need to balance language diversity with accessibility, ensuring that non-native speakers can still fully engage with the story through subtitles or other means.

## Shorter, High-Impact Series

### Brevity and Impact:

As attention spans shrink and content consumption patterns evolve, there is a growing trend towards shorter, more concise miniseries that deliver high-impact storytelling in a limited time frame. These "micro-series" might consist of just a few episodes or even shorter, episodic content designed for quick consumption. Writing for these shorter formats requires a focus on economy of storytelling, where every scene, line of dialogue, and plot point must serve a purpose. Writers will need to master the art of creating compelling narratives with minimal filler.

### Episodic Flexibility:

With the freedom offered by streaming platforms, future miniseries might experiment with varying episode lengths, where episodes are as long or as short as the story requires. This flexibility allows for more dynamic pacing and a greater emphasis on storytelling rather than adhering to traditional time slots. Writers will have the opportunity to tailor the structure of each episode to the needs of the narrative, whether that means a 90-minute pilot or a 10-minute episode that delivers a concentrated burst of story.

## Environmental and Social Consciousness

### Eco-Themed Narratives:

As environmental concerns become more pressing, there is likely to be an increase in miniseries that tackle ecological themes, whether through dystopian settings, speculative fiction, or stories grounded in current environmental challenges. Writers may explore how environmental issues intersect with human stories, creating narratives that raise awareness and provoke thought about the future of the planet.

### Socially Conscious Storytelling:

Miniseries that address social justice issues, including topics like racial inequality, gender identity, and political corruption, will continue to be a significant trend. These stories not only reflect the times but also contribute to important cultural conversations. Writers will need to approach these topics with sensitivity and depth, ensuring that their stories are both impactful and respectful of the real-world issues they address.

## Advanced AI and Data-Driven Storytelling

### AI-Assisted Writing:

Advances in artificial intelligence are beginning to influence the creative process, with AI tools capable of generating story ideas, suggesting plot developments, and even writing dialogue. While AI will not replace human creativity, it can serve as a powerful tool to assist writers in overcoming creative blocks and exploring new narrative possibilities. Future miniseries might be developed using AI-assisted brainstorming sessions or data-driven insights into audience preferences, helping writers tailor their stories to better meet viewer expectations.

### Personalized Story Experiences:

Data analytics and AI can also enable personalized storytelling experiences, where the content is tailored to individual viewers based on their viewing history, preferences, and engagement patterns. This could lead to miniseries that offer different narrative paths or perspectives depending on the viewer's choices or interactions. Writers will need to consider how to craft stories that are flexible and adaptable, allowing for multiple interpretations or outcomes that still deliver a coherent and satisfying narrative.

## Continued Emphasis on Representation and Diversity

### Inclusive Storytelling:

The push for greater representation and diversity in media will continue to shape the future of miniseries writing. Audiences are increasingly demanding stories that reflect a wide range of experiences, identities, and cultures, and writers are responding by creating more inclusive narratives.

Future miniseries will likely feature more diverse casts, explore underrepresented stories, and challenge traditional narratives, contributing to a richer and more varied television landscape.

**Authentic Voices:**

There will be a growing emphasis on authenticity in storytelling, with a focus on ensuring that stories about specific communities or experiences are told by writers who belong to or deeply understand those communities. This trend supports the idea that authenticity leads to more nuanced, accurate, and powerful storytelling. Writers will need to engage in meaningful research, collaboration, and self-reflection to ensure that their work contributes positively to the representation of diverse voices.

## Serialized Podcasts and Audio Miniseries

### The Rise of Audio Storytelling:

Serialized podcasts and audio dramas are experiencing a resurgence, offering a new platform for miniseries storytelling. These audio-based miniseries allow for immersive, narrative-driven content that can be consumed on the go, making them an appealing format for busy audiences. Writers can explore the unique possibilities of audio storytelling, such as creating intimate, character-driven narratives or experimenting with soundscapes and voice performances to enhance the story.

### Cross-Media Adaptations:

Successful audio miniseries may be adapted into visual formats, or vice versa, creating opportunities for cross-media storytelling. This trend allows stories to reach different audiences through various channels, expanding their impact and longevity. Writers working on audio miniseries will need to consider how their stories might translate across different media, ensuring that the core narrative remains compelling in any format.

The future of miniseries writing is bright and full of potential for innovation. As technology, audience preferences, and cultural dynamics evolve, writers will have the opportunity to explore new formats, experiment with interactive and personalized storytelling, and contribute to important social and environmental conversations.

# The Impact of Streaming Platforms on Miniseries

Streaming platforms have revolutionized the television industry, profoundly impacting the production, distribution, and consumption of miniseries. These platforms have not only changed how audiences watch television but have also influenced the kinds of stories that are told, the way they are structured, and the creative freedom afforded to writers and directors. In this chapter, we will explore the various ways in which streaming platforms have shaped the miniseries format, examining both the opportunities and challenges they present for creators.

## The Rise of On-Demand Viewing

### On-Demand Flexibility:

One of the most significant impacts of streaming platforms on miniseries is the shift from scheduled programming to on-demand viewing. Audiences no longer have to wait for a specific time to watch their favorite shows; instead, they can watch whenever it suits them. This flexibility has changed how miniseries are consumed, with many viewers choosing to "binge-watch" entire series in one or two sittings. This shift has influenced the pacing and structure of miniseries, with creators often designing their narratives to sustain audience interest over extended viewing sessions. Cliffhangers, tight pacing, and continuous story arcs have become more common as a result.

### Binge-Watching Culture:

The phenomenon of binge-watching has encouraged streaming platforms to release entire seasons of miniseries at once, rather than airing episodes weekly. This release strategy allows audiences to immerse themselves fully in the story, creating a more intense and cohesive viewing experience.

Writers and directors must consider how their story will unfold in a binge-watching context, ensuring that the narrative remains engaging across multiple episodes viewed back-to-back.

## Creative Freedom and Experimentation

### Fewer Content Restrictions:

Streaming platforms often have fewer content restrictions compared to traditional broadcast and cable networks. This freedom allows creators to explore more mature, controversial, or unconventional themes without the need to conform to network standards and practices. Miniseries on streaming platforms can push boundaries in terms of language, violence, sexual content, and complex storytelling, appealing to niche audiences that may have been underserved by traditional television.

### Innovative Storytelling Techniques:

The creative freedom provided by streaming platforms has led to a surge in innovative storytelling techniques. Writers and directors are experimenting with non-linear narratives, hybrid genres, varying episode lengths, and unique visual styles that might not have been viable in a traditional TV landscape.

This environment fosters artistic risk-taking and encourages creators to break free from conventional formats, resulting in more diverse and original miniseries.

## Global Reach and Diverse Storytelling

### Access to International Audiences:

Streaming platforms have made it easier for miniseries to reach global audiences. A miniseries produced in one country can be made available to viewers around the world simultaneously, breaking down geographical barriers and expanding the potential audience base. This global reach has encouraged the production of miniseries that reflect a wider range of cultures, languages, and perspectives. Creators are now more likely to consider how their stories will resonate with international viewers, leading to more diverse and inclusive storytelling.

### Cross-Cultural Collaborations:

Streaming platforms have facilitated cross-cultural collaborations, where creators from different countries and cultural backgrounds work together on a single project. These collaborations can result in unique, multi-faceted stories that draw on a variety of cultural influences and appeal to a broader audience. For example, Netflix's *Money Heist* (*La Casa de Papel*), a Spanish-language series, became a global sensation, demonstrating how a story rooted in one culture can resonate internationally.

## Economic and Production Impacts

### Increased Investment in High-Quality Content:

Streaming platforms have significantly increased investment in high-quality, original content, including miniseries. With their deep pockets and global subscriber bases, platforms like Netflix, Amazon Prime Video, and HBO Max are able to fund ambitious projects that might not have been feasible on traditional networks. This has led to a rise in miniseries with high production values, star-studded casts, and cinematic storytelling. The competition among streaming platforms to offer exclusive, premium content has elevated the overall quality of miniseries available to audiences.

### Data-Driven Content Creation:

Streaming platforms have access to vast amounts of data on viewer preferences, behavior, and trends. This data is increasingly being used to inform content creation decisions, from the types of stories that are greenlit to the marketing strategies employed. While this data-driven approach can help ensure that content aligns with audience interests, it also raises concerns about creativity being driven by algorithms rather than artistic vision. Creators may feel pressure to cater to data-driven insights rather than taking creative risks.

## Shifts in Audience Expectations

### Demand for Quality and Originality:

The abundance of content available on streaming platforms has raised audience expectations for quality and originality. Viewers have access to a vast library of shows and miniseries, making it more important than ever for new content to stand out. As a result, creators must focus on developing unique, compelling stories that offer something new to the audience. The competition for viewers' attention is fierce, and only the most engaging and well-crafted miniseries are likely to succeed.

### Emphasis on Representation and Inclusivity:

Audiences are increasingly demanding more representation and inclusivity in the content they consume. Streaming platforms, which cater to diverse global audiences, have responded by commissioning miniseries that reflect a broader range of voices, experiences, and identities. This trend has led to more stories featuring underrepresented groups, whether in terms of race, gender, sexuality, or cultural background. Creators are encouraged to tell stories that resonate with diverse audiences, contributing to a more inclusive television landscape.

## The Role of Limited Series in the Streaming Era

### The Appeal of the Limited Series Format:

The limited series format, which is closely related to the miniseries, has become increasingly popular on streaming platforms. Limited series offer a complete story arc within a set number of episodes, making them an attractive option for viewers who prefer self-contained narratives over ongoing series.

Streaming platforms have embraced the limited series as a way to attract high-profile talent and tell complex, high-impact stories without the long-term commitment required by traditional series.

### Flexibility in Format and Length:

Streaming platforms allow for flexibility in the format and length of miniseries and limited series. Creators are not bound by traditional time slots or episode counts, enabling them to tailor the structure of their series to the needs of the story.

This flexibility has led to a greater diversity of formats, from short, intense miniseries with only a few episodes to more expansive series that explore intricate narratives over multiple installments.

## Challenges and Considerations for Creators

### Navigating the Algorithm:

One of the challenges for creators working with streaming platforms is navigating the influence of algorithms on content decisions. While data can provide valuable insights, it can also lead to homogenization if too much emphasis is placed on catering to existing trends.

Creators must find a balance between leveraging data to enhance their work and maintaining the originality and integrity of their creative vision.

### Sustainability of the Streaming Model:

The rapid growth of streaming platforms has raised questions about the sustainability of the current content production model. As platforms continue to invest heavily in original content, there is concern about whether the demand for constant new releases is sustainable in the long term.

Creators may face increasing pressure to produce content quickly, potentially leading to issues with quality and burnout. Balancing the demand for fresh content with the need for thoughtful, well-crafted storytelling will be a key challenge moving forward.

### Maintaining Creative Integrity:

While streaming platforms offer unprecedented creative freedom, there is also a risk of over-commercialization. The pressure to create content that appeals to a broad audience or generates buzz can sometimes lead to creative compromises. Creators must navigate these pressures while staying true to their artistic vision, finding ways to tell stories that are both commercially viable and creatively fulfilling.

Streaming platforms have had a profound impact on the miniseries format, offering new opportunities for creative freedom, global reach, and high-quality production. The shift to on-demand viewing, the rise of binge-watching, and the use of data-driven insights have all influenced how miniseries are written, produced, and consumed.

As streaming platforms continue to dominate the television landscape, the miniseries format is likely to evolve further, with new trends emerging in response to changing audience preferences and technological advancements. For creators, the challenge will be to harness the potential of streaming while navigating the pressures and complexities that come with it, ultimately producing miniseries that resonate with audiences and stand the test of time.

# Final Thoughts: The Legacy of a Great Miniseries

The legacy of a great miniseries is one that transcends its initial broadcast or release, leaving a lasting impact on audiences, the television industry, and the broader cultural landscape. A great miniseries resonates with viewers on a deep level, sparking conversations, inspiring future creators, and often influencing the direction of the medium itself. In this final chapter, we will reflect on what makes a miniseries truly great, explore the elements that contribute to its enduring legacy, and consider how creators can aspire to leave a meaningful mark with their work.

## The Elements of a Great Miniseries

### Compelling Storytelling:

At the heart of any great miniseries is a compelling story. Whether it's a historical drama, a psychological thriller, or a character-driven narrative, the story must captivate the audience from start to finish. A well-crafted plot, rich character development, and meaningful themes are essential components that elevate a miniseries to greatness. Great miniseries often tackle complex issues or explore the human condition in ways that resonate universally, regardless of the genre. The ability to weave together intricate narratives with emotional depth is a hallmark of a truly memorable series.

### Strong Characters and Performances:

Memorable characters are a key ingredient in the legacy of a great miniseries. These characters are often multifaceted, flawed, and deeply human, allowing viewers to connect with them on an emotional level. Their journeys, struggles, and transformations are what make the story impactful. The performances that bring these characters to life are equally important. Great miniseries are often remembered for the standout performances of their cast, where actors fully embody their roles and leave a lasting impression on the audience.

### Cohesive Vision and Direction:

A great miniseries is often the result of a cohesive vision, where every element of the production—writing, direction, cinematography, music, and design—works together to create a unified and immersive experience. This requires strong leadership from the director and showrunner, who guide the project from concept to completion. The direction of a miniseries plays a crucial role in shaping its tone, pacing, and overall impact. A director with a clear vision can elevate the material, ensuring that every scene contributes meaningfully to the story and that the series as a whole leaves a lasting impression.

### High Production Values:

While a great story and strong characters are essential, high production values can enhance the viewing experience and contribute to the legacy of a miniseries. Attention to detail in set design, costumes, special effects, and cinematography can create a visually stunning series that transports viewers into its world. Production values also extend to sound design and music, which can evoke emotions and underscore key moments in the narrative. A miniseries that excels in these areas is more likely to be remembered for its craftsmanship and artistic quality.

## The Impact on Audiences

**Emotional Resonance:**

A great miniseries has the power to evoke strong emotions in its audience, whether it's through moments of joy, sadness, tension, or revelation. This emotional connection is what makes the series memorable and what keeps viewers thinking about it long after the final episode has ended. When a miniseries resonates emotionally, it can leave a profound impact on the audience, prompting them to reflect on their own lives, beliefs, and experiences. This emotional depth is often what distinguishes a good miniseries from a great one.

**Cultural and Social Influence:**

Many great miniseries go beyond entertainment to influence cultural and social conversations. They may address important issues such as race, gender, class, politics, or morality, prompting viewers to engage in discussions about these topics and consider different perspectives. A miniseries that sparks cultural dialogue or contributes to social change can leave a legacy that extends far beyond its original airing. It can become a touchstone for discussions about the issues it raises and inspire other creators to explore similar themes in their work.

**Lasting Impressions:**

The lasting impression of a great miniseries is often seen in how it is remembered and referenced in popular culture. Quotes, scenes, and characters from the series may become iconic, finding their way into everyday conversations, memes, and other forms of media. This cultural footprint ensures that the miniseries remains relevant and continues to influence future generations of viewers and creators.

## The Influence on the Television Industry

### Setting New Standards:

A truly great miniseries can set new standards for the television industry, whether in terms of storytelling, production quality, or thematic exploration. It can challenge other creators to push the boundaries of what is possible in the medium and inspire them to take creative risks. Miniseries like *Roots* (1977), *Band of Brothers* (2001), and *Chernobyl* (2019) have all set benchmarks in their respective genres, influencing how subsequent series are conceived and produced. These series demonstrate that television can be both artistically ambitious and commercially successful.

### Inspiring Future Creators:

The legacy of a great miniseries is often seen in the work of future creators who were inspired by it. Writers, directors, and producers may draw on the techniques, themes, or styles of these miniseries in their own projects, creating a ripple effect that shapes the evolution of television. By pushing the boundaries of the medium and exploring new ways to tell stories, great miniseries pave the way for innovation and creativity in future productions.

### Revitalizing the Miniseries Format:

In an industry where long-running series often dominate, a great miniseries can demonstrate the power and potential of the format. It can revitalize interest in limited-run storytelling, showing that a concise, well-crafted narrative can be just as impactful—if not more so—than an extended series. The success of high-profile miniseries on streaming platforms has helped to re-establish the format as a viable and prestigious form of television, encouraging networks and platforms to invest in more miniseries projects.

## Leaving a Legacy as a Creator

### Staying True to Your Vision:

One of the most important factors in creating a great miniseries is staying true to your artistic vision. While it's important to consider the needs of the audience and the realities of production, the most memorable miniseries are those that reflect the unique voice and perspective of their creators. Trusting your instincts and taking creative risks can lead to work that stands out and leaves a lasting impact, even if it challenges conventional norms or expectations.

### Collaborating with a Talented Team:

Great miniseries are often the result of collaboration between talented individuals who bring their expertise and creativity to the project. Surrounding yourself with a strong team—whether it's writers, directors, actors, or designers—can elevate your vision and ensure that every aspect of the series is executed at the highest level. Collaboration also involves being open to feedback and ideas from others, recognizing that the collective effort of the team can enhance the final product.

### Focusing on Quality over Quantity:

The legacy of a great miniseries is often tied to its quality rather than its quantity. Rather than stretching a story over multiple seasons, focusing on crafting a tight, impactful narrative that can be told in a limited number of episodes can result in a more memorable and powerful experience for viewers. This approach allows for greater attention to detail, ensuring that every episode contributes meaningfully to the overall story and that the series as a whole is cohesive and satisfying.

**Creating Something Meaningful:**

Ultimately, the legacy of a great miniseries is rooted in its ability to create something meaningful—whether it's through the emotions it evokes, the ideas it explores, or the conversations it sparks. A miniseries that touches on universal themes, challenges the status quo, or provides insight into the human experience is more likely to endure and be remembered. As a creator, focusing on the deeper purpose of your work can help you craft a miniseries that resonates with audiences and leaves a lasting impact.

The legacy of a great miniseries is one that endures long after the final episode has aired. It is remembered for its compelling storytelling, memorable characters, and the emotional and cultural impact it has on audiences. A great miniseries sets new standards in the television industry, inspires future creators, and contributes to the ongoing evolution of the medium.

For creators, the challenge is to craft a miniseries that not only entertains but also leaves a meaningful mark on its viewers and the industry as a whole. By staying true to your vision, collaborating with talented individuals, and focusing on quality and depth, you can create a miniseries that stands the test of time and becomes a lasting part of television history.

As the television landscape continues to evolve, the potential for great miniseries to shape the future of storytelling remains immense. With each new project, creators have the opportunity to contribute to this legacy, pushing the boundaries of what is possible in the medium and leaving behind work that will be remembered and celebrated for years to come.